PRAISE FOR *MAN FAST*

"Natasha Scripture's quest for independence and self-definition in the face of pressure to conform to traditional ideas of femininity will be familiar to women everywhere. Presented with brutally honest and wry insight, *Man Fast* will provoke readers to rethink their choices in the best possible ways."

—Soraya Chemaly, award-winning writer, media critic, and activist

"A gorgeous testament to the pure power of slowing down and going deeper. Natasha Scripture has learned the divine order of manifesting: first we attune, then we attain."

—Danielle LaPorte, creator of *The Desire Map* book and planners

"A funny, courageous, and inspiring memoir about one woman's journey into the unknown. Scripture shows us her unraveling against the backdrop of exotic landscapes and emerges from her grief-stricken journey with a new sense of purpose and a deeper understanding of love. It becomes impossible not to root for her."

—Elisabeth Eaves, author of *Wanderlust:*
A Love Affair with Five Continents

"I was immediately absorbed by this raw, self-aware and humorous book. Natasha Scripture takes us on an emotionally charged journey, and leaves us with a greater understanding of ourselves and the world. *Man Fast* is a book for anyone who has worked through unmanageable grief and come out the other end."

—Jessica Alexander, author of *Chasing Chaos:*
My Decade in and out of Humanitarian Aid

"Smart, searching, and soulful, Natasha Scripture's *Man Fast* is an absorbing read for any woman thinking about a change of place, or heart. Exhausted and overwhelmed by her gut-wrenching work as a humanitarian aid worker in the most devastated places in the world—not to mention everyone's expectations that she get married and have a kid already—Natasha takes a sabbatical, and a break from men. Her travels span many exotic countries—India, Tanzania, Italy—as she searches to find herself at home and at peace with herself. She's an engaging guide for a spirited and spiritual journey."

—Laura Fraser, *New York Times* bestselling author of *An Italian Affair* and *All Over the Map*

"Contemporary, lyrical, funny, inspirational, sometimes painful, and always intellectually rigorous. This beautifully written book demonstrates the emotional complexities and struggles facing many modern women today, while also underscoring how women are exercising agency and continuing the solid fight against stereotypes and gender prescriptions. Natasha lends a fresh voice to the inventory of emerging feminist authors."

—Meghna Pant, author of *One and a Half Wife*, *Happy Birthday!*, and *The Trouble with Women*

"Natasha Scripture takes us on a heartfelt quest to explore the meaning of love, in all its multi-armed wisdom and splendor. Her travels are varied and intense, but more so, her internal journey—circling around the world to find the truths within herself. Beautiful, honest, vulnerable, and compelling, *Man Fast* is a spiritual travel memoir for anyone who has chased after success and wondered if perhaps there was more to life and living."

—Lavanya Sankaran, bestselling author of *The Red Carpet* and *The Hope Factory*

"Utterly captivating! In her thirtysomething years on this planet, Natasha Scripture has lived many lifetimes—all of them juicy. As an international aid worker in some of the most devastated regions, Natasha shares highlights of a journey that sent her swinging between the upper limbs of adrenaline and compassion and descending into the sacred depths of grief and self-inquiry. A vital aspect of her self-directed vision quest was the practice of letting go of the search for conventional partnership in favor of fully showing up for her own true self. Smart, funny, and deeply wise."

—Mirabai Starr, author of *God of Love: A Guide to the Heart of Judaism, Christianity and Islam*, and *Caravan of No Despair: A Memoir of Loss and Transformation*

"*Eat Pray Love* reimagined for a spiritually seeking millennial audience. Important, resonant and touching on a woman's essential journey."

—Eleanor Mills, editorial director of the *Sunday Times*

"We all want to be part of a bigger story, something beyond ourselves that allows us to serve the world while finding personal fulfillment and a sense of wholeness and well-being. Natasha's journey shows us how we can ultimately transcend the idea of wanting to give or receive love—to learn how to actually *become* love itself, to tap into a deeper wellspring of the love, wholeness and beauty that ultimately lives within, which connects us with the rest of existence. Written with authenticity, boldness, and vulnerability, this is a remarkable story of a truly remarkable journey within, of returning home to one's own self. A powerful, poignant read."

—Ananta Ripa Ajmera, author of *The Ayurveda Way: 108 Practices from the World's Oldest Healing System for Better Sleep, Less Stress, Optimal Digestion, and More*

"Scripture reminds us of the secret we can't be told, the one we have to experience in order to know; that love cannot be found in any single sacred text or in any far-off temple dripping in gold. The love we seek and eventually find is the love we start with, that's left unnoticed in our own heart. *Man Fast* is a must for any woman ready to find not just love but the source of love itself."

—Meggan Watterson, author of *REVEAL* and *How to Love Yourself*

"Natasha Scripture's *Man Fast* is as well-written and deeply felt as one could hope for in such a memoir. It digs deep and inspires me to do my own intensive spiritual work."

—Jennifer Keishin Armstrong, *New York Times* bestselling author of *Seinfeldia* and *Sex and the City and Us*

"An engaging memoir with life lessons all along the way. Natasha is a great writer, and this is the kind of book you may find yourself staying up to read long into the night."

—Sharon Salzberg, author of *Real Love*

"*Man Fast* is a delight: honest and funny, truth-telling and wise. And it's a salve and a guide for any of us who are questioning who, how, and when to date or marry. Scripture reminds us that it's simple: look inward and you will find what you need."

—Elizabeth Flock, author of *The Heart Is a Shifting Sea: Love and Marriage in Mumbai*

MAN
FAST

MAN
FAST

a memoir

Natasha Scripture

Published by Little A, New York

www.apub.com

Amazon, the Amazon logo, and Little A are trademarks of Amazon.com, Inc., or its
affiliates.

First published in Great Britain in 2018 by Piatkus

ISBN-13: 9781542091183 (hardcover)
ISBN-10: 1542091187 (hardcover)
ISBN-13: 9781542091190 (paperback)
ISBN-10: 1542091195 (paperback)

Cover design by Adil Dara

Printed in the United States of America

First US edition

In loving memory of Mark Rowland Scripture

Whatever inspiration is, it's born from a continuous 'I don't know.'

—Wisława Szymborska

Contents

AUTHOR'S NOTE

I have relied upon my memory of these events from this time of my life to the best of my abilities. However, I have changed the names of some places, and the names and identifying details of many individuals to protect their privacy.

Prologue

"Any cute boys?"

It was midnight in Pakistan. My sixty-four-year-old Indian mother was at the other end of a choppy Skype call some seven thousand miles away in a cushy suburban enclave of Washington, DC, doing her usual interrogation around my love life. She was wearing her favorite paisley kaftan, drinking orange Gatorade out of a Redskins glass, and reclining on the living room sofa with *Law & Order* on in the background. Her cozy setup seemed a far cry from my own precarious situation as I suffered through a bout of dysentery made worse by a nonresponsive air conditioner, evidently only placed in my tiny, airless room for aesthetic purposes; the mushroom-colored machinery perched lifelessly above my bed almost in derision. These two happenstances had the combined and unwanted effect of making me lose what seemed like half my body weight in sweat even as I raced to catch up by chugging what some might consider an alarming quantity of water. At the same time, CNN International was airing breaking news about a kooky American pastor in Florida threatening to ignite a bunch of Qurans. Not the best time to hold an American passport in the Islamic Republic of Pakistan. As I considered my circumstances, I felt a nostalgia for the days at *Glamour* magazine in New York, when I was a freelance fact-checker and the biggest threat to my existence was getting busted pilfering cosmetics from the beauty closet.

But that was at least eight lives ago.

———

The year was 2010. I'd been dispatched to Pakistan as an emergency spokesperson for one of the United Nations agencies after heavy monsoon rains caused floods that ravaged swaths of the country and uprooted millions of people. As is standard on these types of assignments, my job was to work the communications front lines: answer questions at press conferences, fly around on deafening military helicopters with story-chasing journalists and deep-pocketed donors documenting the delivery of supplies, traipse across flood-gouged areas to take photographs of the wreckage for use in digital fund-raising campaigns, and churn out press releases to raise awareness of the lack of basic necessities—water, shelter, food—and the money required to pay for them.

The needs *always* outweighed the available resources, at least at the beginning of any humanitarian disaster, so everything was always harried, tinged with desperation. An aid worker's body carries a certain angst, too, a heightened anxiety folded into its bones, but I was accustomed to skidding into survival mode, able to function all day on nothing but the ever-reliable supply of Pringles, lukewarm Fanta, and cigarettes to quash the hunger that rose at the most inopportune moments. Yes, the human body is incredibly resilient and adaptable—at least mine proved to be. While I never felt prepared enough, somehow I moved through the intermittent showerless, foodless situations as if they were my new normalcy, which they were for a while. This did not come naturally but rather was a useful skill I'd picked up months prior when a huge earthquake rocked Haiti and I was deployed to Port-au-Prince for several sleepless weeks with thousands of other aid workers and journalists (followed by an entourage of celebrities and donors). That was the job: gritty, unpredictable, intense. But it was worth it. At the time, it felt like the most meaningful way to spend my days.

Yet in Pakistan there was an uneasy feeling I couldn't shake. I was technically in my mother's birthplace, where my ancestors had lived for centuries, which meant I thought I would feel at *home*, like I was returning to my roots.

But no.

The anxiety I felt was likely due to the bomb blast. We lost five colleagues when our Islamabad office was the target of a suicide-bomb attack the previous year. While I hadn't known any of the victims personally, when it happened I was assigned the grim task of writing the press statement from headquarters, which made it feel more real than it would have otherwise felt—two degrees of separation from death, or maybe even one degree? The idea that this could happen to people who shared the same email server on which I fired out hundreds of emails across the world from my BlackBerry daily had a disquieting effect, even though I was safely lodged in Rome at the time. We'd since moved to a squeaky-new building in the Diplomatic Enclave where austere-looking security guards sporting spiky facial hair routinely waved metal detectors under our vehicles. We used our fingerprints to enter the building after proceeding through airport-like security and pat-downs, but there was still the underlying sense that danger was lurking, even in a city as subdued as Islamabad.

Fortunately, the basement bar of the Marriott hotel helped take the edge off. It was one of the spots where non-Muslims could legally drink without a special license. A jumble of aid workers convened there on buttery August evenings for alcoholic beverages alongside the hotel's usual suspects, mostly foreign businessmen. The liquor was numbing and helped burn down frustration, apprehension, and any general malaise. We all drank way too much, generally, in this line of work. I definitely did, though I am not sure why (fear? habit? thirst?). On the nights I abstained from Johnnie Walker Black, however, I was back in my room in a nondescript guesthouse, which I'd been placed in for security reasons. I could never really remember where it was located, because every day, the van that picked me up would take a different route to the office, just to be safe, and would also come to take me and my colleagues home at different hours so that our schedule was not predictable to whoever might have unfriendly intentions toward unsuspecting foreigners. While I appreciated the extra caution, it was all pretty disorienting, and the only thing that grounded me was Skyping with my parents at night to let them know that I was safe, even though I couldn't be sure that I was. With the shudder of each vehicle outside my guesthouse, the whole place quivered, its foundations seemingly as weak as a stack of graham crackers. This would invariably cause several geckos to dart across the cracked ceiling, where a dust-coated fan cranked in lethargic circles, drowning out Christiane Amanpour's voice in the background.

"Tashie?"

"I'm here, Mom."

I knew what she'd say next. It was just a matter of time before she mentioned his name, but it always came up.

"I just don't know why you can't meet a nice guy like Federer." She sighed.

And there it was. Through no fault of her own, my mother, Pramilla, lives in an imaginary world where handsome celebrity tennis stars are easy to come by or in a Nora Ephron movie where good-looking people bump into each other at the tops of skyscrapers or in bars when they're least expecting it. That had actually been her reality. She never searched or dolled up for hundreds of awkward dates with virtual strangers; instead, she chanced upon a fine-looking Yankee in a now-shuttered DC lounge called The Cave, on Valentine's Day, of all days, when she was only twenty-four—a freshly minted immigrant to the US. My parents fell madly in love and became one of the first generations to intermarry, in spite of the fact that they lived at a time where diners in places as close by as Virginia refused to serve my mother because of her skin color.

Their love story was, in a word, *storybook*.

My path, however, had been more of a zigzag. Not one big story but rather hundreds of nonsensical romantic threads that led nowhere except to greater self-reliance (which of course is nothing to sniff at). In any case, the likelihood of me encountering a Swiss tennis star, or anyone remotely like that, where I was headed the next morning—a former Taliban stronghold, the very place where Malala was shot in the head by a gunman two years later—was kind of slim.

The charismatic, menthol-cigarette-wielding woman who birthed me in the latter part of the twentieth century only wanted to see me "settled" and happy (preferably to a kind, sporty multimillionaire who never seemed to tire of procreating). I get it, as antiquated as it is. Parents of that era, especially the immigrant ones, still want their daughters espoused, for protection, security, and companionship. Yet her obsession with Roger Federer had created tension between us as she compared every potential love interest I had to him. Put simply: nobody made the cut with the bar so high.

Clearly the stars align on the romance front for some; others have to slog their way through a bunch of misfits and hope that the person who makes sense, who feels right, will eventually emerge (something that has become, ironically, notoriously difficult with the advent of dating apps and the proliferation of choice). Like any other woman who grew up on a gargantuan, nonpaleo diet of rom-coms, which included both Hollywood *and* Bollywood, I assumed everlasting romantic love would find me eventually. Reaping the benefits of feminist inroads from generations past, economically I didn't actually *need* a partner, and like many women, I had an emotionally rich life already, with deep friendships and healthy relationships with my own family and with colleagues who'd become *like* family (there's loads of bonding among expats, especially among the aid-worker crowd). Pramilla, on the other hand, had strong, unsolicited opinions on the subject. "South Asian men have unreasonable expectations of their wives," she chimed into the silence, as if she had experience being married to one. As if at that very moment, in that hot, dreary guesthouse amid the crumpled packets of rehydration salts, I was considering a marriage proposal from one. I was too preoccupied to explain to her, for the umpteenth time, that it was nearly impossible to find a husband while doing short-term stints in refugee camps, war zones, and natural-disaster areas, and that I wasn't looking for one anyway!

There were *always* men, of course—Norwegian water-sanitation experts, Italian logistics officers, Kiwi photojournalists—but the kinds of romantic trysts that transpired in these environments were often as short lived as the postings themselves. These men were often married, or in open relationships, or vagabond James Bond types always after the next fix, kind of like I was. We were already married—to adrenaline. We were seeking momentary connection, but not much beyond that.

That's a result of all the transience and instability that comes with being an aid worker (or working in any industry that demands near-constant uprooting)—relationships tend to fall by the wayside. At the time, it hadn't felt like a sacrifice, because the work itself was electrifying. It had an addictive quality that deluded those of us who did it into thinking we were saviors of some sort. As if we were actually *saving the world*. In a way, some of us probably did it, at least in part, out of self-interest, because it made us feel good and important. Not that we didn't care—we definitely cared—but many of us were also trying to escape something: a pedestrian life, our own stuff, stillness. I didn't realize this then, but that is what people do and why some lives are bursting with chaos and distraction. We are uncomfortable with how naked stillness makes us feel. Instead of slowing down to look inward, where all the real work casually waits to be done, it is much easier, much safer, to run away from quiet.

The globe-trotting, highly kinetic nature of the work also meant that childbearing was put off or skipped over entirely. Admittedly, I had started to question my life choices in this regard, especially as I began to notice the abundance of single, childless, fortysomething women in my profession, sometimes referred to as "humanitarian widows," posted in countries like Syria and Afghanistan. Women who were much braver than I was, women who had taken on the riskiest of postings with gusto, for years on end, something I had not yet done and didn't feel I had the nerves or constitution for. It required a hardiness I didn't think I could muster. I had colleagues who had been doing that kind of work for decades, whereas I'd only worked on emergencies for a handful of years, dipping in and out of places. But staying on for years—that kind of job takes a real toll after a while. Being stationed in a "hardship duty station" like Kabul for a longer period entailed exhausting work, though there were usually some added perks—hazard pay and an unconventional, no-holds-barred extracurricular life that usually involved sex with rugged, heavily tattooed strangers, if that was your thing. I had decided not to do the long-term field postings, as I'd started to feel some internal anxiety about the whole child/relationship thing. I didn't feel empty or as if anything was lacking until I reached a certain age. At that point, society at large had deemed me incomplete in the most subversive way. I was feeling the effects of subtle and antiquated but very real external forces, slowly changing social structures that continue to relegate a woman to spinsterhood if she doesn't pair up on the same timeline as everyone else (or perhaps ever, for that matter). Facebook had begun to make me feel like I hadn't followed the right script, the one that had been laid out for me as a woman, who also happened to be the daughter of a woman who came from a country that glorified marriage. I was thirty-two, and people my age were nesting. Babies were popping up in my newsfeed, whereas all I had to offer were shots of myself in distant lands poking my tanned and windblown head out of Range Rovers while careening down dirt roads (something that surprisingly never got tiring). Neither was better or worse, but *babies*. Babies smell good.

But I couldn't argue with Pramilla. Not then, not in that state. The generational divide was too titanic to cross, the cultural rift too taxing to navigate via Skype. Besides, considering my current circumstances, this could have been the last time I spoke to my mother—ever. What if our final conversation had been about something as absurd as my relationship status?

The following day, I was whisked deep into the heart of war-torn Swat Valley in an armored vehicle to document the dire effects of rampant flooding across farming communities in the northern parts of Pakistan. There I videotaped crackly faced farmers planting the very seeds my employer had provided and captured their beaming smiles with my clunky Canon digital SLR. I later wove all the visual magic into success stories for the donor newsletter and the corporate website, with interview quotes wrangled only after my translator, Waleed, stopped flirting with me for thirty seconds and actually translated something. I became irritated at him and then smugly pointed to the hijab encasing my head (though not expertly secured, which meant it kept sliding off as I filmed). It was the garment that was supposed to transform me from an irresistible sex object into an untouchable, respectable woman. It pretty much said, *Off limits, bucko,* or at least it was meant to. I certainly wasn't encouraging him. And yet later in the day, when I sat down with some Pashto-speaking women in their cool yurt, sipping cardamom chai offered to me with exquisite hospitality, Waleed surfaced wearing his toothy grin and bearing a question I did not want translated.

He, along with the rest of the village, wanted to know if I was married. My relationship status was all anyone anywhere seemed to care about.

Chapter 1

ALLOWING

Don't stop at the tears; go through to truth.

—*Natalie Goldberg*

A single sweet truth: growing up, I had a lot of love in my life, so I didn't need to look for it in the form of a boyfriend or relationship. From the get-go, I had that stable, loving male figure in the form of a very present father. My parents were the epitome of a devoted couple. They never argued or yelled, which meant home was a utopian safe space, barring my older brother's tireless pranks involving hermit crabs, batteries, and small fires. Like most people, only in hindsight do I realize how lucky I was and how much of my youth was squandered on wanting to be older. Only later did I recognize the sumptuousness of my childhood, the wall-to-wall affection and solicitude from my parents that cordoned me off from the rest of the world. We lived in an eclectic East-meets-West household in suburban Washington, inside the beltway, a large house tucked at the end of a leafy cul-de-sac where children with braces scooted around on brand-new bicycles. "I want you two to have everything," Pramilla would say when I asked her why she came home from the office late. My father worked for Singapore

Airlines, which meant we sometimes traveled first-class free across the world—to India, to Singapore, to Hong Kong—but my mother was the breadwinner in our nuclear family, toiling away as the vice president of a defense-contracting company.

As a child in what was then Bombay (now Mumbai), all my mother had in her possession was a single doll and a few starched gray uniforms, part of the mandatory dress code at the private Protestant school my grandmother sent her to. The Partition of India had forced my grandparents and entire extended Hindu family to flee their homeland over half a century ago with my infant mother and scant belongings in tow. In August 1947, India won independence from the British after nearly two hundred years of Britain asserting its iron will over the subcontinent.[1] This was the result of a nationalist struggle lasting nearly three decades and the devastation of Britain's economy, which could no longer afford to hold on to its overextended empire. The outcome was two independent nation states—Hindu-majority India and Muslim-majority Pakistan—resulting in one of the biggest forced migrations in human history with nearly fifteen million people violently displaced from their homes. My family never returned to their sprawling bungalow in Karachi, a city on the coastline of the Sindh province in the southern part of the country. The oil paintings of our ancestors were left dangling on the walls to be caked with dust or burned along with the Persian rugs, furniture, and whatever else was too large to shove into the cars—all left behind in haste when machete-wielding angry mobs stormed down their wide boulevard with blood dripping from their hands (at least, that's the story I was told by my relatives who were old enough to remember it).

We were opposites: my mother was a refugee as a child, whereas I was an overindulged American with too many Cabbage Patch dolls. I had security, both financial and emotional, which made me fearless. By the time I hit my late teens, I harbored the belief that I could do anything and the world would catch me with its cushiony tongue, like some sort of trampoline. I gorged myself on small adventures: skydiving, bungee jumping, body piercing, psychedelic mushrooms. But the high from these thrills was short lived. As my graduation from New York University approached, I was anxious about what my career would be, especially as I'd been attracted to theology and designed my own college major around spiritual studies. My dissertation was focused on the rising popularity of new-age figures like Deepak Chopra, who was becoming a big deal in the 1990s, a time when the self-help industry was coming into its own. I'd been taking a compendium of philosophy and spirituality courses, but how would any of that translate to an actual job? All I knew was that I wanted meaningful adventure where I would be giving to the world instead of just taking from it.

Journalism seemed like the right path at first because it ticked the boxes: travel, adventure, gravitas. An internship at the BBC's Washington Bureau kicked off my ephemeral career. There, I had the unglamorous role of lugging bulky noncompliant cameras and tripods around Capitol Hill. I freelanced at CNN on *The Situation Room*, where I handled the intellectually rigorous role of disseminating scripts, mic'ing up guests—everyone from political talking heads to the Polish president—and on unlucky days, undertaking the nerve-racking duty of working the teleprompter, the magical device that allowed Wolf Blitzer and other anchors to read a script while maintaining eye contact with viewers. Even though I wanted to be like Christiane Amanpour, there was a ton of dues-paying that needed to happen before I was rocketed to some war-torn land and stuck in front of a live camera. In the end, nothing about working in TV news felt right; an off-putting bitterness permeated the industry. I also hated being in the control room and hearing uncharitable comments from the burrito-glazed lips of producers directed toward unsuspecting correspondents, their faces freighted with makeup as they waited for the camera to pan to them for their segment. I knew my skin was too thin, that I would have been timid and self-conscious on air, fumbling for the right words, incapable of communicating to a live audience in coherent sentences. I was an introvert disguised as an extrovert: being on live television every day would have frayed my nerves.

When I realized TV wasn't the way forward for me, I turned to print media. For a brief period, I freelanced in the Condé Nast Building when it was in Times Square. I navigated the crisp halls of *Glamour* and *Teen Vogue* without any ease whatsoever, cowered from the editors and their blowouts as they sashayed by, and knew I was not remotely fashionable enough to exist in that world. I left when the emptiness around me made me feel like I was hollowing out.

In desperate times, I did a handful of reporting assignments for financial news outlets—a subject I was totally unqualified to write about given my kindergarten-level grasp of anything related to finance. It also made me feel like I was treading the margins of some shadowy world. When I miraculously landed at *National Geographic* for a yearlong editorial stint, I thought it was the first step toward my new dream job of becoming a photojournalist, but quickly realized my role was entirely desk based and consisted of writing photo captions. I had a windowless office with a single overhead fluorescent light. I hammered away at my job until I found out that the traveling gigs were for veterans and I'd have to put in some serious time—like a decade—before I saw an African savanna or a melting iceberg. I was an idealist in my twenties; what I really wanted was to be *in the world*, active in it, not to read about it passively, not to be inside an office withering away when I had much to offer—or so I thought.

In between journalism jobs, I floated. I started an MFA in creative writing in LA before realizing I was too inexperienced to write anything poignant. I moved to San Francisco to work at a start-up just when the internet bubble burst. I went to India and studied Hindi. I was a paralegal for the US government for four drawn-out months with big plans to become a human-rights lawyer, but quit once I realized (after perusing a colossal book entitled *LSAT for Dummies*) that trying to pass the Law School Admission Test, and the eventual bar exam, would be a joyless endeavor.

I was restless and itinerant—that's for sure. My free spirit thrived on constant change, was addicted to not knowing what was next (it was more exciting than committing to one thing for a potentially interminable time frame). Every time I left a job that I could have stayed at, I felt tsunami-sized ripples of anxiety at the thought of being unemployed forever, but in the instances when I didn't have something already lined up or cooking, it felt as if I had to leave in order to figure out what I wanted next.

I later realized the discomfort many of us feel when we are *in between* places is actually the most fertile ground. Those unchartered interludes when I felt lost and insecure were when I grew and expanded the most (sadly, you don't grow in the same way when you're happy or insouciant).

During this time, I had a few overlapping relationships with men who were older than me. It began with an off-and-on, long-distance relationship with my first-everything—a soulful thirty-year-old British surfer named James, a fellow free spirit. I'd been interning for a music festival one summer in Paris as part of a yearlong study-abroad program. A break-in at my apartment in Le Marais caused me to move out, break up with my not-serious French boyfriend, and backpack south through the deepest parts of Spain and Portugal. I met James in the Algarve. He lived near Oxford where he was an electrician by trade and the lead singer in a popular local rock-and-roll cover band. He had come to Lagos on a surfing trip with his friends. We fell madly in love on a beach, and I gave him my virginity in Paris weeks later in the middle of a star-spangled summer night with *la tour Eiffel* in the background. We stretched out our unconventional relationship for three years and met up in different parts of the world—London, New York, Baja, Mexico, Los Angeles, Verbier, the Florida Keys, Biarritz, and San Francisco— sometimes for weeks at a time. Our relationship ended, ironically, on

Valentine's Day in Paris, when I realized I had outgrown him, or us, and I couldn't pretend anymore. He spent the whole night curled up in a ball on the floor crying, and even though I still feel guilty about the way things ended, I knew I had to live honestly, even back then. Another Englishman came into my life for a period of three years, a divorced advertising executive fifteen years my senior, whom I met while temping in San Francisco. Ashley was sexy and smart, loved dogs, and had a taste for the finer things in life. That relationship eventually ended, however, because he was cold and standoffish, which I later realized were symptoms of being afraid of emotional intimacy; besides, at twenty-five, I still had a bad case of wanderlust that precluded me from settling down. There was also a fling with an eligible bachelor in Mumbai that comfortably transitioned into an enduring friendship. And there was Niall, a rugged, poetic, old-souled Irishman I'd met in New York. He was a twenty-nine-year-old certified public accountant and part-time rugby player I'd met through a friend, and the one person who could look at me and see the whole of me, even when I could not, who knew who I was before I did. But at the time, I wasn't looking for that; I wanted to go off deep into the belly of the world instead. I was too young to appreciate when a person could see more of myself than I could, who loved me without overquestioning or overcomplicating things or fearing my free spirit. It was a rare, pure, grounded kind of love that wasn't imprisoned by expectations.

No doubt, beyond travel, beyond romance, I was also searching for something greater—a sense of purpose, but I didn't know what I was supposed to be doing exactly. I was equipped only with a vague sense of the direction I was going in and that it would involve writing in some capacity, the only thing that came relatively easily to me besides sleeping.

In retrospect, being a refugee's daughter had instilled some things in me: a deep connection to others facing hardships comparable to the one my mother's family went through, and a feeling of having to do something with the education I'd been given, the relative life of privilege I was born into. Even though she had no firsthand memories of fleeing the newly created Pakistan because she was only a baby at the time, the story of my family's sudden departure was repeatedly told to me by her older siblings—one of her older brothers and my beloved late aunt Devi, whom I lived with in Mumbai after college—and it had a haunting effect.

Also, I had been exposed to poverty at a young age, not as a victim but as an involuntary bystander during my childhood trips to India, a country where destitution goes largely unconcealed and is often more conspicuous than in other parts of the world. I remember wondering *why* people were living in the alley behind our apartment in Mumbai—half-clothed families sleeping, bathing, and eating on the street in squalor—and why we could see them doing all of these intimate activities from our balcony. As my brother devilishly pelted pomegranate seeds at any pedestrian who had the misfortune of walking underneath us, I was uncomfortable with the disparity I was witnessing, even though I obviously didn't understand any of it back then.

As nonsensical as it sounds, in the years after college, I'd reached a point in life where I was trying to step out of privilege and *into* suffering. While suffering does not discriminate based on socioeconomic status, I knew that I'd never really experienced deep suffering in my life, that I was too protected in my upper-middle-class bubble. It was almost as if some part of me craved, or needed, the entire human experience in order to feel complete. I wasn't looking for something as simple as love and a happy marriage—those things were too benign. In a way, I felt undeserving of them because I had already been given more than my fair share of fortune, and deep down I knew they wouldn't complete me in the way I wanted to be completed; they wouldn't round me out with the experience I needed to grow. For reasons beyond intellect, I needed to suffer and then, eventually, hopefully, make sense of it all. Or at least try to.

Eventually I was drawn toward humanitarian work. The United Nations soon rose to the top of my list of places to work, and I needed more qualifications to get a job there, so I moved to London where I got a master's degree from the London School of Economics (LSE). While Pramilla wanted me to focus on finding an eligible partner in grad school (LSE, attended by the sons of dignitaries and the well-to-do from all over the world, could be viewed as prime hunting ground for women who were ambitious that way, which I was not), I rebelled by dating a self-described entrepreneur who didn't go to LSE, an English guy from Essex—someone who was sharp yet mysterious in a sexy-dangerous way. I was pretty sure he worked for British intelligence. My parents met him when they came to visit and were not impressed, with Pramilla remarking after one particular dinner that he was "a master of fiction." In any case, that relationship fizzled out when I left London and tried to get a job at the UN in New York, which involved many failed attempts in spite of industrious networking, a bit of social capital, and a (quintessentially American) belief that if you want something badly enough, you will get it if you persist, especially if you come from the privileged place of having an expensive degree. I eventually made my way into the World Bank in Washington, DC, as a consultant and finagled an assignment that sent me to Lima. A couple of years later, I leveraged my experience in Peru to get a job in Rome at the UN. In Italy, I was a spokesperson liaising with the media against the backdrop of the deepening economic crisis of 2008, which meant the cost of food in many countries had skyrocketed and pushed the total number of hungry people in the world to over a billion. Angry mobs were rioting, looting bakeries and food trucks from Haiti to Bangladesh. It was a global crisis. I hit the ground running, challenged on every single front—intellectual, emotional, physical, and even spiritual.

Six years after deciding I wanted to work at the UN, I'd finally gotten there. At that point, I poured myself into my work and made it my primary focus—not love, not finding a relationship; that was all ancillary. When I left DC, I'd ended a relationship with a Swedish painter who was brilliant and kind, yet wild, overly attached, and in the middle of a drawn-out separation. Shortly after I landed in Rome, I was introduced to Alessandro, a Roman film director twenty years my senior, at a dinner party thrown by a colleague. While he was seductive and intellectual—and lived a life of leisure—I was moving up the career ladder, dealing with what seemed like a titanic amount of responsibility. Even though we dated for many months, I didn't have much time for la dolce vita beyond our nightly bottles of wine and occasional jaunts to the Teatro dell'Opera, which consisted of dreamlike evenings zipping across Rome on the back of his *motorino* with the wind whooshing through my hair, my arms snugged around his leather-jacketed torso. But most evenings, I came home late. "You live to work," he used to say in a slightly accusatory manner, while he leaned back in his armchair with a wine glass in one hand, a cigarette in the other. He may have been onto something. Unlike my mother, who had worked so hard for us, I wasn't really sure what I was working for or if I was actually making a difference at all. I *loved* it, though—the pace, the travel, the way it made me feel important—and I wasn't ready to make a commitment to anything else. I loved fully participating in an unruly, wild, aching, beautiful world.

I'd finally landed my dream job.

But dreams, of course, change.

———

Two years after the Pakistan floods and seven years after leaving New York, I was back. I moved to a less frontlines-focused job at headquarters, an office job where I could easily return to see my family in DC and keep a close eye on my father, who was suffering from a chronic lung condition that had taken a turn for the worse. The prognosis from the doctors was not encouraging—his lungs had almost entirely deteriorated from decades of smoking, and he was on oxygen. The year before, a real scare had landed him in the hospital and on a ventilator while I was posted on the Tunisia-Libya border during the war, which meant I had to travel the twenty-five hours it took to get home frozen in a state of anxiety. It was touch and go for a while, and I frantically checked status updates from my brother via text message all the way home, until I got to the intensive care unit at the hospital where I could hold my father's dry, familiar hand and watch the rise and fall of his chest against the chilling sound of equipment. He came through that time, though I knew I couldn't afford to stay so far away nor endure that type of panic-ridden journey across the world again. The truth was, my father needed me near him, in a safe place, living a normal life like other people's daughters, not traipsing around the world in danger's way.

Being back home in the US after several years overseas had assuaged my parents' anxieties, but mine escalated in a different way. His illness made me feel like I was running out of time. I wanted him to see me happily married, to meet my unconceived child. To walk me down the aisle like Steve Martin does in *Father of the Bride*. These are not things that he said he wanted, but I latched on to this absurd notion, probably as some sort of coping mechanism. In fact, while he worried about the occupational hazards that came with me traveling, often to sketchy places, he understood that appetite for adventure; I'd inherited it from him. He was proud of my accomplishments and never once mentioned that I should think about marriage or kids. Yet despite the growing number of women who were childless by choice, I felt that, at the very minimum, exploring the idea of becoming a mother was an important part of my path. I figured if I didn't start prioritizing, I might miss my chance. As much as I relished my freedom and my globe-trotting career, I also started to fear I would end up old and alone with straggly gray hair, living in the outskirts of Kathmandu, childless, grandchildless, hand-building wind chimes as a hobby, or gilded with tattoos and living in a hut made of coconut shells on a beach in Goa surrounded by hundreds of stray dogs. Even though I'd been happy on my own all these years, choosing freedom and career aspirations over relationships for the most part, the urge to settle down had kicked in. It was partly biological, partly social conditioning, partly cultural, but mostly driven by the mortality of the person who meant everything to me. The quiet apprehension that I'd been feeling about my love life while abroad suddenly surfaced, and I felt compelled to do something about it, to prioritize it for once so that everything could fit into this narrative of perfection. So I did what any twenty-first-century woman would do, something I'd never really actively done, or done in such a goal-driven way: I started to date, *a lot*.

I embarked on what I now realize was a monomaniacal boyfriend/husband-hunting mission that took me from Wall Street to the Upper East Side, across the Williamsburg Bridge, and into cyberspace. Even though my heart wasn't in it, I engaged in online dating, signed up for free high-end matchmakers (where, strangely, men in a city oversaturated with single women *pay* big bucks to meet single women *under thirty-five*), and subjected myself to the indignities of awkward blind dates. I said yes to every social event and likely incurred severe liver damage owing to the countless vodka martinis I imbibed while keeping an eye out for that special someone in between sips of Ketel One. I even joined a fancy gym, not because I intended to work out or enjoyed doing so, but on the off chance that I might meet someone special pumping iron next to me. All that ended up coming out of this was a continuous yearlong hangover and several uncomfortable incidents with an elliptical trainer.

I never thought it would be so ridiculously difficult to find love. I never thought I would have such a hard time meeting someone I liked, because I always used to meet people so easily. In my anxiety over my supposedly dwindling marriageability and fertility, I tried talking myself into suitors whom I would never have considered in my twenties. But in the end, *I would not, could not settle*. Even though that *New York Times* bestseller tells women to settle for Mr. Good Enough, I felt like throwing up at the idea of being with someone I didn't want to be with. It had to feel right—why would anyone do anything that didn't feel right in the gut? Yet the pickings seemed slim. There was something wrong with everyone, and it felt like the universe was conspiring to keep me unattached. Any single, dating woman in New York (once she has grown tired of the short-lived novelty that accompanies the early adventures of dating in the city) usually concludes that it can be a soul-destroying endeavor often involving creeps, players, social climbers, commitment-phobes, and way too much intoxication.

Where, oh where, was this elusive, heart-centered man, this tall and intelligent Indiana Jones, who also happened to be funny, clean, employed, multilingual, emotionally astute, and super deep? An old soul who exuded confidence, honesty, and patience and didn't feel an iota of insecurity around a woman who had maybe traveled more than he had? Where would I find this kind, democrat cowboy, who drank green juice, watched foreign films, and read the *New Yorker* but could also change flat tires and slay dragons if the occasion arose?

After months of hopelessness, I did happen to meet someone special, when I wasn't looking, of course. I'd just finished a rather rowdy game of billiards at the Gramercy Park Hotel and was about to head home when his group of friends approached my group of friends. I fell into conversation with a perfectly adorable, blue-eyed, fluffy-haired Frenchman named Jean-Claude. I was not into him at first, but he persisted in that Frenchman way, and we started dating. Here, in the flesh, was a guy who was kind and unjaded, who could do things like install air conditioners. A guy who made me laugh and was generally delightful to hang around with. But I wasn't the nicest, most charitable version of myself. By that point, my crazed manhunt mentality had taken its toll upon poor, unsuspecting Jean-Claude, whose only offense was his being ten years younger than me. I made him feel like he wasn't good enough for me, bruised his ego, and ended up sabotaging the whole thing. One day he looked at me with his soft blue eyes and said with a puppy-dog sadness, "I have nussing to offer you." Basically, he dumped me, and I was crushed.

A few months later, I started dating someone new who ticked a few superficial boxes: he was handsome, smart, and successful. There were some red flags that I foolishly chose to ignore, such as him admitting to having been a philanderer and self-identifying as selfish, as if it were a special religious community he was proud to be a member of (note to self: people tell you who they are). He was going through a divorce and living at the Crosby Street Hotel, across the street from where I was living at the time. But he broke up with me just days after the worst thing that could ever happen to me actually happened to me—my father died.

———

They say that traumatic moments can either drive us away from or toward our true selves, that it usually takes some sort of trauma or catalyst to push people where they need to be pushed, where they've been resisting going, and I needed to go very deep inside in order to come back out in one full piece.

If the death of a parent doesn't call everything into question, then I don't know what will. I reached the end of my role as my father's daughter, which felt, at least in part, like a stripping away of part of my identity. According to Carl Jung, midlife, somewhere near forty—then considered halfway between adulthood and the end of life—is a critical transitional point in our lives. He defined it as a period in which the true or essential self, the spirit inside us, begins a process of *separation* from the ego. The quest for meaning and purpose, and thoughts around mortality, take center stage. Apparently it is pretty common for people at this stage of life to get involved in some sort of physical or spiritual pilgrimage to find a deeper meaning in life, a symbolic holy grail.

After my father's death, I found myself breathing very shallow breaths as if I didn't want to breathe at all. Breathing meant living, and living was too sad. There was also anger underneath that grief: at life, for being unfair, for taking away one of the kindest human beings ever to grace this universe, yet allowing all sorts of broken, selfish, mean-spirited people to live. There was anger toward myself—I had failed to meet someone, which meant my father would never meet my child because I was selfish and hadn't made it a priority early enough. And my child would never know my father, know this amazing man who had existed; my child would see photographs of him, but never understand how significant he was in the whole scheme of everything. But the most anguishing part was knowing that I would never again nuzzle my face into his warm neck and smell the comforting, familiar whiff of 7-Eleven coffee, tobacco, and the sports section of the *Washington Post*. Never again hear his deep, reassuring voice, laugh at his sense of humor (dry jokes that could sometimes slip by if I was distracted), listen to him recall quotes from his favorite author, Mark Twain. I buckled under the realization that he was really gone: this gentle, well-loved human being who had been my rock for more than thirty years was no longer going to answer the phone with his cheerful hello when I called, or wait for me in anticipation in front of the house, in front of our red door, when he knew I was coming home. That was no longer my reality, and I wanted to wind the clock way, way back. The only tiny redeeming thing that kept me from disintegrating was that I had loved that man in the biggest way possible and had always made sure that he knew it.

Sometimes it felt as if we shared one soul—that we could communicate without even saying anything, and when he died, I had the sensation that he had melted into me, the way the tide gets absorbed into the sand, the cycle of nature. I was there in the exact moment, holding him as his body slumped into my arms. Days later, it was almost as if he hadn't gone anywhere because I could still hear his voice in my head. The scent of his Old Spice aftershave permeated the house as though it had just been pressed into his clean-shaven face, but of course he had gone, leaving behind little white pieces of paper on his desk, scribbled with some of his last musings. He, too, was a poet, a quiet one; he didn't advertise it or need attention for things like I did; he didn't need any external validation. It was the sight of these little things—like his handwriting, which had become shaky from all the medication—that would make me stiffen into a semicatatonic state, without knowing if I could ever find my way out of it. Even now, when I see my father's handwriting on the paper over by his computer in the office—all left untouched, all of our cell phone numbers, the number to Deer Park water delivery, his computer password written down in case he forgot it, the RadioShack caller ID, a dusty mug of mismatched pencils—I stop breathing for a few seconds. Then there is the plastic cup that I could not throw out. His favorite blue cup, a sheer blue, always half-full of water. I couldn't even throw out the water that he had sipped the day he died (and it finally evaporated—did it go where he went?). It was light to carry around, that cup. He liked the girth of it. He was very particular about the things he used, very minimalist. He liked that one cup only. He liked simplicity. As he got older, he had a visible nostalgia for his youth, which was largely spent outdoors in upstate New York, even in the bone-cold winters, playing by the Mohawk River with his older brother and their Great Dane, Helga. He encapsulated this period of his life in a self-published memoir, a series of "Cold Stories" entitled *Letters from Upriver* that he wrote because he wanted my brother and me to have these treasured memories of his. His writing had a playful, humorous style, and when I read through his stories again, there they were—all the things I was starting to yearn for myself, almost as if he were living through me now: a return to simplicity, the wholesome web of nature, and a heightened ability to live in the present, as if time were slowly rolling and nothing had to be done. The more complicated life was, the faster it went, the less happy I felt, and the more I felt like something was off, that I was on a path parallel to my real path and

I needed to cross over, somehow, but wasn't sure how. The questions started to come: How to uncomplicate life while still being a part of the world. How to live without compromising the authenticity of the soul. How to move forward without moving so fast that I would miss everything sacred.

I felt some sort of change happening inside me, but it was noiseless, invisible, like a new moon, there but not. I wasn't sure what was going on, but I was intuiting something. It was like looking up at a starless night sky—seeing nothing, but feeling something.

Back then, at my lowest point, as I hunched over my bed breathless from crying, I felt something subtle, intelligent, and powerful inside me. I didn't understand what it was, but I could tell that it was wise and that it could revitalize me in some way.

This is what I knew for sure:

whatever it was, it was good.
I needed to pay attention to it,
to cultivate its presence, even if I wasn't sure how.

On a visceral level, I knew this thing would save me. Or rather, *I* would save me, because it was a part of me—a piece of god or spirit or the universe, whatever you want to call it. Sometimes we call it *intuition* or our higher power. Whatever that mystical thing was, it was making itself known, and I needed to be wide open to it.

Darkness, it turned out, would be my ultimate teacher. The Buddhists consider suffering to be the ultimate gateway to awakening, and mine had brought me to a crossroads of sorts. One road was paved and would take me along a more conventional route. It was the more popular road because it was simpler to navigate, well lit, and easier to tread (and faster, even though there was more traffic). Here people had faces and everything was orderly and sterile. There was a solid framework, and things were done in certain ways and did not stray from those ways. The other was scarier, darker, less familiar, with shadows and turns and faceless beings and mountains to scale, but with a whole lot of mystique, with varying shades of light and wind that spoke, blowing in different directions and making everything feel circular rather than linear. It was the more unpredictable road, easier to get lost on, obscured with brambles. This road beckoned me, tugged at my heartstrings, but I hedged, afraid of losing everything familiar to me, of alienation. I feared I would become some lonely, ghostly figure. It was safer to stick to what I knew, but the familiar was no longer comforting to me.

———

Three years after my father's death, I still hadn't fully tended to that presence inside me. There was an invitation. It had been soft at first, though it seemed to gain power the sadder I felt. It was inviting me to let go of who I knew myself to be in order to allow for the possibility of who I might become.

It was inviting me to descend into the darkness to understand the expansiveness that was mine to be had, but I was deliberating.

Even though I'd been called to turn down that road, I was afraid of being alone with my grief, afraid it would eat me up and I would just be bones and sadness. I knew there was something rising in me, a flame almost, but I tried to douse it with distractions until it burned through those distractions. Maybe I didn't think it was time yet. While I was still functioning—working, breathing, living—my sense of hope and my normally cheerful disposition had dissolved. I didn't trust the universe anymore, even though I desperately wanted to free myself from the clutches of despondence. My career started to feel less impactful, being far removed from the places and people I wanted to help. The distance spawned a sense of helplessness that made the work feel less gratifying, and I didn't care about adding more accomplishments to my already unwieldy CV. I also felt a mild yet pervasive sense of discontent from living in a country that seemed more politically divided and hostile than ever before, as well as from the overly masculinized paradigm of how the world that I was trapped in functioned. If the world was the same shit-show it had always been—or if things were getting worse, people cared about each other less, and nothing was salvageable—then what *was* my purpose, what was the whole point of my being here on this planet? If big true love wasn't in the cards for me, if I wasn't going to do the whole distracting marriage-and-procreation thing, but still had to endure the loss of loved ones and the general pain that comes with empathetic living, I wondered what the point of everything was and how I was going to go on and find some measure of inner peace.

Viktor Frankl, who survived the Holocaust, said that we can't avoid suffering, but we can choose how to cope with it, find meaning in it, and move forward with renewed purpose.[2] That is where the meaning is hidden—in the suffering. It's the beating heart of life, without which everything feels arbitrary and numbing; otherwise, there's too much coasting without the undulations that make *life*—the lows low, the highs high. I had not experienced the horrors of Auschwitz. I was not a refugee. I had so much to be grateful for, but I did have my own pain. Instead of diminishing it, I knew I had to own it in order to struggle through it and make it to the other side. I started to realize that's the great human project: facing our suffering, moving through our struggles, and forging toward some kind of happiness and meaning.

I hated to think of myself as old, but clearly I was knee-deep in some sort of midlife crisis and hadn't even known it because I'd always associated it with older white men with sports cars. My only solace was that crossing this threshold was a pretty universal thing. I kept thinking of the opening line of Dante's *Divine Comedy*: "In the middle of the journey of our life I came to myself in a dark wood where the straight way was lost."

I decided to try to let go of whatever I thought my life was *supposed* to be and let it live out the way it felt like living itself out, without all the constraints and measurements I'd lined up against it. I was about to make a first attempt at surrendering, a small step forward and inside. There was an inner shifting, wordless, quiet like snow. I was at the beginning of the road—some kind of severance from the past, a change that was needed—at the start of a newer leg of my journey and, simultaneously, at the precipice of moving deeper inside. The path outside was beginning to mirror the path inside, but I did not know that yet. My intention was to find meaning in the suffering that I'd experienced and to consider how I could design my life so that I would feel whole, no matter what, and continue to carve my own genuine path without feeling like something was missing, especially *if* it was going to be me and only me forever. How could I, if love never came along, be content with myself, fill my life up so that there was no emptiness? How could I return to this sense of wholeness that was rightfully mine, just by virtue of being human? I'd grieve the stuff—the plans, the constructs—that was holding me back, a process of destructuring and deconditioning, and free myself from the tangle of expectations of whom I should be as a woman or where I should be in my life by now, and instead focus on becoming the person I was becoming.

Women are always asking the world what we want or need—measuring ourselves against the masculine paradigm of success, our quiet wants buried under the behest of the dominant social order—instead of asking ourselves what will fill *us* up. Well, I was asking myself now. And behind that question was a search—raw and unbending—for a radiant kind of truth.

I had no idea at the time, but I was about to start doing a different kind of saving—and it didn't involve saving anyone but myself.

Chapter 2

SURRENDERING

Forever—is composed of Nows.

—Emily Dickinson

"Good luck with that!" said Mads, blowing smoke directly into my face when I first told him I'd given up men for a while to focus on other things. Mads was my cantankerous boss, a gay chain-smoker from Denmark who was amused by the idea of a man-free self-discovery mission, as well as my deepening fixation with spiritual matters and overall well-being. Most of our meetings were held on the sidewalk in front of one of the UN office buildings owing to his tiring nicotine addiction. Crankiness aside, Mads's personal cocktail of sarcasm and cynicism was laced with an endearing affection for me. He had become faintly supportive of my self-help shenanigans, a pastime he used to ridicule mercilessly but of which, in recent months, he had become less disparaging. He was even intrigued by my project, which for the sake of brevity, I'd blithely called a "man fast," though that term would become painfully ironic.

In the three years since I'd lost my father, I'd still been looking for "true love"—for the man of my dreams to replace the man who had meant everything to me—even though I knew this was not just a tall order but, in fact, impossible. I'd had a string of unremarkable encounters over coffee or glasses of wine, but nothing stuck. There was no coup de foudre with any man the way I had it with James on the beach, no kind of physical attraction with a guy like I'd had with Ashley. James had long ago disappeared from my life. Had it not been for my photo albums, which showed us smiling and bronzed by the sun with our surfboards on various beaches, it would have been as if he'd never existed. Ashley and I were on friendly terms, but that was all. He'd had a vasectomy and was committed to living a bachelor's life with a rescue dog as his only live-in companion. Niall had moved to California with his wife and children, though they had recently decided to separate after ten years of marriage. We saw each other a handful of times over the years after he reconnected with me when he heard me being interviewed on the radio once for work. "You really did it," he said. "You made your dream come true." When he said that, I couldn't remember what my dream had been in the first place.

Back in New York, there were multiple dinners with a Norwegian guy, an Australian guy, a Canadian guy, and others—all met through work—but they were all disqualified for varying reasons: too cheerful, too morose, not deep enough, *too deep*, not intellectual enough, overly cerebral, too insecure, too arrogant.

You could argue that I'd been disqualifying plenty of men in New York even after a first date for arguably trivial reasons:

for licking his fingers after we ordered yucca fries (both hands, multiple times),

for repeatedly calling me by the wrong name (Natalie),

for not knowing where Addis Ababa is,

for eating meat off a stick,

for carrying a large wad of one-dollar bills in his pocket,

for being my height (5′3″),

for having a face slightly paralyzed by Botox,
for not having heard of *burrata*,
for wearing a beanie at dinner,
for having a visible herpes simplex virus breakout on his lip,
for snorting coke in the bathroom between courses,
for wearing a tooth around his neck,
for being on Atkins,
for reviewing the bill like he was studying for the bar exam,
for not having eyelashes,
for wearing raspberry-colored trousers,
for asking me for a blow job,
for telling me he dreams of a Range Rover full of offspring.

The list goes on. Maybe I was exhibiting signs of being a shallow person. But I didn't *feel* like I was shallow. Maybe being picky and having high expectations was one of my largest flaws, the thing standing between me and what I thought I wanted. Maybe I was trying to find someone like my father and was bound to be disappointed over and over again because there was no one like him. Maybe keeping my options open (a very New York thing) had left me with no options. It was the Barry Schwartz conundrum—the wealth of choices in the modern era can actually be a major source of distress for us, and when we're faced with too many choices, we become almost paralyzed by options and simply don't decide on anything.

Or maybe I'd eliminated everyone on purpose because I wanted to be alone. Perhaps, on a subconscious level, I knew there was work to do that I could only do by myself.

Besides, the search for that perfect partner felt much less meaningful after my father died. I knew I needed to accept that invitation to go inward, which meant disengaging from the superficial external world of dating. I couldn't do the internal work I needed to do, the reflective, powerful contemplation, while having trivial conversations with strangers I'd met over dating apps—or even with people I knew—when I wasn't ready to reveal what was going on inside because I didn't even *know* what was happening to me.

In fact, giving up men for a while opened up new space in my life. I had channeled my grief into poring through indiscriminate stacks of spiritual books, and the poetry of the mystics had lost its resonance. There is only so much comfort one can get from reading—the experiential component of healing is also necessary. I didn't know what that would be for me or how to do it, only that it had to be lived to be understood. Weekend workshops at brand-name self-help retreat centers like Esalen, Kripalu, and Omega did not do much to alleviate my existential angst. I needed something . . . different? More? Deeper? I needed to spend less time trying to absorb someone else's formula for enlightenment and more time prying open doors and windows into the neglected and dark places within myself, by myself, on my own terms—whatever those turned out to be.

I was also wary of cultism, having met people at retreat centers who, in desperation, had handed over their power to a so-called spiritual leader without even realizing it. I did not seek a guru outside of me— only my internal guru, and I needed time to find her. I needed to find healing, nourishment, and inspiration after the years of grief, romantic disappointment, and working in zones of catastrophic suffering without time to process what I'd witnessed. I thought of a Rumi verse that asked, "And you? When will you begin that long journey into yourself?" With every breath that tumbled out of me, I felt myself trying to answer back, *Now. Now. Now.* More than ever, what I needed was a pilgrimage to the center of myself, and I couldn't get there by swiping on Tinder.

But when I tried to explain it all to Mads, I struggled to find the right language.

"What I'm saying is that this is not *just* a dating detox," I told Mads. I'd searched for the right words to describe something that was, in actuality, ineffable. "It's a period of self-inquiry, an exploration of my whole way of being." It all sounded silly and esoteric when I tried to verbalize it. I didn't even know what I was trying to explain!

Mads rolled his eyes. He had very little patience for what he termed my "new-age bullshit," though it all felt more old-age to me. I told him not to worry about it, that it was a *cleanse* of sorts. At least now he would stop calling me a love addict—an accusation that put me on the defensive only because there was more than a kernel of truth to it. Admittedly, I was addicted to the idea of love, to the tantalizing yet punitive search for romantic love, more than the actual reality of what a relationship entailed. Like many, my hesitation was in part because I wavered between too much aloneness and the fear of engulfment, of descending too much into myself and total suffocation by another, and I'd been in that in-between space for some time, using writing people off as an excuse (though in my defense, many of them deserved to be written off).

I knew why he didn't get it. People who were open to the subtle mystical persuasions of the universe, which are as pervasive as the gravity that keeps us from rising into the sky but are largely ignored—they got it. My closest female friends who, by no coincidence, were walking their own spiritual paths in some form—they got it. *Yes!* They would say. *Do it,* whatever *it* was. When I told my friend Camila, a feisty Ecuadorian living in London who moonlights as my life coach, what was going on with me, she quoted a Chinese proverb: "Pearls don't lie on the seashore. If you want one, you must dive for it." I took that to mean that if I wanted to unearth some answers inside me, I couldn't just skim the surface of myself. I had to go deep.

Like many people, 90 percent of the time, Mads seemed lost in the crushing responsibilities he held at work or his nonstop relationship sagas. I was prone to falling into the same trap. My mind was always somersaulting way ahead of where I actually was or jammed up in something, perhaps to distract myself from the piles of grief stuck inside me. Eckhart Tolle says stress is caused by being "here" but wanting to be "there." It was true: I strained to appreciate the moment. The moment has a menacing quality to it. It allows everything to surface that we might not feel ready to confront. That was something that *had* to change in the coming months.

When I thought about it, getting off the dating merry-go-round was only a part of what I needed to do, but it was a necessary first step. Stopping the hunt for someone else to magically make my life what I thought it was *supposed to be* was the prerequisite for what I was beginning to see as a recalibration, a quixotic experiment in self-redefinition. A rebirth. I was in an in-between place, and it was delicate. I had to remove myself from the male world for reasons that were deeper than I understood. I had to reconnect with my hungry feminine side, the neglected parts of me that had recently come to meet me out of nowhere as soon as I looked their way, calling on me to run off to the art store to buy oil paints and canvases and spend all weekend alone painting monstrous, misshapen sunflowers; to take a course in the Japanese healing arts; to go on a rampage buying sea salts and essential oils to make large jars of salt scrubs for friends; to sit in a room with a bunch of strangers and chant in Sanskrit on a Friday night instead of going to a bar; to write poetry and streams of consciousness on any open surface, in the margins of my journal, not for any other reason than for self-expression.

Evidently the path forward still felt unclear to me. Yet I was pretty sure this whole exploration was going to require time, and space, to reap any benefits. Like most women with full-time jobs, however, I found free time in short supply. Every woman I know has bucketloads going on career- or family-wise or both, maybe because they have to work harder to get to the top, or because they have to prove themselves, or because they have to pick up the slack from their partners, and yet— with all that external stuff going on, the climbing the corporate ladder, the scheduling of playdates—they often forget to take the time to truly meet themselves.

By keeping myself busy, I didn't have to feel any sense of loss; I could be safely sealed in a pseudocollective trance. At times, I was frantically active in a way that swallowed up the existence of a meaningful inner life, almost as if I had been afraid to have one. My relationship with my inner world was estranged, namely because I was always focused on what was next in my conquests. Yet if I was going to discover what would be truly *enlivening* for me, what was healing and enriching, I would need to slow down and do the whole mindfulness thing for real.

A chance fortune cookie told me to be brave enough to live creatively, so I tried. I cut back my hours at work (though doing so induced recurring nightmares of destitution and homelessness). Switching from a full-time position at the UN to working as a consultant allowed me to unclench some psychic muscles for what felt like the first time in years. I also redirected my efforts from the near-frantic pace of emergency humanitarian response to the slower-paced but still important support for global health issues. This shift gave me more flexibility to choose how to focus my time. I even moved out of my one-bedroom apartment in Manhattan and into a friend's three-bedroom share in Brooklyn to save money on rent—a mammoth adjustment after living on my own most of my adult life.

Pramilla was worried. "Just remember, employers are less likely to hire you at forty," she remonstrated when I told her that, at thirty-eight, I was going to switch to part-time freelancing for a year, or for as long as I could afford it. Even though I wasn't sure she was right about the HR prospects, I tried to reassure her that the change was temporary. I was going through a wee midlife crisis, that was all. Nothing to worry about.

"I refuse to make fear-based decisions," I countered, with a surprising degree of calm, even though I was scared by what was happening inside me. "Osho said that fear is the antithesis of freedom. That it degrades my humanity."

Pramilla did not give two hoots about the teachings of a controversial (and now dead) Indian mystic. Like any mother, she wanted me to have a solid grasp on my own financial security, especially if I was going to remain single—all too possible given my track record. While the notion of dying alone in poverty because I was disorganized and impetuous made my heart quiver, and not in a good way, I knew that if I was really down and out, I could scoop up an assignment in Sudan or Yemen, places no one wanted to go. Although that prospect darkened her mood even more, deep down she trusted me to make the right decisions for myself. She was a dependable oasis of emotional support, even if she had no clue why I had to make everything so flipping complicated.

Neither did I, but I knew I needed to find out.

———

Anxiety can snake out from so many corners of us, and I understood where my mother's anxiety came from. The early years of her life were shaped by a depth of insecurity that most of us would find unfathomable. The aftereffects of India's Partition were catastrophic for the family. Her father had been a prominent barrister in Karachi but was forced to rebuild his career from the ground up when the family fled their homeland. Those social, economic, and personal ruptures drove my grandfather to a nervous breakdown. Two years after Partition, he went to Tripura in northeastern India, where he had found some work through his legal connections, leaving his wife—my grandmother Bhabhi—and their six children in a two-bedroom apartment in what was then Bombay. Months went by with no word from him, so Bhabhi and her oldest son set off to find him. Following a word-of-mouth trail, they eventually located him—at an ashram in the famed tea-producing region of Assam, in the foothills of the Himalayas. He had completely changed. As a young man, legend goes, he'd been a bit of a playboy, fond of drinking and smoking, but after Partition, after the ashram, he became quieter, withdrawn. Perhaps that was his midlife crisis, triggered by geopolitical events out of his control. He developed Parkinson's disease and died before my brother and I were born.

My grandparents' marriage had been arranged for them, a standard for the time. Sometimes I sit in our hallway and leaf through formal black-and-white portraits of them stored in an antique chest, and I wonder what their marriage was like. Their postures have an almost-military stiffness in the photographs, as if they were fulfilling duties assigned to them, without objection. Their lives were expected to be about family, community, safety in numbers—rarely about the solitary self. That was extravagant.

So I was intrigued to discover that my grandfather had spent time at an ashram after he lost his home, as I had after my father died. I passed a month at a sparsely populated spiritual center in upstate New York ensconced in a galaxy of maple trees. Evidently, my grandfather had gone looking for something too. I suspected we were kindred spirits and found myself wishing I'd known him.

Perhaps he had also discovered that it can become impossibly difficult to remain in a familiar structure—whether a family or a profession—when something inside you is demanding to get out. Maybe for some souls the clamoring subsides with time, diminishes into a vaguely muffled dissatisfaction, and whatever was struggling to become real remains unmanifested. For others, maybe the clamoring becomes persistent, deafening, impossible to ignore. That seems to have happened to my grandfather. I felt it happening to me, and I was frightened by what had impregnated me and was driving me toward unusual choices and pulling me in mysterious ways. Tending to it felt like an indulgence, but of the most crucial kind.

On the one hand, I was acting entitled and irresponsible by leaving a more secure path for an insecure one, yet I was call-heeding. Given the choice between freedom and security, freedom would always win with me. Creating space and carving out time were investments in my well-being. While a lot of women simply cannot leave their jobs just because they're unhappy, or change something that desperately needs changing or launch some great adventure because tight finances or unyielding personal obligations stand in the way, sometimes the barrier is truly a fear of the unknown. Paring down to the basics can be uncomfortable, but it can create room for a different kind of abundance.

Slowing down and reaching for freedom can be surprisingly scary because it opens up a space in which we *fully emerge*, whether we mean to consciously or not. We can fear the truth of ourselves, the power we have.[1] We are afraid that wielding that power will transform the way we know ourselves to be, our identities, demand new visions for the landscape of our lives, and it will. It changes who we were becoming or had planned to become.

I was ready, even as I felt shadowed by mountains of fear about every aspect of the journey before me. I had no choice but to put my essential self before my professional self. It was a matter of self-preservation. I didn't know exactly what I was going to do, but I was absolutely certain that I needed to do something, and that was enough.

And thus I accepted the invitation, still there, yet stronger and louder, from some place beyond anything I knew, and the scariest part was that it was asking me to sever myself from my ordinary world in order to grow. The deal it seemed to be making with me was twofold: If I wanted to reclaim myself, I had to let go of the things that made me feel secure. Likewise, to go in and expand back outward, I had to let go of the narratives in my life that were disempowering. I had to let go of what I didn't need and what I was not; it was a real disrobing.

And if I wanted to learn to trust the universe again, I had to move forward with a peaceful, questioning kind of faith—and leave everything else behind.

The change I needed to explore all of this stuff, nebulous as it felt, was to get away. I was burned out. My acupuncturist, Lian, a radiant Chinese woman, was always imparting advice: Put chia seeds in your water. Eat simple foods. *Leave New York.* That was her big thing for me, though she was only repeating back to me what I'd been wanting to do for some time. "You don't want to become one of those high-stress career women," she'd warn me, as if I hadn't been already. Some people thrive on stress and busyness, or *think* they do, reveling in the projection of importance it gives them. Inconveniently, given my current home base, I was not one of those people. She introduced me to her husband, a martial arts practitioner from Puerto Rico who taught Qigong—an ancient Chinese form of moving meditation—in the East Village (yes, they are the most aligned couple). In one of his classes, he mentioned wu wei, a Taoist concept that basically means doing nothing or going with the flow. Action that does not involve struggle or excessive effort.

"We train our mind to allow our actions to be in alignment with the flow of life," he explained. "We merge with what we are doing."

When there's too much thinking going on, we can't reach this state. It's big in Taoist ideology, the not-struggling thing, and I was fully on board, though I didn't know how to jump from struggling to not-struggling, to flow. I wasn't sure if I could step into the flow in New York; the river seemed to circle around the city, not through it. Maybe it was just a matter of finding the right entry point. Maybe I had to leave and come back in at a different angle.

"Go off into the wilderness and find the love you're looking for," urged Lian, as she poked needles across my torso. "This city is not for you right now."

I wasn't looking for love, I reminded her. I was taking a *break* from love, I said in earnestness, to which she just smiled.

Truthfully, I'd long wanted to work remotely anyway, preferably somewhere without fluorescent lighting. I suppose most of us dream now and then of escaping the lockdown of our office environments to work on our laptops from artisanal coffee shops, claw-foot bathtubs, or a Greek island. Telecommuting was becoming a norm across several industries, though the UN seemed eons behind on that front. I adored my colleagues and the familial vibe at the office, the aroma of hot grease on Waffle Wednesday, and the reassurance of having people who noticed my whereabouts, who would hopefully call the NYPD if I didn't show up to work for several consecutive days. But the growing need to get away, at least for a while, so that I could find something that could be best described as *clarity*, overpowered the comforts of a familiar environment and the security of being surrounded by a network of friends. There was something rising in me, and where I was, there was not enough space to let it come out. I had been trying to leave New York for months but kept getting pulled back by various things—and one major thing, or person—but now it was time.

I hadn't even "properly" processed the death of my father before I jumped, or fell, into a relationship that made me question everything I thought I knew about love. It was fast and unknowable, and it had ended. This particular loss had split me open at the navel, and I had to stitch myself back together and grieve yet another loss. This would require an escape, because New York is not the kind of place to walk around with raw wounds, with organs dangling off the sides of us, the heart wild and red and thumping in the sooty heat of the subway platform. I had to be far from the source of that sorrow. I had to reconcile the outside of me with the inside of me, and I needed to retreat somewhere, anywhere but where I was, to reach those distant places inside me that, in the end, turned out to be closer than they seemed.

I had worked hard for Mads, delivered every kind of brief imaginable, sat through marathon meetings and conference calls, and churned out editorials, talking points, and press releases at the drop of a hat. I could manage my workload from anywhere with a decent internet connection, and I could easily make the case that to be able to communicate powerfully, to do any compelling form of storytelling, I would need to be out in the field collecting stories and interviewing people, taking photographs and giving new faces to age-old problems like poverty and discrimination.

But I didn't really need to go down that road—I knew Mads didn't have the will to face the grueling bureaucratic process of bringing on someone new when I was already immersed in multiple projects. I was good, or at least good enough, and I was a known entity, tried and tested—that gave me a lot of leverage.

On a chilly day in November, while he was on a work trip in Uganda, I decided to send him an email. I did not beat around the bush—my subject heading proclaimed, "Can No Longer Live in New York." I knew it would have been better to do it in person, but he was gone for weeks on end, and the New York winter would soon take on a frigid, merciless shape. The winter before, I had found myself accidentally locked out of my apartment during a blizzard the media had named Snowmageddon. As snowflakes nestled themselves into my eyelashes, I'd vowed to myself,

This is my last winter in New York.
This is my last winter in New York.
This is my last winter in New York.

Yet there I still was, on the verge of allowing another winter to make my bones brittle. In my email to Mads, I proposed that I work remotely from India, where we had a substantial portfolio of projects, for an indefinite stretch of time. I made the case that I would be in a better position to advocate for them from within the same time zone. To my advantage, life in Mumbai would be hot, spiritual—and free, because my family still had an apartment there, in my grandfather's name. It would be a bridge to the next world, and maybe a way to get over to the other path I could faintly sense. Even though India was hardly unfamiliar, *I was approaching the change of environment with the intention of transformation.* I knew I would lose something, but I had to lose it to gain what was meant to be gained, even though I had no clue what that would be.

Mads relented. He agreed to let me telecommute for several months, providing that the arrangement didn't disrupt my workflow and that I made myself available at hours that suited New York. I figured being on a conference call at midnight was a small price to pay for freedom. For all his sassy and cutting jabs, I suspected he had an almost brotherly kind of affection for me. He had picked up on my angst; he saw it because he, too, had it (many of us have it but don't necessarily understand the roots of it, instead trudging along in a permanent state of mild discontent). I'd once read, "Monotony collapses time; novelty unfolds it," and this can make our lives seem longer than they are.[2] Our lives are meant to be expansive and enchanted—something we understood as children but often lose sight of as adults. I wanted to come back to that. I was also searching for a regenerating experience that would allow me to walk in the sunlight again without denying the darkness. I needed space to do that. In Japan, there is a word for it: *yutori*. I was asking for spaciousness.

Even though I didn't know what this quest would reveal about myself, even if I was going down some path that I couldn't turn back from, the moment had come to step off the moving walkway of my life. When I thought about what that meant, I felt weightless, as if I was being lifted out of my old life and floating somewhere in the ether. The space was intimidating, like swimming for the first time. Yet the request had come from the bottom of my soul, and because it came from such a raw, honest place, and because the stars and planets decided to conspire in my favor, I got the green light to go to India, to step into what would eventually come to feel like an inexplicable *flow*.

———

India is a maddening place, but it's my second home. I have been going there since before I could even crawl and staying at the same family home in south Mumbai, sometimes for long stretches at a time.

The country can be mind-blowingly spiritual, but it can also be the opposite—congested, noisy, fast-paced, and chaotic. As a sort-of Indian woman, I was never "allowed" to have the hippie-backpacking experience of India or an eye-opening spiritual experience like the Beatles had; I never smoked hash in an ashram in Rishikesh or rubbed shoulders with a self-proclaimed guru. The mere notion of that kind of traveling was always frowned upon, and relatives repeatedly warned me of the risks for a woman traveling alone in India. On past visits, I was typically saddled with family obligations: relatives tried to plump me up on chutney sandwiches while interrogating me about my lack of a husband. I tried to explain that I had a flourishing career, but interest in my professional accomplishments waned quickly, and the conversation always veered back toward the question of settling down. While part of me found these exchanges amusing, they did niggle at me by making me feel incomplete. Another part was frankly pissed off: I'd covered more of the world than most people ever would, but I was still seen as half a person because I hadn't shacked up with some dude. I couldn't consider marrying anyone I didn't already love, but in India, it was understood that love comes after marriage.

For an unmarried woman, I am now considered downright ancient by Indian standards. This is a huge relief as I don't have to face any more ad hoc introductions to putatively eligible Indian men by extended family members. Also, many of the most energetic attempted matchmakers have passed away, or age has left them too busy tending to their own aches and pains to meddle in my romantic affairs. To them, I am a lost cause no doubt, a Western woman with Western values (whatever those are). As my aunt Devi used to say to me, "You have chosen to become a career woman instead of a married woman." She didn't say it in a negative way; she herself had never married, which was unusual for her generation, especially in the land of arranged marriages, though she certainly dished out loads of unsolicited advice on the subject. She used to tell me that the best kind of husband would have "the five melons": health, wealth, wisdom, character, and education. "I'm only sixteen," I reminded her the first time she introduced me to the melon concept, which was, according to her, some sort of Sindhi legacy, the genesis of which no one seemed to know (which meant she probably made it up).

Aunt Devi ran public relations at Air India in the 1970s when aviation was glamorous and its jobs coveted. She globe-trotted with India's elite, regularly meeting celebrities and often showing up on our doorstep wrapped in a flamingo-colored sari and bearing a suitcase stuffed with ashtrays, bath towels, and other paraphernalia branded with the airline's iconic mascot, the maharaja—a chubby, turban-capped Indian prince with a distinctive mustache.

While Aunt Devi was a witty storyteller whose company I relished, the label *career woman* did not sit well with me. Something about it sounded very selfish, in a 1980s pantsuit kind of way. I understood that she came from a generation of women who thought in such binaries, but I argued that a woman could have both—love and a career—as her sister Pramilla did. Of course today a woman can have even more than that—be a wife, or have an open relationship or a polyamorous relationship, or stay single—arguably without quite as much scathing judgment, though they still use the term *spinster* in a nonsatirical way in India. That's the beauty of being in an age of tremendous transition, where new forms of family are more often becoming the norm. In that sense, we are all reinventing the landscape, crossing an uncharted territory plush with choice. Yet Aunt Devi remained obstinate: her view was that while my father may have been completely comfortable with my mother being the breadwinner, *most* men were threatened by a woman's intelligence and success, and if I were to pursue that path, I would have to dumb myself down in front of them. Simone de Beauvoir said essentially the same thing.

I didn't follow that advice, and I wasn't married.

The path that I had chosen was different, but it was my own. What was meant to be a circle became a weird shape I'd been making my way around for years, with detours that allowed me to live life more deeply than I would have had I stayed on the expected path and played it safe.

Eventually, I hoped, I was going to close in on why.

———

Pramilla tagged along for the first month. She needed her annual dose of the motherland, both to visit relatives and to check on the apartment, where the tropical climate reduced everything to a perpetual state of crumbling and the need for repairs was constant.

My mother is a warrior: she is, hands down, the most resilient person I know. She has lost three brothers, a sister, both of her parents, and her husband, yet she still manages to get up every day, to run her own business, to be generous and huge-hearted with others, and to elude the temptations of bitterness. There is an underlying darkness in her, a palpable sadness that I can detect because I know her, but she forges on because that is what the human spirit beckons us to do. If rebuilding my strength was a goal to pursue in these first couple of months away, then it made sense to begin in the company of someone who had long set a powerful example.

The other remarkable thing about Pramilla is that she is a revolutionary woman without even trying to be and without having any self-awareness that she actually is one. At age one, she was a refugee; at age nineteen, she was sent far from home—all the way to the US, to live with older brothers who had emigrated before her—by my grandmother when it was suspected she was seeing a boy from "the wrong kind of family." In her new world, she lived with one of her brothers, went to college at night, and worked part-time during the day. At age twenty-four, she wrote to her parents and told them she had fallen in love with an American man and was going to marry him. They sent a frenzy of blue aerograms, slender and tissue thin, which fluttered through her mailbox each week, seeking to dissuade her, but she did not budge. In fact, she flew to India with my father in tow and forced the family to accept him.

When Pramilla went to meet her new in-laws in upstate New York, it was the first time she had ever seen snow. My father's parents, a landscape architect and a teacher, were taken aback by her; not only did she have a lively personality and flashy fashion sense, but she was one of the few brown-skinned people back then to pass through the small, mostly white town. Fortunately, they were progressive and big hearted—they immediately welcomed her into the family with open arms.

I often wondered where my mother got her strong sense of self, especially at such a young age. They say most women grow up to become their mothers. I welcome that. I hope for that. Yet my younger self felt much more whimsical and flighty, unarmed and sensitive to the point of near paralysis. Anything could make me cry. I was often sad as a child, when I had zero reason to be, none at all. This is where I wonder if epigenetics plays a role in our characters, if we can carry sorrow from our ancestors, held in our bodies like a yolk is held within an egg. It doesn't know why it is there, but it just is. As I matured and adapted to the world of humanitarian work, I slowly realized the strength in vulnerability, that emotion and empathy were powerfully human, not weaknesses. When seen as drawbacks, they can feel crippling, but when their quiet power is allowed, they become the key to connecting with others.

Pramilla was tough, though. She had her shield and her weapons. I'm pretty sure she was some sort of benevolent dictator in a past life. She mellowed with time, but growing up under her parenting elicited feelings of terror in my brother and me. She had a very short fuse. If we misbehaved, she would threaten to leave us and move back to India. Sometimes she even went into her room to start packing, which made us hysterical. Then my father, the peacemaker, would intervene and calm everything down. While she was warm and beautiful, the kind of woman your eyes would land on in a crowded room, she could be temperamental and domineering—always fiercely protective of my father, self-identifying as a tigress when it came to him. When she was seven months pregnant with my brother, she went to a Christmas party with my father where booze was free flowing. Some drunk started to pick a fight with him, which was unusual because he was even-tempered and good-humored, not the type of person people got upset with. As the man became aggressive, my mother stepped in between them with her big belly jutting out and pushed the man to the floor.

In other ways, she was conservative and traditional. There were some things you just didn't talk about, which is very Indian. For example, she never told me about sex (what it was, how to do it). Nothing from my father either. Everything I knew about sex as an adolescent came from a large illustrated version of the *Kama Sutra* I had discovered in a dust-covered box in our basement one rainy summer afternoon when I'd tired of Paula Abdul videos and started poking around for something to do. When I came across this glossy semi-instructional book, I felt I'd hit the jackpot. I showed it to my brother, to which he responded, "Ew! Put that back. It must be Mom and Dad's." We barfed in unison. I skulked back downstairs but continued to leaf through it. Sex was a mysterious adult thing like taxes and politics but, unlike taxes and politics, not necessarily negative. It apparently involved contorting your body into very strange yoga-like positions, however, so I avoided it for a long time because it looked so uncomfortable.

Likewise with love. I avoided it until I decided not to anymore. But when I'd started searching for it back in New York, I was perplexed at how something so familiar could seem so elusive.

Just like my mother. She was familiar to me of course; there were pieces of her in me, and there were equal pieces of my father in me, and perhaps their ancestors, but there was a whole other mysterious part of me—of all of us—that didn't belong to anyone. This shared landscape perplexed me. I'd caught a glimpse of whatever it was, once, on psychedelics. If, biologically, I came from two people, then I wanted to know what this unknown piece of me I was carrying around was all about, why it was there, and if, maybe, perhaps, it held the answers to the questions I didn't even know I'd had.

I'd heard that India was the place to do that kind of searching.

———

Embarking on a mindful, more balanced, and healthier approach to living took concerted effort, focus, and sobriety, and at every moment I felt that it could be derailed in Mumbai even more easily than in New York. While I had more physical space—a welcome change from the series of minuscule, misshapen apartments I'd inhabited in New York—my mental space was constantly under threat. Trying to tune out the perpetual hammering, sawing, and construction sounds in the building, along with the clouds of dust that seemed to torpedo in from nowhere, proved challenging. A string of inconvenient but necessary visitors arrived throughout the day, announced by our shrill doorbell, so startling it could wake someone up from a coma: the *dhobi wallah* to collect dirty laundry, the Bisleri guy to collect plastic bottles for recycling, the trash guy for his weekly tip, the grocery man delivering a weekly supply of vegetables, and various repairmen to fix the never-ending stream of broken things—pipes, outlets, stove burners—though never all in a single day, of course. That was the charm and exasperation of India. The evenings brought their own sonic assault: it was wedding season, and our apartment is behind the Cricket Club of India, which doubles as a popular wedding venue, so most evenings were marked by hours of Bollywood music blaring through antiquated speakers and megaphones. Only around three in the morning can you experience a delicious pocket of silence in Mumbai. The crows that caw like maniacs all day long fall silent, the incessant honking of taxicabs subsides, the bone-rattling construction sounds cease, the random wails in Marathi are fewer, and the street sweeping stops. All that is left is the warm embrace of a city promising to spill into another day of sweat, dreams, and chaos.

Despite such petty grievances, I forced myself to review my inventory of reasons to be grateful: not to have to hustle in the morning and commute to an office, not to face snowstorms and subways, not to pay rent, and to be in a place that was more spiritual by default. Taxicabs carried shrines dedicated to various Hindu deities, and the green lawn of the Cricket Club of India became a massive outdoor yoga space each morning, which meant I was awakened by three resounding oms instead of the alarm on my phone. The internet, while sluggish, did not let me down, so I could carry on with necessary work remotely. And I was certain that it was only a matter of time before I felt *spiritual*, before I felt connected to that subtle, intelligent, powerful thing inside me, the one that I knew was there, that had softened its tenor and was now speaking to me in a hushed tone, like the wind, that I could hear only if I was listening for it.

Increasingly drawn to anything in the so-called mystical arena, especially as I inched closer to forty, I made an appointment with a shadow reader—a kind of fortune-teller who reads shadows—a couple of weeks after I arrived. I was hoping he would say something to make me feel less lost, cook up a prediction that would assure me that I was on the right path, moving in the right direction, that good things were coming, that I'd eventually tap into that sense of peace inside. According to what I read, this fellow could glean a lot about my life based on detailed calculations of the dimensions of my shadow on the pavement when I stood in the sun. Judging by our conversation over the phone when I booked the appointment, I knew I would need help with the Hindi. Pramilla, who has superstition in her DNA, likes the theatrics of this kind of thing and happened to be a die-hard fan of *Long*

Island Medium, the reality television series starring Theresa Caputo, an Italian American woman with distractingly long nails and a knack for communicating with deceased souls in New Jersey. After briefly feigning resistance, Pramilla agreed to come along and serve as my translator.

Before we even entered the building, we were both keen to turn around, as the entire edifice seemed to be disintegrating before our eyes. An emaciated cow meandered through a large pile of colorful waste in front of the entrance, her long tail flicking at flies as she chewed on a heap of discarded potato peels. Pramilla, chic in a wrap dress, wanted to go straight to the Taj Palace for the Sunday Champagne brunch, but I assured her that the scuzzier the building, the more authentic the reading. This one might give me insight into some important aspect of my life and the spiritual journey I was on. When she remained unconvinced, I stooped to dangling Roger Federer: perhaps this mystical man knew where his clone was hiding.

Gingerly, we climbed broken staircases and refrained from touching the dirt-caked handrailings, careful to step over the stray kittens splayed on the landings. When we entered the room at last, the shadow reader and his son, both of whom were adorned in high-necked white *kurtas* and had matching hairy knuckles, hugged us like long-lost relatives. The son then guided me up a very wobbly ladder to a grimy rooftop in the pressure-cooker heat and instructed me to stand still and face into the blinding sun while he measured my shadow for a painstaking quarter of an hour, something he'd apparently been trained to do since age three. Back inside, the father-son duo seated us in rickety chairs as they began their analysis. The sun streamed in through the clouded window as papa shadow reader spent an hour telling me what was in store for the rest of my life in five-year increments up to age seventy-five, after which he could "see" no further. His predictions were pretty clearly pieced together from information about me he'd managed to wrangle out of my mother while I was sweltering on the rooftop. The baby shadow reader sat silently as his father droned on. I stared at a pearly yellow Ganesh, or elephant god, resting idly in a glass contraption, reading a book of sorts. I should have brought my small wooden Ganesh statue along with me on the trip. Ganesh, also known as Ganesha or Ganapati, is the god of wisdom and good fortune, and mine was swaddled in wool sweaters and stashed in a storage unit in the Bronx with the rest of my belongings. Ganesh—one of the most worshipped Hindu gods in India, a deity whose images I've been looking at in various incarnations since childhood—reminds us to tap into our own wisdom, something I wanted to do more of but continued to prove unusually bad at, even so.

I was jolted back to the present when papa shadow reader pulled out a stack of thin sandalwood cards covered in Sanskrit and proceeded to mumble in Hindi as if presenting a homily of sorts. I understood one out of twenty words at best, and glanced at Pramilla to see if she could make out what he was saying. He stopped speaking and looked up with a grave expression.

"He says you're a pure soul," she said with finality, the way she does when she wants to shut down what she assumes will be a cascade of questions from me.

"It sounded like much more than that."

"He says you'll never have any financial problems," she continued, her voice dry. "In the long term. And that you're very spiritual, that you'll write books about it."

Not bad. Not preposterous. I could live with all that.

Then her expression changed from skeptical to despondent. The shift was slight, but I perceived it.

"What is it?"

She paused.

The room stilled. Even Ganesh looked somber sitting on his rat.

"He says you won't marry."

The remark cut. It cut because I was supposed to get married, even though the logical, fiery feminist in me knew that marriage was an antiquated institution that perpetuated patriarchal ideals and largely discriminated against people of sexual orientations that veered from the established heterosexual norm. But that had secretly been the plan all along—silly old marriage—that it would eventually happen as one of the inevitable stages of womanhood or whatever. If it did not happen, it would surely be owing to some failure on my part. Certainly it was a failure by Indian society's standards. After all, when I was nine years old, a very authentic-looking swami working at the back of a restaurant in Jaipur had preordained matrimony for me. "She will marry very well, to a rich, handsome boy from a good family," he assured my mother while holding my small hand with his knobby fingers and pocketing a twenty-dollar bill from her with his other hand. (Had he lied to us?)

It cut because now it made me feel that that wouldn't happen, that I would have to think of a new plan or vision for my future, one that might involve several cats, and I don't even like cats.

It cut because it made me feel I was being gluttonous. Perhaps I'd already received my quota of love for this lifetime, if there was such a thing, and I was being greedy by expecting more when some people hadn't even had any.

It cut because I wanted to have the fairytale romance my parents had—or nothing at all, nothing blah or mediocre—and I was slowly starting to realize not everyone gets that. Not everyone gets to meet a conscious, heart-centered, emotionally astute and spiritually advanced person and wed them.

It cut because I was disappointing my mother, even though I knew she just wanted the most basic thing in the world: for her children to be happy.

While there was no logic behind any of this, no rational reason to believe a strange man I found through a paperback guidebook who claimed to predict the future by measuring people's shadows for an exorbitant cost, it cut because it tapped into my deepest fear: that I would be alone, unloved, forever. That I had become unlovable because I was incorrigible and eccentric, too contemplative, too restless and flighty, too sensitive to be normal, too complicated to be easygoing and light-hearted—like my dentist, for example, a perennially cheerful woman who simply met some guy on Tinder, liked him, and married him soon afterward with her perfect teeth in her perfect dress, and now they live in the suburbs. I envied her. She did not question things in the way that I did. Or even if she did, I doubt she was prone to falling into an existential stupor the way I was. Why ask big questions when you could stick with small day-to-day questions and spare yourself the intellectual and spiritual hassle? Sages have long warned about getting started on a spiritual path—according to them, there is no turning back. When you start questioning things, you can't really turn around. Why make things more complicated than they need to be? Why not just floss, pay your taxes, and have fun?

It cut because it surfaced some truth: I had become too comfortable in my aloneness to let anyone in. Letting people in is scary. Being vulnerable is scary. It is easier to stay alone and not be completely known by someone than to be fully open to someone and risk rejection. It is easier to date someone you already know is unavailable, since there is no risk of losing yourself in them because they are not actually open to having you.

It cut because I realized that I was not who I thought I was. Something had transpired in the months before I left New York that made me question my entire identity. I hadn't been able to speak openly about it to anyone beyond a very few trusted friends. Pramilla did not know, and I thought it best to keep her ignorant, both for her protection and for the sake of my nerves. But by not sharing it with her, I had this doomed feeling that I wasn't living my truth.

"He says you may meet someone, depending on the decisions you make this year, and he will be a good partner," Pramilla said, cutting into my reverie. She and the shadow reader had continued speaking while I was lost in thought. It seemed papa shadow reader had turned to a more sycophantic approach, wanting to ensure his baksheesh.

Experience had likely taught him that the more positive the prediction, the bigger the tip.

"That's the last time we see a fortune-teller," I said as we stumbled out of the building into the blistering heat. "They say the real ones don't charge anything anyway."

The car slowly lurched its way through the Colaba traffic. Shoe wallahs stood in the shade smoking *beedis* and waiting for customers. Bright-skinned tourists toting bulky Nikons congregated by the Gateway of India. *Hijras*, or eunuchs and transgender people, once respected spiritual figures now facing discrimination and living in communes on the fringes of society, swarmed the scene in colorful garb. Tears began rolling down my cheeks. Of course I was lucky. Of course I was enough on my own, but all the struggling, searching, and not-knowing had worn me out. I wanted love as much as Daryl Hannah wanted that lobster in *Splash*. As insane as it sounded, I wanted a baby so I could reincarnate my father, but I was scared to do it on my own. Knowing how important my father had been to me, I didn't want to deprive my child of a father's love—yet I didn't want to settle for just any father. Maybe if my own had still been around, if he had been healthy and thriving, I wouldn't have cared about any of this. Maybe I'd been trying to fill a void—the huge black hole of his physical absence, a gulf—and was going about it the wrong way. Maybe there *was* no void. Maybe *that* was the ultimate illusion.

"Aw, don't pay attention to him, Tashie—he's a crook!" Pramilla insisted as she wiped my cheeks with her hand, her gold bangles clanking together. "I don't know *why* we waste money on this stuff."

I knew she was right. But it still felt good to surrender to my emotions. I'd gotten so good at containing them. That's one of the handy tricks you learn in humanitarian emergencies: you either keep your shit together or fall apart entirely. You take all the sadness and horror you feel, squish it into an invisible, emotion-proof box, and bury it at the bottom of your gut where it stays like a meal that cannot be digested. Of course everyone copes with the exposure to bereavement differently—some folks develop a dark sense of humor, others self-medicate or do something else to desensitize themselves, and some suffocate their emotions. The problem is that when you dare to let a little out, it *all* comes out. I didn't even know exactly what I was crying about. Everything?

I had no reason to cry. I was simply too demanding of life. I thought about our neighbor across the hall in our apartment building, a forty-year-old woman crippled from some mysterious nerve disease the doctors didn't fully understand, who couldn't get around without a walker, slowly and painfully. She rarely went out of the house because she was self-conscious. She lived with her mother and her brother and would never travel or have romantic love. Her condition was deteriorating. I sat with her one afternoon to keep her company. She had recently had a stroke, and her jaw wouldn't even close, which meant it was nearly impossible to understand what she was saying unless she was lying down, and even then it was a near-incoherent mumble. I managed to make out she was too depressed to watch TV, too depressed to read. She couldn't even eat the chocolates I brought over—they had to be melted so that she could swallow them.

I asked her, "What can I do, what can I do?"

"Find a cure," she told me.

When I thought of her, I felt angry at myself. I was keenly aware of my good fortune. My work had taught me that, to the point where I felt guilty whenever I got upset about anything that was not life-threatening or that could potentially be labeled a first-world problem. I'd seen dead bodies, met families made homeless by war and natural disaster, known people who had lost those they loved to earthquakes, combat, famine, and the bleak arbitrariness of fate. I'd spoken to people living on the poorest, most destitute margins of society. I'd witnessed such concentrated human suffering on such a grand scale that I deliberately quashed my emotions. If I did not feel anything, I could continue whatever I was doing without unspooling, even though part of me feared that I absorbed some of that human pain (how could I not?), even if it was not my own.

But now, for some reason, I started releasing. I realized I couldn't keep a stranglehold on my emotions. They'd been brewing, and they weren't going anywhere. I didn't have to keep everything in order and contained. I could be disorderly like the world around me. I started to give myself permission to truly grieve, to honor my own suffering instead of brushing it under the rug. It was significant, at least to me. Suffering is one of the shared human experiences, and I certainly had my fair share: over the loss of my father, over my friends and family who'd died young, over what I'd seen as an aid worker. I had grief over my unborn child who hadn't been conceived, who only existed in my imagination, and whom I feared I was going to lose because I wasn't doing anything to bring him into being. I could feel the warm bundle in my arms, the sweetness of his scalp, the stickiness of his thumbs. I had grief over relationships that had been joyous but had petered out, love turning into the mundane so that I wondered if it was really love in the first place, over losing the deliciously soft innocence of childhood. And I had grief over her.

Yes, over *her*.

———

When I met J., she was married. We met for coffee through a mutual friend. She was new to New York, a journalist on assignment, and didn't know many people in town. I didn't think much of that first encounter. We talked about our mutual friend, who was living in Islamabad. We talked about our jobs, briefly. Mostly we spoke of how she was adjusting to being in New York after years of living in Istanbul. I remember her being warm and amiable, someone I could be friends with. She was tall and attractive, with long ash-blond hair and gray eyes. Nothing else stood out about her except for her ability to hold eye contact with me, whereas I tend to dart my eyes around while speaking, a habit I was trying to break. Half an hour passed, and we went our separate ways. I forgot about her, not deliberately but because life happens and you forget people.

Two years later, our paths crossed again at a United Nations Correspondents Association event. We chatted casually about her two young girls, about work. She invited me to another event, and then we agreed to meet again. We were intrigued by each other, almost as if there was a subtle pull between us, but I didn't understand why. She was divorced from her husband at that point; I had decided to give up men, at least for a while, to focus on anything and everything else.

But something unexpected happened: I started to think about her in a nonplatonic way. I'd lie in bed on the weekends and find my thoughts drifting to her, fantasizing about her, her body, her lips. I was surprised, to say the least. I'd had same-sex experiences in my twenties, like many other women, but they were whimsical, experimental, and there was usually a large quantity of alcohol involved.

This was different. This was sober, willful fantasy about a woman several years older than me—a mother, a woman who had been married to a man who had left her for another woman (though at the time I couldn't see how that could be possible). I figured the feelings would dissipate, that I was bored or going through a phase. Perhaps it is true what they say: when you close one door, another one opens. But I had never felt this way about a woman before, and I didn't know how to make it go away.

Of course it didn't. When I would meet up with J. and she would greet me with a hug, I would flush with embarrassment. She had such a presence that I could almost feel her before I saw her. Did she know? She had a way of seeing through my eyes, into my throat, down my esophagus, and into my stomach. She was warm with me; she watched me, complimented me. Was it flirting, or just a woman being nice to another woman? I could tell she wanted to be my friend, but I didn't know why. I started to believe that what I was feeling was mutual, but it didn't make sense. I told a friend.

"It's all in your mind," she said, when I shared the feeble evidence of mutual affection. "You're just bored since you've gone off dating apps," she informed me.

Maybe I was going crazy. We were both self-identified straight women who had been in serious relationships with only men. Even if I was often more impressed with the women I'd come across in my adult life than the men, I never gravitated toward lesbianism, probably because I was conditioned not to. If I looked at a woman, it was usually to look at what she was wearing, not because I desired her. Until J.

Why her? Why now?

I started to surrender to my crush. Fighting it was too exhausting. I looked forward to seeing her. Yet at the same time, I didn't want to see her because she was intimidating: she left me flustered and breathless and unbalanced. I always sounded dumb around her, at least in my head; my sentences sounded short and clumpy when she was smart and articulate, with a smooth voice punctuated by a soft South African accent. Even though I'd started a regular meditation practice—fifteen minutes of stillness in the morning, rain or shine—even though I sucked at it and was still a slave to my head, to the crushing boredom and inanity of my thoughts, even though I'd been reading all sorts of spiritual books that were teaching me how to get better at the internal arts (practices *like* meditation), J. had the power to make me feel wildly vulnerable.

Yet when I didn't see her, I felt empty. Who *was* this woman? It was like she came into my life to test my commitment to the spiritual path I'd slowly begun to tread. Whenever I casually mentioned a kundalini yoga class I'd gone to, or the Reiki certification I'd received, she scrunched up her nose, gave me a half smile, and looked at me like I was the weirdest person she'd ever come across. I felt a little bit of myself collapse when she did that. She liked getting drunk and going to comedy shows. She liked nightclubs and eating steaks. She was a wild party girl at heart. We couldn't have been more different, but I only learned this in bits and pieces, and by then it didn't even matter.

Then it happened. After hours, in a bar, at some media event happy hour she'd invited me to. There was alcohol. I remember her drinking three vodka martinis in the space of an hour, eating all of the olives first, her mouth suctioned around the toothpick, pulling them off one at a time, deliberately. I remember sitting next to her on a velvet couch, leaning in to her neck as I was talking to carve through the bar music flooding over us, her signature fragrance, Poison by Dior, climbing into my nostrils. I was tipsy. I remember the crowd I knew dispersing at some point in the night, into the music, into the mild evening, the world outside. There remained only two people with us, and they were engrossed in conversation several feet away. I remember her smile, and how it gave her a tiny spray of lines around her eyes, her dimples deepening, her head cocked back. Did I say something funny? God willing. Make a woman laugh, and you are halfway there, though I didn't even know what I was trying to do. And then there was that moment when everything shifted. Out of nowhere, for no good reason whatsoever except that I couldn't hold it in anymore, I confessed: she made me question my sexuality. I stopped breathing and waited for her reaction. She half frowned in surprise, and I thought about running out of the bar, quitting my job, and moving countries, but then her expression softened, and she smiled and placed her hand on the inside of my thigh. The next thing I knew, we were outside and I was running down Park Avenue after her. She was barefoot, giggling like a schoolgirl, holding her platform sandals in her hand. She had run off without paying for her drinks and had left her colleague with the bill. She was bad that way, but no part of me could stay away. She was drunk. She needed to be put in a taxi. We stood face-to-face, body-to-body, on the corner. Cars thundered by, but it felt like we were the only two people in the world. She grabbed my hand and told me she liked me. She wanted me to come home with her. Her hand was cool, smaller than mine. I wanted to be clear.

"Like me like a sister?"

"No."

"Like a friend?"

"No."

We were quiet for what seemed like a long while. She stared into my eyes, and I stared back into hers without looking away. A warm wind tousled her hair. It was the kind of summer night when you wanted to be outside forever. When you wanted time to stop, because nothing feels better than the moment when you realize you have been madly in love with someone and that that person might, maybe, hopefully, possibly, love you back.

———

After a month in Mumbai, I was already feeling stronger. I had sleep, the great healer and strengthener, to thank for that, and wearing *chappals*—the ubiquitous Indian slippers designed to make you shuffle along as if you can't be bothered to actually lift up your feet, which encouraged a slower pace. Instead of eating delivery food or dining at restaurants, home-cooked vegetarian meals were prepared for me by a feisty cook determined to make me fat, because obviously that was the reason I'd "failed" to get married. "Too skinny," she scolded me in Hindi as she thrust a chili-laden omelet onto a plate. This was hardly the case, but Indians have a totally different body-beautiful ideal and scale of fatness. Pramilla had left, and for the first time, I was alone in Mumbai for a long stretch, without staying with family, without any really close friends. I descended into my solitude, surrounded by the armor of noise that hugged the building. I still struggled to concentrate on work, feeling the chaos around me that was Mumbai, but unlike New York, it wasn't the kind of chaos you felt you had to be a part of or you'd miss out on something important.

I didn't feel like I was racing against time; I was closer to just *being*. I was working, but it did not feel manic. On my days off, I started volunteering part-time for a couple of local nongovernmental organizations (NGOs) in Kamathipura, Mumbai's red-light district, working to rescue and rehabilitate women who had been trafficked into prostitution. These were mostly girls from poor small villages in the northern part of India or on the border with Nepal who had been sold into sexual slavery as young as nine years old, beaten, raped, violated, and imprisoned. This was emotionally exhausting, but an issue I'd long felt passionate about. Not having any self-determination, having your human rights stripped and violated so completely, affected me in such an acute way. Being with them, I felt almost ashamed of all the freedom I had; how could the world be so unjust? Some nights my cousins would pick me up and take me to a private club for dinner, a striking contrast to the conditions I was working in during the days I was volunteering, and it would make me feel almost sick. I thought about the cops I questioned on the gritty streets of Kamathipura and how dismayed I felt by law enforcement in general, how they could blindly look the other way with all of these human rights abuses happening right in front of them.

It would make me want to be alone even more. Some days I'd walk along Marine Drive, treat myself to a coconut, and drink it while sitting on the parapet, looking across the Arabian Sea, and contemplating everything. One afternoon, I stopped into Pramilla's favorite jewelry shop to buy a present for a very dear friend who was turning forty, and the salesman recognized me, as my mother was his favorite client—as a fellow Sindhi, but mainly because he always talked her into buying more than she had intended (she was a sucker for buying presents for people). I had more self-control and chose only one thing, a bracelet for my friend. When I made to leave, the man gave me a pocket-size Ganesh made of marble, a painted swirl of red, gold, and blue. "Keep this with you. It will bring you luck, especially if you believe in it," he said, his hair white, his eyes tender, as I held the heavy deity in the palm of my hand, already thinking of how lucky I was, even more so to have him gift me a Ganesh when I'd left mine in New York. I tucked it in the side pocket of my purse and decided I *would* believe in it.

Days like these gave me the space to cultivate awareness. I knew a million people in New York, but everything always felt rushed there, squeezed into slivers of availability. There was never any gradual unfolding of time. We were addicted to efficiency, but distance helped me realize that efficiency is not a pace humans are meant to keep up, day after day after day. The moments felt too pressed together, with no time to digest anything in between. "Beware the barrenness of a busy life," Socrates had warned. Besides, how could I reach any level of mystical enlightenment, or even become fully aware of my deepest inner needs, if I was hustling all the time?

Being interminably busy does not translate to living life to the fullest. I was revolting against advice from the likes of Facebook CEO Sheryl Sandberg, who had called on women to *lean in* to their careers. I had decided to lean out of my career, almost to the point of falling backward—a bend that was becoming a circle into myself. Like *Urdhva Dhanurasana*, or wheel pose in yoga. I'd lost my hunger for external achievements; it was replaced with something base: a thirst for some deep and rumbling wisdom. This inner journey, this intimate, soundless, invisible revolution—no one cares about it except for the people who are on it. There are no cheerleaders lined up watching in anticipation. No one wants to be friends with someone who is disconnecting. It is weird. Even though I felt nervous about breaking away, I welcomed the idea of retreating into myself. We all go through periods of introversion, when we feel less social. I wasn't in the mood to fritter life away. I was cracked open and gazing within, not without some hesitation.

"Make a decision and stay with it," my aunt Devi used to tell me when she was exasperated by my constant wavering, over whether to go to graduate school, over whether to take a job in Bangkok. "It's the process of indecision that's exhausting, but once you've arrived at a choice, stay there and don't look back," she would say with perfumed authority.

Leaning in to myself was a choice I'd made; no point in looking back. I wasn't sure where it would take me, but I had to believe that decisions made from the bottoms of our souls are ultimately the decisions we don't regret.

I also harnessed a faint belief that if you're on the right path, the world conspires to deliver what you need to get the job done or to get you where you need to go. At first I was confident that my remote-working situation was proof of that, though an unexpected admin glitch at work a month into my trip undermined that smug certainty. A sudden flurry of emails indicated that there was an issue with moving forward with my contract extension. As it had been impossible for me to save money in New York, I was completely dependent on my current income and feared that at any moment the auspicious remote-working scenario I'd somehow finagled would fall through, and I'd be forced back to headquarters or left jobless. Suddenly I was in a dream from which I felt doomed to have a rough awakening. As it was hard to tell from the email traffic what was actually going on, I became paranoid and heard the unhelpful mutterings of my very insecure ego: perhaps the powers that be were doing away with me. Perhaps someone better had sauntered into the office who didn't share my aversion to cubicle life, who also volunteered another skill, like reflexology foot massages, cake baking, or horoscope reading, things I'm pretty sure would win my team over. Mads assured me, however, that it was only going to be a short contract break. "We're not firing you, trust me," he declared over FaceTime. "Why don't you just go on a yoga retreat or whatever you new-age types do out there?" I feigned disappointment, and then swiftly booked a cheap ticket to Kerala, the southern Indian state that locals call God's Own Country. Work would be waiting for me when I got back.

I'd been planning on making my way down to Kerala at some point. The plantation-rich state is the heart of Ayurveda, a sophisticated approach to wellness practiced in India for at least five thousand years. Based on the early Vedas, the oldest scriptures of Hinduism, Ayurveda—which translates to the *wisdom* or *science of life* in Sanskrit—is not an *alternative* practice in Kerala but a holistic way of living deeply embedded in the culture, comprising science, religion, and philosophy.

While I was no stranger to Ayurveda, I was not an expert. I planned to dig deeper both as part of an exploration of my Indo-Aryan roots and as part of a detox of sorts. In recent years, naturopathy, self-healing, and the use of plants and nature as healing medicines—all the so-called alternative health stuff—had started to gain more traction in the ecosphere, intriguing me and many others on similar paths of exploration. Ayurveda's underlying mission statement of "returning to wholeness" matched my own goals for the coming months. I was looking for the lost pieces of myself—the dismembered parts—that had made me feel out of sync with myself or that had gone missing in the fray of life, in the unconscious race to achieve things. I'd already noticed that in syncing more with the feminine—the internal, the heart over the mind—with creativity, with stillness, and with surrendering, I was connecting to a vast ocean of power, strength, and flow.

I was sold on the idea that total well-being comes not just from physical health but from mental and spiritual health as well. I was starting to realize that if we don't pay close enough attention to our various parts through meditation, focused awareness, and other contemplative practices, or sadhana, through living in a mindful way—living with awareness about what we put in our bodies and the thoughts we think, making conscious decisions about how we spend our time and the pace at which we do things, and plunking ourselves in the wild, our natural habitat, at regular intervals—our parts drift apart and we feel out of whack. Technology overload can also add to that sense of imbalance and is partly to blame for making us feel scattered and, ironically, *disconnected*.

I also hoped Ayurveda could restore my sense of control. Many aspects of life are out of our hands—climate chaos, humanitarian disasters, the dead-end tribalism clutching the world, the death of loved ones, the dystopian political landscape. Part of my avoiding despair and moving forward was surrendering to that and shifting my focus to things that were within my scope of action. It wasn't an easy change to manage, though, and I began to realize why Reinhold Niebuhr had asked the Almighty for help with this particular process in his well-known Serenity Prayer:

> God, grant me the serenity to accept the things I cannot change,
>
> Courage to change the things I can,
>
> And wisdom to know the difference.

There were things I had power over. Certainly my diet and physical self-care—and so maybe my fertility, to an extent—were in my own hands. Ayurveda, like other natural health systems, provided insights that made me feel like I was doing something enlivening for myself. There was something empowering about taking care of my body by paying attention to the actual biology of it. Also, through the lens of Ayurveda, the act of slowing down is seen as fundamentally antiaging and the foundation of good health in general.

Ayurveda sees all life in nature as constantly evolving toward a higher state of consciousness, and it seeks to connect us with nature's intelligence through practices such as yoga and meditation, in addition to the use of herbs and structured nutrition. It is by no means dogma and is not only for those interested in mystical matters. In fact, it considers each human being to be a miniature universe. A huge component of Ayurveda is simply about syncing with nature, something I clearly wanted to do more of. The Vedas were written in an ancient era when people were more in touch with things like changing seasons, unlike today where city dwellers in manmade environments have access to food from different parts of the world year-round.

The underlying principle of Ayurveda is that balance is the natural order, and disease is a manifestation of disorder or imbalance. Part of working with Ayurveda is getting in touch with how our constitution goes in and out of balance and what to do when we are out of balance, which is probably most of the time, at least for many of the people I know, including myself. It is a rather delicate thing actually: my eating habits, lifestyle choices, relationships, environment, and even my job had the ability to create emotional, physical, or spiritual imbalances in my system that could make me more prone to illness.

According to Ayurveda, diseases manifest from an imbalance of our *doshas*, the bio-energies of the universe that govern the body and make up our individual constitutions. In a nutshell, there are three *doshas* made up of the "five great elements," which, according to Hindu scripture, are earth, water, fire, air, and ether. Every substance in the universe is made up of these five elements, the building blocks of life, though there is usually a predominant one. A human has a mix of these five elements *plus* the immaterial self, which is distinct from the body (and a whole other ballgame). The three *doshas* are known as *vata* (air/space), *pitta* (fire/water), and *kapha* (water/earth), and they can be assessed through an examination of physical and personality traits. Diet and lifestyle choices can either balance the *doshas* or make them go out of whack.

Trying to adopt an Ayurvedic lifestyle can be overwhelming at first. It is said to become intuitive with practice, though I was far from that stage. Before I'd decided to go to India, I had sought counsel on navigating the complex Ayurvedic landscape from Dr. Anjali, a highly recommended practitioner randomly located on Wall Street. A rotund, sixtysomething Indian woman, her main piece of advice for me was to "avoid the hurry, worry, and curry in life," which made me wonder if she ever left her office and actually walked around the city. As sincere as my intentions were when I first met with Dr. Anjali, her elaborate eighteen-page lifestyle plan and diet felt a dash unrealistic. Sure, I could keep fresh flowers in my bedroom and toss some pearls and moonstones into my handbag—those were easy add-ons. Refraining from being judgmental and critical of myself, also prescribed, was no easy undertaking, but I could sure as hell try. But then it got logistically challenging: I was supposed to spend time at waterfalls and water reservoirs wherever possible, take lengthy naps in the middle of the day, and go for glorious long walks in the afternoon (and I imagined she did not mean threading my way through midtown Manhattan at rush hour). The morning ritual alone was enough to make me want to climb back into bed and pull the sheet over my head. For starters, I was instructed to wake up before sunrise so that my body could begin to synchronize itself to the rhythm of the sun.

> On waking, lie in bed for a few moments and become aware of how your body is feeling and of your attitude toward the new day. Remember the divine reality that is our life. Think about all levels of your being and your part in universal creation; start with kind and loving thoughts about yourself and for all beings.

"Try to carry this attitude of awareness into all your daily activities," she advised. There was an entire sequence of things I was supposed to do, before breakfast even:

> Wash your eyes with cool rose water, and massage the eyelids gently by rubbing them. Blink your eyes seven times, and then rotate your eyes in all directions: side to side, up

and down, diagonally, clockwise and counter-clockwise. Then take four or five ounces of warm coconut oil and rub it all over your head and body. Gently massaging the scalp with coconut oil can bring happiness into your day as well as help prevent headaches and slow balding and graying of your hair. Scrape your tongue using a tongue scraper, gargle twice with warm coconut oil: hold the oil in your mouth, swish it around vigorously, and then spit it out. It will strengthen the teeth, gums, and jaw, improve the voice, and remove wrinkles from the cheeks.

At the time, I concluded that either Dr. Anjali had wildly unrealistic expectations of her clients or I was some kind of degenerate for not being ecstatic about this elaborate presunrise ritual. But away from the bustle, with my own schedule to man, with each languorous day melting into the next, it didn't seem so far-fetched. With time taking on a more elastic quality since I'd left New York, I'd started to relish the idea of slowly unfolding into the day with all of these small ritualistic steps designed to enhance my experience of living and heighten my awareness of pretty much everything—from my surroundings to how I felt physically to how I felt emotionally. It helped set the tone for the day by allowing me to choose, for example, that I would have a good day and do that by beginning it with such intimacy with myself and the moment. In fact, *Brahma muhurta*, or the early morning period about ninety minutes before sunrise, is considered to be the best time for spiritual practice. I experimented with waking up while the sky was still dark, and while it was at first disorienting and a touch spooky, when I opened myself up to the experience, emptied myself of thought, I felt a weightless harmony with something immaterial. That's what happens: when we become conscious—aware of our surroundings, aware of ourselves on a deeper level—we connect with flow. I would wake up feeling like the only person awake in the world, and then when I settled into it, I would feel like everything was awake inside me.

Dr. Anjali also told me that there were two *doshas* predominant in my constitution. While not uncommon, this dual nature made optimizing both my diet and my sleeping schedule less straightforward. I was categorized as a *pitta-vata*, with an imbalance of fire, air, and space. So basically, Ayurveda was calling me fiery and spacey, which I couldn't honestly disagree with, but the list of foods that I should and should not eat grew fairly labyrinthine, and I was lost. The only thing I knew for sure was that I was supposed to avoid chilies because apparently I already had too much fire. While *pitta* ignited the intellect, people predisposed to a *pitta* imbalance had a tendency to take on too much and then *burn out*. Sounded all too familiar.

When I told her of my India trip, Dr. Anjali emailed me recommendations for Ayurveda ashrams in Kerala. Annoyingly, they were all full, and I secretly cursed the fact that Ayurveda was moving more into the mainstream (even if that was probably a good thing for humanity). While my short contract break was welcome, the last-minute nature of it meant that I had to scramble to find an Ayurveda center with an opening. Luckily I found an available place on the internet and booked a reasonable package, not knowing what I'd be getting into but forcing myself to trust that whatever it would be, I needed it.

———

I arrived at the wild, ungroomed grounds of Ginger Tree in Varkala, a beach town north of the unpronounceable city of Thiruvananthapuram, after a dust-infused, unair-conditioned hour-long journey in a rickety Tata cab. When we sputtered into town, signs for *pancharkarma* were everywhere. Ayurveda's signature treatment, *pancharkarma*, which translates to "five actions," involves detoxifying the body and strengthening the immune system through five individualized regimens, such as a variety of oil massages, skin brushing, herbal enemas, and therapeutic vomiting. That was what I was about to put my body through.

I took a few minutes to circle the property, wander past a smattering of sticky-looking Westerners weighed down by the humidity, and take in the chaotic jumble of plants and trees that were an incandescent, almost supernatural green, before Dr. Jossy, the ashram's Ayurvedic doctor, started peering into my eye socket and taking my pulse. A mild-mannered man with a good command of English, he asked me if I had any physical ailments. I said, "No, only tiredness," but everyone I knew was tired; it appeared to be the normal human condition. When Dr. Jossy asked how long I had felt that way, I admitted it had been a few years. He stared at me without blinking and then scribbled feverishly in his notebook.

After a brief chat, the doctor weighed me on what appeared to be a prehistoric scale and placed me on a customized Ayurvedic meal plan. I was relieved to focus on my body, something I actually had control over, instead of anything outside of me—the weather, people, death, war, planetary alignments, or whether the cast of *Downton Abbey* would ever come back for a reunion—all of which I had zero jurisdiction over. *Love*—no control there either. It forces us to bend to its will when all we want is to be in control.

While my college friend Erika, a PETA-indoctrinated animal rights activist, had succeeded in turning me into a vegetarian twenty years earlier, that didn't mean I wasn't prone to countless food indiscretions, especially of the cheesy, crispy, deep-fried, or chocolaty kinds. But at Ginger Tree, there was only the good stuff: bowls of fresh papaya and pomegranate seeds; coconut-infused vegetable curries; spiced salads made of thinly shaved cabbage, carrots, and red onion; warm porridge with shaved coconut, bananas, and cardamom seeds; cauliflower roasted in cumin and mustard seeds; all sorts of light, nourishing vegetable soups; and *idli sambhar*, a southern Indian specialty consisting of rice patties and a golden lentil stew, considered to be the ultimate breakfast because the rice and *urad dal* complement each other, forming a complete protein. I also ate loads of *kitchari*, Ayurveda's staple meal of split mung beans and rice, often used in the ancient practice of fasting, known as a *kitchari* cleanse, because of its detoxifying effects.

Being in the hands of a kindly, avuncular medicine man—who dwelled in an overgrown garden like an enlightened gnome—was right up my alley. He was a guardian of all sorts of ancient Vedic knowledge that I could jot down in my journal and take with me to the end of time. Whether or not following his advice would make me feel different on any level remained to be seen. At the very least, I was trying, surrendering to the little piece of me that whispered, *Slow down and chill out.* I was doing what my friend Camila calls "meeting the universe halfway" by nourishing myself.

I was learning, too—always a good thing. For example, according to Dr. Jossy, I had been drinking water wrong all my life. Chronic dehydration, of course, is one of the main causes of tiredness. According to Ayurveda, tepid or room-temperature water is to be *sipped* throughout the day so that the body absorbs it slowly. Swigging ice-cold water shuts down the central digestive fire, or *agni* in Sanskrit. *Agni*, considered to be the cosmic force of transformation, is often compared to a burning fire and, like a fire, there is a balance to maintain—if the flame is doused or too low, food won't cook. If it burns too hot, the food will be charred. Traditional Chinese medicine, which shares plenty of similarities with Ayurveda, also discourages drinking cold water, as it slows down the metabolism. When I first learned about the water-sipping thing, my immediate reaction was, *Who has the time and discipline to sip water?* Which revealed a lot about my lifestyle, and not in a good way. Apparently, I even used the wrong vessel—neither glass nor plastic would do. Ayurveda recommends the use of copper to store drinking water because of its many "anti" properties: antibacterial, antimicrobial, antiviral, and anti-inflammatory. Evidence also shows it can slow aging, make skin glow, and prevent cancer. That was enough to convince me to scout out a copper thermos at a local shop.

In Ayurvedic terms, my lack of vitality was likely owing to depleted *ojas*, which stabilize the body and mind and provide immunity against stress and disease. They're like the human equivalent of a bee's honey: a refined essence we produce from the plants and other vital nourishment we absorb. Potato chips and martinis don't enhance this biological energy. Fresh, unprocessed foods do. A person with good *ojas* has a healthy glow that has less to do with using that shimmery Laura Mercier foundation and more to do with eating well, meditation, yoga, deep breathing, and *surrendering*. I'd often read that when you struggle against the moment, you struggle against the entire universe—saying no to *what is* can cause all manner of woes. I had to try: I'd been doing the other stuff with due diligence for months, but maybe surrendering was a missing piece of my current puzzle.

So I surrendered, with my body at least: every day, a woman exactly my size but twice as strong slathered me in warm medicated oil and rubbed my body vigorously for over an hour in a dusky, candlelit room, while the ravenous squawks of crows echoed in my ears. After these sessions, I was given two shot glasses filled with purple-black liquids. "Herbal medicines, not narcotics," Dr. Jossy clarified when I asked if I would start hallucinating at any point. I scrunched my nose, drained the mystery juices, and hoped for the best. I never found out *exactly* what was in either of them, though when I'd casually mentioned my desire to stay fertile as long as possible, Dr. Jossy wrote down *Shatavari*, a species of asparagus common throughout southern Asia that he said had been used as a fertility-boosting tonic for women in India for centuries. The name literally translates to "she who possesses a hundred husbands," which made me a smidgeon nervous as I wasn't even sure if I wanted *one* husband. One of the medicines also contained Ashwagandha, a powerful herb used in Ayurvedic healing. The Sanskrit name translates to "the smell of a horse," and the herb apparently brings about stallion-like strength in people who ingest it. Like ginseng, Dr. Jossy explained, it wipes away fatigue with its rejuvenating and immunity-boosting properties. While one potion was slightly sweeter and gooey like a dark caramel, the other akin to cough syrup, both contained ghee, or clarified butter, which loosens impurities; jaggery, an Indian sweetener made from boiled sugarcane that cleanses and acts as a digestive agent; and amla, or Indian gooseberry, an Ayurvedic superfood and powerful rejuvenator.

This is what I'd begun to believe: a cleaner body aligns better with the rest of our pieces—the soul part, the mind part. In fact, Hindus believe that their lives are stages in the progression to enlightenment, that the mind is the cause of bondage and also the agent of its release. With less residue clogging the body, it is able to inform the mind and the soul; the pathways of communication between the three pieces are not blocked by things like chocolate-frosted doughnuts (tasty as they are). I hoped that by gently nourishing my body instead of pushing it to extremes, I would eventually start making decisions with my body, leaning on its innate intuition, getting in touch with the somatic wisdom of it, instead of always turning to my fickle mind, which never seemed to have my best interests at heart but catered exclusively to my attention-grabbing ego. Not drinking alcohol made me feel more connected to my body. The reasons for abstaining became more and more compelling, even though I had a general weakness for dirty martinis.

Each meal at the ashram was eaten in solitude, engulfed by jungle, as I was chewed on by various visible and invisible bugs. I followed the principles of *upayoga samstha*, the art of eating in Ayurveda: I consumed warm food as it is better for digestion, unlike food that is too hot or too cold; I took my meals at the same time each day, sitting down in a calm, quiet atmosphere, where I did nothing else *but* eat; I sipped warm water thirty minutes before my meals and nothing during; and I ate with my hands instead of silverware.

Eating with your hands offers surprising benefits. For starters, you have to pay attention to what you eat, which discourages shoveling everything into your mouth at lightning speed without tasting a thing. Eating with the hands also improves digestion in the most curious way: research shows the nerve endings on the fingers direct the body to release digestive juices and enzymes as soon as they feel the texture and temperature of the food. At the ashram, I also tried to align myself with a basic Ayurveda consumption rule—eating the equivalent of two hands cupped together, or two cups of food, filling my stomach 50 percent with food, 25 percent with liquid (from before), and leaving 25 percent empty for digestive action. I had no idea if I was getting the proportions exactly right, but I felt like I was *feeding my body*, which was not a feeling I had when wolfing down a Pret A Manger wrap in my cubicle. I even started to keep a food diary to support this way of eating, taking little notes in the margins to describe how I felt after certain meals. When you force yourself to (honestly) document what you eat, you eat better, and you get a better sense of how your body responds to individual foods (and might be able to detect potential allergies).

It felt valuable to focus on this crucial aspect of my life, namely the substances I put into my body to ensure its best possible functioning. Maybe it was simple, small in the grand scheme of things for sure, but also pretty foundational. There was something starkly therapeutic about it: I liked the act of homing in and the control I felt from starting at the center and working my way outward, to the more overwhelming stuff. Maybe I couldn't fix the world, but I could fix myself. I once read somewhere that everybody wants to change the world, but nobody wants to change. What better way to change than to start from within, on a cellular level? Start micro, and then move to macro. I'd been doing the reverse for years. Pramilla had always told me, "You have to help yourself before you can help others," an idea I dismissed when I was young, but now it made more sense than anything. Before, I was trying to save the world externally—doing the Band-Aid work, picking up the pieces after disasters—when the real work that I needed to do was to turn inside. That is a very hard task. No one wants to do it. For some reason, everyone wants to run away from themselves and point fingers at everyone else. It could almost be a parody if it weren't so tragic.

Sure, all of it felt self-indulgent, but again it was for self-preservation. If I wasn't going to take care of myself, who would? If I ended up alone, a fear the shadow reader had forced me to face, then where would that leave me?

It would leave me with me.

Basically, that relationship—the one with myself, the one anyone has with themselves—has to come before anything else.

———

My efforts to slow down enough to process the world around me, suffusing my day-to-day existence with mindfulness—through eating the Ayurvedic way, meditating more, and experiencing those coveted, short-lived glimpses of bliss, or just being still without anything on the agenda—were opening me up not only to deeper, wider, softer kinds of love, namely self-love and love of nature, but also to a deep respect for the present moment, the *now*. That was where the bounty was, where I felt I was at the center of something, but I didn't know what that something was. Grace? I steeped myself in its aliveness, its richness as long as I could. It was like being so wrapped up in the present moment that you almost disappear. The more I was slowing down, the more of god I was feeling. The more I tempered my frantic pace, the more it felt like something was listening to me.

Silence—when the mind ceased momentarily, when my surroundings emitted only the sounds of nature—started to feel like a spiritual encounter.

Stillness was *hard*, though, especially for someone who was used to coasting on a wash of adrenaline. I couldn't keep annoying bouts of restlessness at bay. While daily yoga classes were held on the ashram's premises—in a makeshift outdoor studio shaded under a ripped tarp below coconut-carrying *Thengu* trees—I hankered for stimulation beyond crow pose. To that end, a couple of weeks after my arrival in Varkala, I went to North Cliff. I normally give anything touristy a wide berth, but my FOMO (that is, my fear of missing out) drove me to climb into a rickshaw that gasped its way to an area speckled with wandering, hot, pink tourists trying to shield themselves from the sun with flimsy hats. My throat was gritty from the clouds of dirt stirred up by the rickshaws and motorbikes, the hovering exhaust in the air, and the baked sand kicked up by many feet.

North Cliff is perched on fifty-feet-high red laterite cliffs and provides a generous view of Papanasam Beach below, a stretch of sand strewn with coconut shells and flower garlands, where the water is thought to be holy, drawing Hindus who come to make offerings for deceased loved ones and perform pujas, assisted by priests. At one end of the beach, a lone Ganesh statue made of stone faces out to sea. I walked by it several times and can attest to its energetic presence. North Cliff, on the other hand, had the potential to be a pleasant destination, but in reality, it was a backpacker lair littered with a bland jumble of makeshift stalls and poky stores. A stream of unrelenting calls oozed from shop wallahs: "Madam, come see. Special price for you." I thought of a verse from a Hafiz poem I'd once read: "Stay close to any sounds that make you glad you are alive." These were not those sounds. Within minutes of arriving, I regretted leaving the refuge of the ashram and longed to return to the crows, to the banyan trees, to the herbal medicines that were maybe quietly fixing things inside of me. But then something made me turn into a shop halfway down the promenade.

"How much is this?" I held up a cotton tunic with a look of near scorn, to keep the price down. I instantly hated myself for shopping, especially as I'd planned to adopt a Buddhist-chic minimalism to lighten my load on many fronts. I quickly did some internal PR spin and transformed the hate into *self-compassion*, a new term I'd plucked from the indiscriminate library of self-help literature that had been in my possession until I left New York (now on display at a Housing Works thrift shop, being leafed through by fellow soul-searching bargain hunters). I *was* stimulating the local economy, after all.

"Buy a few things, and I give you a special price," said the small shop girl, a young woman wrapped in a canary-yellow sari that made her dark skin glow.

The woman shadowed me as I fingered a row of suspended tops. "Madam, you so pretty. You married?" I'd been assaulted with that question on every visit over the last fifteen years, but for some reason, this time it startled me. I'd been doing so well, living in the moment like a modern-day Buddha, hanging out with birds and stuff, not checking my email, trying not to worry about the future. For all I knew, I was becoming a Kuan-yin reincarnate: bailing on marriage and convention like she did, forsaking the good life—air-conditioning, coffee, and chilies—in order to become what the Buddhists call a *bodhisattva*, an enlightened one. I'd gotten used to the now: it was a pretty chill space that didn't ask anything of me; if I listened closely, if I put my ear down close to my soul and listened hard, as the poet Anne Sexton beckons us to do, I could hear some pretty comforting things, like *Trust in the deeper order of the universe,* which really took a load off.

No, I was not betrothed, I replied to yellow-sari woman. Her eyes opened tea-saucer wide when I told her my age. We fell into conversation. Because of the blood-stopping heat, I was invited to sit on the floor inside the shop where we could barter back and forth in a friendly way and settle on a price for the items I was planning to purchase. I was in no rush and had nowhere to be, which was still an adjustment for me. I once read an article on tinybuddha.com that advised, "Whatever you're doing at the moment, slow it down by 25 percent." I figured this applied to shopping.

The shop girl was named Sita after the consort of the Hindu god Rama in India's most well-known epic poem, the *Ramayana* (a woman who became known for her self-sacrifice). This Sita had been married at seventeen and at twenty-two was already the mother of two children, one of whom stomped around the store, his two-year-old hands digging through my purse and pulling out rupee notes. She scooped him into her arms, squeezing and rocking him at the same time, and I felt it: the ache. It was something I noticed more as I made my way through my thirties. Whenever I saw a mother and her children, I felt a wistfulness and then an anxiety that rose like bad acid reflux. The having-a-child thing: I was torn between doing it on my own, waiting it out, or skipping the whole shebang altogether (wasn't the world going to spontaneously combust from global warming soon anyway?). I had to come to a decision at some point, but I kept delaying it, hoping that time—not my eggs—would freeze while I figured it all out. I could feel Aunt Devi seething over my indecisiveness.

As if reading my mind, Sita asked me if I wanted children. I told her that I did—at least, I thought I did—and it sort of tumbled out that I was thinking of doing it without a man, maybe, perhaps, but I wasn't sure yet. Her eyes widened again. "How is that possible?" She was brimming with awe and questions. While I didn't want to go into it because it made my blood pressure spike, it was also amusing to see her reaction. I tried the best I could to explain the concept of sperm banks and sperm donors, even though I'd only vaguely looked into it as I was sort of in denial about that being a real option (the swami in Jaipur hadn't mentioned it).

To my surprise, Pramilla had come around to the idea of me having a baby on my own. I'd even tasked her with the selection of a baby daddy since she liked matchmaking, or at least the notion of it, and wanted a Viking grandchild for some inexplicable reason, even though my brother had already given her one (a normal, non-Viking grandchild, that is). Encouraged, I emailed her a handful of sperm-donor websites containing thousands of out-of-focus baby pictures, though the last time I checked she hadn't opened them. I didn't blame her—it was overwhelming and kind of terrifying, which is why I was trying to get her to do it. What if I ended up birthing a psychopath? I wanted to be able to blame her for choosing the seeds. A nice, living, breathing guy whom I'd actually want to be in a relationship with was the obvious alternative, but time was ticking, and I'd long suspected all the nice guys were in Montana or San Sebastián, two places I never went to.

Months earlier, before I let go of my staff job with comprehensive health benefits, I'd gone to a Chinese fertility specialist to get the low-down on my egg situation. She did a full examination and said that while everything looked fine and dandy, she would not advise me to wait, because of my age. When I told her I was considering a sperm donor, she seemed startled. "It's New York City!" she crowed. "Just go out and have fun!" She was telling me to *get laid*. The problem was, there was no man in New York I wanted to get laid by, which is why I used to grumble to Mads that as a gay man, he had it easy. Of course he thought my standards were impossibly high. According to Mads, a baby daddy needed to meet only three criteria: he should be good-looking— "You want a baby that's easy on the eyes," he said—be intelligent, and have no major diseases in the family.

"What about a baby daddy *plus*?"

"I know you just made that up."

"A baby daddy plus is a baby daddy who shares my values, whom I respect, whom maybe I even want to be with beyond co-parenting," I said, waiting. "In other words, what about *love*?"

"Fuck love."

Sita was also coming from a practical place, though she struggled with the sperm donor concept I'd inadvertently raised.

"So you get these sperms, and the doctor puts it in your stomach?" Sita giggled, pulling me back into our conversation.

"Well, not really your stomach. Do you know what a turkey baster is?"

"The bird?" she asked in horror.

"Yes—I mean no, the baster. It's a thing people use to moisten meat before they cook it." This instrument, of course, had no relevance in southern India, which is largely vegetarian. Having never used one myself, I wasn't really sure how it worked, but I knew squirting was involved. I struggled to explain the exact process of insemination and may have unintentionally misled her into believing that sperm banks are the same ones as those that people put money in, with sperm being dispensed through an ATM mechanism. I gave up and told her to watch *The Back-Up Plan* with Jennifer Lopez, that it would explain everything.

"But it makes more difficult. Easier to get a husband. That way, he can help you." Sita gave me the Indian head wobble that means yes, no, and everything in between.

Reality check: a two-parent household is easier than one, perhaps more so in Western society where it is not ingrained in the shared psyche that extended family serve as a support structure. But I'd always believed that having no relationship was better than enduring a mediocre one; that it was better to be alone than entangled with someone who drove you half-mad, whom you had to be in touch with until the end of time because you shared spawn; that it was healthier to be on your own with loving friends and fun lovers than to force yourself into some monogamy mold that plenty of sociologists cogently argue violates human nature.

"I just haven't met anyone I like enough to go all the way with," I explained to Sita, not without thought. I wanted to say so much more: that it can be hard to meet someone we want to be with in the long term, that we have so many choices now, which ironically makes it harder, and that so many stars have to align for a synergistic pairing to happen (though of course it happens all the time). I wanted to say that I think it boils down to timing and readiness and openness with a sprinkle of destiny and that the best matches are when two whole people come together, two individuals who are profoundly connected to themselves and are then able to connect to each other. That it's all a delicate balancing act; that being in a relationship is hard work requiring heaps of patience and a willingness to compromise. That it could all topple at any moment, and it often does, and that I was afraid of that toppling. I wanted to tell her that sometimes I think it's just way easier—and more interesting—to stay single. But I didn't share any of this. Instead I said, "It's hard to find someone to love."

"When you love someone, you love through them to yourself," she said, gently tugging on her son's leg. "Love can only be good."

She made it sound so simple. Was it? Having a partner would certainly make the child part easier. Maybe that's why it literally takes two to tango and you can't get pregnant from masturbating, but then why hadn't I chosen someone already? True, I'd passed on some decent-enough guys. Mostly, though, I wanted to find someone like my father, with a kindness and goodness that was otherworldly. But can I blame my father's perfection for my not being able to find a companion who felt right? He was not your typical traditional male in that he wasn't the breadwinner, more of a stay-at-home dad later in life, but he was the anchor. He was a feminist but also a gentleman—the best of both worlds.

Sometimes, though, I believed I was single purely because of Pramilla and her expectations of the quality of person I should end up with—Federer, a prince. I once called her after a coffee date with a lawyer who was cute, had been outside of the country, seemed thoughtful, and, according to him, read the *New Yorker*. While I tried not to fixate on it, I was troubled by the fact that he closed his eyes every time he took a sip of his Americano. It was the strangest thing: he would lift the cup to his lips and then close his eyes, like one of those dolls. If I asked a question mid cup-lifting, he would lower it to the table while he answered my question. I thought that maybe he had difficulty multitasking. Could he not do two things at once? Sleep and breathe? Laugh and walk? I knew men were terrible at multitasking, but this was a potential deal breaker. I was scared to see him take on solid food.

"Maybe he is just savoring his coffee," Pramilla remarked.

Okay, I like that notion, I thought—someone who appreciates the small things. I could cope with that. I needed *more* of that in my life. Yes—he could become my teacher in that regard.

"Maybe you're right—I'm being too harsh," I said, relenting.

"Where does he live?" she asked.

"Queens."

"Forget him."

Yet she often conspired to set me up in such bizarre, slapdash ways that it made me worry about her sanity. As I never heeded her advice to simply loiter at Tiffany's—where she envisioned the "kind of men" I'd want to meet would linger, just waiting to meet me—she sometimes took matters into her own hands. She called me excitedly once to tell me that she had seen, while driving, the finest specimen walking down the street. "So tall and handsome!" She was convinced, from that cursory glance, that he was my soul mate.

"So?"

"So, I honked at him as I drove by, and he looked my way," she said with a giggle. The image of my senior citizen mother soliciting random men from her silver Toyota Camry as she flew across Chevy Chase, her neighborhood in the DC suburbs, was too much to bear. I called my brother with growing concern.

"She's just bored," he mused. "Your love life is a good distraction for her."

"Glad to be a source of entertainment," I said, though I wished she would take up bridge instead.

———

"My parents chose, you know," Sita told me. "I met my husband once, and then we got married. That is how it is done in my community." Sita tugged on her gold *mangalsutra*—the necklace the groom ties around the bride's neck on the day of the Hindu wedding ceremony, one of the many markers of a married woman in India, alongside bangles, toe rings, nose rings, and a red bindi, the decorative dot worn in the middle of the forehead. In marriage, Hindu culture is collectivist to the core, and the bride and groom are not only united, but their families are as well—it's basically a kind of bondage that is pretty impossible to snake your way out of. Being forced into marriage because of custom and culture is not unusual. The fact that I took my freedom for granted was definitely not cool.

Marriage is also considered a rite of passage in the West, at least in the US where puritanical ideals are still largely ingrained into the nation's psyche. The journey I was undertaking was partially about getting comfortable stepping beyond social constructs—freeing and disassociating myself from them, expanding myself beyond them. It would take some time to do away with more than three decades of social conditioning and brainwashing. For centuries, women lacked the economic opportunities that would allow them to be financially independent, which meant they pretty much had to get married and depend on their husbands for pocket money and everything else. Legally, they were often treated as property. Under the doctrine of coverture, a woman was considered to be "the chattel" of her husband. Oh, and don't even start on the major social and economic tolls for women who had babies outside of wedlock. These days, many of my European friends skip the marriage part, choosing to raise children and build lives with their partners without religious approval. In many countries, the notion of eternal marriage has grown largely obsolete. In France, marriage rates have plunged more than 30 percent, even as population and birthrates are rising. Some couples simply opt for civil unions, if anything, skipping the old-fashioned matrimony part. In Italy, according to the

Italian National Institute of Statistics, a downward trend in marriages there began in 1972. Rebecca Traister, author of *All the Single Ladies: Unmarried Women and the Rise of an Independent Nation*, which in part traces the history of unmarried and late-married women in America, says that the likelihood of women under thirty being married is now "astonishingly small." I do question why we allow the government to be in the business of sanctioning or affirming our love through a legal contract. Of course, there are practical reasons for it, such as tax gains and health-care benefits, but without those perks I wonder why we would want to go through all that paperwork when divorce rates hover between 40 and 50 percent in the United States alone[3] (which may explain why anthropologist Margaret Mead popularized the idea of temporary marriage, suggesting that we match up our love lives with our developmental stages at different ages).

In fact, plenty of Marxist feminists argue that there is an economic capitalist side to modern marriage that never skewed in favor of women's empowerment. They believe that capitalism needs social structures like the nuclear family—a term that first appeared in the early twentieth century, though historians say this family structure was in existence in Western Europe and New England as early as the seventeenth century and in England as early as the thirteenth century.[4] This is why keeping women at home was seen as integral to the progression of capitalism: industry needs labor, and women are the reproductive engine for future labor. Through this lens, capitalism essentially gets two workers (husband and wife) for the price of one. In her well-known article "The Political Economy of Women's Liberation," Margaret Benston argues that the nuclear family acts as a stabilizing force in capitalist societies because employees find it difficult to stop working if they have families to support (and women are rearing the future workforce at little cost to the capitalist class, thus preserving patriarchal inequality). Furthermore, capitalism, from this perspective, has a vested interest in ending the larger extended family model, which includes multigenerational households. By stripping away that support structure, industry can thrive by making men dependent on their jobs to support their families. When women began to enter the workforce in greater numbers, this started to shift, but the nuclear family model is still an aspirational social unit for many.

But the nuclear family structure can be lonely and isolating, says American anthropologist Helen Fisher. Two people must take care of themselves and their family rather than benefit from the strength of larger communities. Once the adult children move away, imagine the loneliness when the husband or wife dies, leaving their widowed partner behind. Interestingly, numerous studies show that premodern hunter-gatherer tribes operated on an egalitarian basis in an extended community system, where both sexes were powerful and autonomous (and child-rearing was a shared community responsibility).[5] This fact is widely unknown, and historian Stephanie Coontz says that the notion that women in this era were solely dependent on a man's hunting prowess for survival is nothing but a projection of 1950s marital norms onto the past.[6] This all changed of course with the emergence of agriculture in the West, which witnessed the decline of women's participatory power: gender-based divisions of labor during industrial agriculture led to a cultural belief that it was the man's job to work outside the home, not the woman's, and it all went downhill from there.

In spite of all of this, I am not against marriage—it can be a wonderfully sublime long-term partnership, which is what I witnessed between my parents. I'm not even against the nuclear family model; I am the happy product of one, though I do wonder if being a part of an extended family clan or community is better for human beings in general, economics aside. What I really *am* against is the *pressure to marry that continues to dominate certain communities and affect women's choices and sense of self-worth*, as well as the subsequent pressure to make the marriage work because of the stigma of divorce in certain cultures, such as in India.

"Acha ladka hai?" I asked Sita if he was a good guy.

"He is okay," she said, looking down. "He is better now."

I didn't pry. She smiled with resolve and changed the subject.

"I never traveled. I want to travel," she said. "You been to Goa?"

"Yes," I said, not without guilt.

"So lucky," she said, her eyes lighting up. "I want to go."

I knew she would probably never get to Goa. And suddenly freedom didn't seem like such a bad thing.

You have to work with what you have, so they say, and what I had just then was a little bit of anxiety and a whole load of freedom.

Maybe then, just maybe, I could give myself permission to recognize my wholeness even in the absence of that fairytale ending. I no longer bought into the myth that we are all incomplete, wandering halves looking for our other halves. This wasn't Plato's *Symposium*; this was my life, and I wanted to be in love with my freedom. That in itself was a noble wish, and more, it was wholly mine. Maybe this was what it felt like to slough away at the callused surface of something and see what was gleaming underneath—the golden slate of purpose: to be in love with our destinies.

———

In the spirit of freedom, the next morning I decided to go surfing. I was on the Malabar Coast, after all, and water is considered healing and balancing in Ayurveda, a baptism of sorts—it washes us, cleanses us, quenches many kinds of thirst. I was trying to stick to the Ayurvedic way, as least while I was in Kerala, and carry over whatever I could to Mumbai and wherever I went after that.

I'd surfed a number of times, even impulse-bought my very own surfboard after a particularly promising week in Costa Rica one summer. Yet I couldn't seem to get into the flow that morning, so I signed up for a group surfing lesson organized by a quaint British-run hotel in

Varkala. After meeting at the designated spot at sunrise, we ate small bananas together in near silence, then piled into *tuk-tuks* toward some paradisiacal beach where there were no tourists besides us—just a smattering of local fishermen putting away their nets after a hard morning's work.

My conversation with Sita had brought up some anxieties, and my mind was elsewhere. In the back of my mind, I was questioning my entire past, doubting every decision I had made, instead of practicing what I was supposed to be practicing: *surrendering*. Over and over, I would paddle and then change my mind. Or I would paddle, catch a wave, and then nose-dive soon after, fumbling under the water while my board shot perilously upward. I would haul my body back on the board, and another wave would come—the third in the set, the one I had been waiting for all along—yet I was still recovering from its predecessor, so I would only meekly paddle, breathless, not actually trying to catch it.

The *timing* always seemed to be off.

At some point, I decided to just straddle my board, look over my shoulder, and read the waves—enjoy the freedom of being in the ocean instead of dealing with the mess of trying to catch a wave, the risk of choosing the wrong one and wiping out. I wasn't sure if I really wanted a particular wave. One would look nice but a bit choppy. The one before it would be too big. It was kind of like dating actually: I could find something wrong with every wave that came my way.

When you're alone long enough, it is easier to stay alone, especially the older you get. No doubt I was picky, something I was perpetually accused of, but there was a dearth of single, mentally sound bachelors in the five boroughs of New York; the statistics were evidence enough. Men were flailing in the face of shifting gender dynamics. Many of them didn't know how to *be* anymore, in a way that made most women want to scream, *Step it up, bros!* At least meet me halfway. At least be half as good as I am so I don't feel like I am settling. Beyond issues with *them*, however, there was definitely a huge part of *me* that was terrified to take the leap. Yet if I were to chance upon someone who supported my soul's reasons for being here, what they call "a spiritual partnership," I could not say no. I remember going to a friend's wedding and being captivated by his wife's face every time she looked at him, at the dinner, during the hora dance—the joy and love swept across her whole being. She cried as if she was astonished that she had met the man of her dreams, another human she loved so entirely. I remember thinking, *I want that. That's what I want.* Now that I knew that existed I couldn't settle for less.

While I couldn't imagine anything less than that, I simply didn't feel ready to be so vulnerable with another human being in that way, especially not with the ones I'd come across in recent years, and the one time I had in the last three years, it backfired. I'd tried to communicate this to Pramilla.

"I need to do some more soul-searching," I said.

"How much searching does that poor soul of yours need?" she replied.

I didn't know then, but since leaving New York, I knew I was on my path. The path could take me back to New York. It could take me to a ranch in Taos or to Bhutan, a place that had long held mysterious appeal. At some point, though, I would have to take a risk if I wanted to be in a relationship. If I wanted a baby daddy plus, or if I wanted to feel the way I felt with J., then I had to let myself be fully known by someone. Either way, I would be moving forward. Just like the waves—at some point, I would have to give one of them a try (or I would get all wrinkly or eaten by sharks).

When a juicy, slow, medium-sized wave came along, the adrenaline kicked in, and I started to paddle, but then it grew larger, nearly a tsunami from my vantage point, and I bailed, ducking into it. I'd psyched myself out.

"You must commit to the wave!" yelled Raku, the surfing instructor, from twenty feet away.

I pretended not to hear him. I had water up my nose, and my arms were limp with exhaustion, dangling like the threads of an old coat. I floated on my board with the side of my face pressed against the wax as the sea rocked me in the sun. I thought of the postcard I kept as a bookmark, of a long-haired woman in a wispy rainbow dress lying on a giant sea turtle and grabbing its sides as it swims away from the shore. The side of her head is pressed against the shell, and she is wearing a peaceful yogic expression. Underneath it reads:

SURRENDER
TO THE
JOURNEY

It had kind of become a daily mantra, without the practice of actually saying it out loud. I didn't know what the hell I was doing with my life, nope, but I *was* surrendering—or at least studying the art of surrendering—to this phase I was going through and to some of my boxed-up emotions.

Raku swam over, carving through the water as if he had a motor on the back of his board. His giant muscles pulsated under his tomato-colored rash vest.

"Do you need help?" He grinned, a flirtatious glint in his eyes. "I can push you into a wave."

"No!" I said, resolute. I knew the mechanics of surfing; it was the other part I was struggling with. "It's just that none of these waves are good," I informed him, gesturing toward the rising and falling sea.

"You have to commit to the wave with your heart. Trust it, don't fear it. With God, all things are possible." He smiled, and all of a sudden, I felt I was at church in the middle of the sea.

"But that's just it. I can't seem to commit. To a wave, or to anything!" I said, exasperated. His words had struck a nerve.

It was true: I hadn't held one job for years on end. Had not been the kind of girl who stayed in one place, punching my time card, watching my retirement savings pile up with delight and maybe a touch of smugness. No. I had not done that. I had bounced. With love, too, I was a bouncer, a gleaner, an experience collector. I wanted a taste of several things, not just one, like a flight of wines. It was a privileged place to be. I wanted to experience the flight of life. When I chose, I chose wrong. I was perpetually making poor choices—at least that's what a therapist would tell me if I were to claim I was seriously looking for a life partner. I chose unavailable people and impossible, sexy, short-term relationships because I was secretly addicted to my own freedom, to not knowing what was next. Because I myself was a commitment-phobe. It was pretty textbook.

Many women are commitment averse but don't realize it, because we're always told that men have issues with commitment, men have the midlife crises. It's a narrative that needs to be discarded. We have a right to the same messy stuff, even if we don't want it. Besides, I'd known all about the beautiful, perfect-forever relationship because I watched one play out between my parents. For a while, I sought something else, not permanently but just to see what that *else* was. I was driven by a curiosity about the other, a desire to know what lies on the other side.

———

I found J. on the other side. I wasn't looking for her; she just emerged. I saw her light, a light that masked a darkness, but it didn't matter. We all have both in us. That first warm summer night, after the multiple martinis, after we slid into a taxi together, sticky thighs squeaking against the leather, she passed out in her bed before anything physical happened between us. I looked down at her breathing body, her hair fanned across the pillow with a tenderness that almost choked me. I loved her before I even knew her. In a way, I wanted to be her. It was not a choice I made.

It chose me. Some things choose us. I already loved her girls too. She took me to their room as soon as we got to her apartment, and I fell for them at first glance. In love with their bundled, sleeping bodies before I had even looked into their eyes. I didn't know it was possible to fall in love with voiceless bodies, with fluttering eyelids, with the smell of someone's sleep. With people before you know them. With a woman. I knew women loved other women, obviously. What was not to love? I'd read everything written by Anaïs Nin. I had lesbian friends. But for some reason, I did not know that *I*, me, the theoretically straight half-Indian woman that I knew as being a certain way for thirtysomething years, could be another way.

It was exciting, all of it. Someone new, a woman, a mother, someone smarter than me, more accomplished, just as traveled, just as independent. A superwoman of sorts. It was like meeting my ideal match, like playing tennis with someone better than me: it would improve my game, make me better. I felt a buzz from being around her. I respected her, something I felt lacking in the dates I'd been on in recent years—nice guys but too many crucial components missing. I wanted to mush them together to create the impossible: the perfect man.

That night I snuck out in the middle of the night, in case J. woke up sober and was horrified by the sight of me, even clothed: in my peach chiffon top, in my pencil skirt, barefoot, lying next to her. By the idea of it all. Before I left, I slipped my bracelet on her wrist. She had admired it earlier that evening. It suited her better. I wanted her to have a piece of me, of this night, in case we were to pretend it away the next time we saw each other. The bracelet was the legacy of it.

We could have pretended, J. and I, avoided, circled back to what we knew, to what was safe. Man and woman (though *was* that safe?). We could have easily waved it away the next time we saw each other. She could have said, *Oh, I was so drunk, I totally blacked out!* I could have said, *I don't even know what happened or how my bracelet ended up in your apartment!* We could have swept our complicity into the gutter.

Instead I left chocolate truffles for her with her doorman. No note, just chocolate truffles wrapped in gold foil. It was an invitation. I was inviting the most unavailable woman in the world into my life, but I did not know that at the time. I did not know then that she was irrevocably sad, reeling from her divorce. That we were both sad, but about different losses that neither of us could understand—she had not lost her father, and I had not lost my husband. I did not know that she, like me, was able to freeze her emotions to keep from unraveling, though I should have seen it. She was surrounded by armor for her own self-preservation, but the armor had cracks. Enticed, she came to the door of me, she knocked (tentatively), she peeked inside, but she couldn't cross the threshold of me. I couldn't reach far enough to pull her inside.

We were full of our own fears, our own sadnesses, J. and I, but we did not know that, and we continued on, dangerously, unready. No one knows anything until later. Underneath her tough exterior, underneath the frustration she felt about how things had turned out for her, if you ever got beyond the sheer force of her presence, beyond her insecure, wounded defenses, all you found was a vulnerable little girl, deeply sensitive and playful, wanting to be fully loved but never feeling like she was worth it. I did not know that all the love that the most sacred part of her craved was blocked by her adult self, which was mired in a deep distrust of the world that had likely been percolating since adolescence. Her adult self had unconsciously constructed a rock-hard wall around her heart, with no doorway to enter, no mailbox slot, no desire to be saved by anyone; total self-reliance without actually tending to various aspects of the self. It was a sham. I tried to commit to a woman who could not even commit to her whole self (and yet had I even committed to my whole self?). I loved a woman who could not love herself, and I could not force her to. And in trying to commit to someone who was unavailable, there were few risks. There was no engulfment.

During the summer when we started to spend time together, I traveled to Lisbon and spent my birthday attempting (and failing) to kite surf under the stewardship of a very sporty German friend who had just started her own company. I found a piece of rose quartz on a delicate chain in the market and bought it as a gift for J. The week after I returned, I gave it to her in the back of an Uber while her baby girl was on her lap looking at me with huge, curious eyes. We were coming back from a mutual friend's barbecue, and I'd purposely waited until I'd had a few drinks in me, because I felt shy about giving her such an intimate gift.

She squeezed my hand and gave me a quick kiss on the mouth, which I felt for several days afterward. I didn't believe that she liked me the way I liked her—none of it made sense to either of us—but she did, or must have, for a little while. A few nights later, I stayed in her bed, tracing her curves in the middle of the night while she slept. I breathed in her breath without anyone knowing, took in the warm air from deep inside her body, the most intimacy I could fathom. Lying naked next to a woman, I couldn't help but compare bodies, and I couldn't understand why J.'s stomach was flatter than mine when she was the one with the kids, or how she could be slender but mountainous at the same time, a bending landscape. I felt frustrated by her body, or my body. No, hers. We fit so well together, yet she couldn't get me pregnant. I still wanted to be the woman. But I wanted her to be the woman too. Her curves were a whole other world I didn't want to leave. There was something so comforting about the softness of a woman after witnessing the hardness of the world; it felt like a physical homecoming. Her skin was translucent next to my tanned skin, and when I held her, everything in the entire world felt complete and right and whole. She held me, too, sometimes, squeezed me so tight one night that I woke up and had to loosen her grip around my stomach so that I could breathe. I told myself that was a sign that she loved me, but maybe she was scared or suffering or holding on for dear life and it had nothing to do with me. I was just a warm body in the world.

She never spoke about her actual feelings, whereas something about her had stripped me raw. She had awakened a sensitivity in me I had never experienced, and it frightened me to be so affected by another person, to be rendered so entirely breathless. Zora Neale Hurston once wrote, "Love makes your soul crawl out from its hiding place." Is that what had happened? I had never been in love with any man the way I was with this singular woman, maybe because I understood her heart, even though it was closed. I desperately wanted to open it. I gave her a Reiki treatment, but she said she didn't feel anything. I bought her self-help books on divorce, but she never read them. I told her to take some time for herself while I watched the girls, but she said ten minutes in the shower was enough. I chose rustic wine bars as meet-up spots, looking for deep romance and deep conversation, but she wanted to get drunk and preferred nightclubs or somewhere trendy. I made her play that "36 Questions to Falling in Love"[7] game that everyone had been talking about, but she yawned and we stopped before we got to the last bit where you look into each other's eyes for several moments and something profound happens.

One night when we were drinking cocktails on a boat-bar off Battery Park, I asked her what she thought the meaning of life was, and she said, "To have fun." My jaw dropped. *How could someone actually think that?* An hour later, when the sky turned navy, I saw a shooting star behind her, but she didn't believe me. I told her it was a sign, but she didn't allow herself to believe in any of our magic. Magic was dangerous, an illusion; it could backfire and leave you in a pile of yourself, your broken-down defenses like a carcass next to you. She didn't like that side of me, only my light, fun, funny side—I had to bottle up my depth and insights and feelings around her. She never wanted to know the whole of me.

Knowing the whole of someone is scary.

In general, though, I pretended to be casual, not that I was very good at it. She canceled on me a few times, and I acted nonchalant about it, telling myself that she was a busy, working single mother, and what did I expect? I didn't want to play games with her; she wasn't some guy. She was precious to me, and I honored her precisely by not toying with her in the way I would have had a man given me the same mixed signals. But I was supposed to be looking at men, dating men, thinking about having children instead of spending all my time being with (or thinking about) an emotionally unavailable woman, someone I was trying to save from herself, which I now realize was a totally futile endeavor.

I wasn't being very strategic. "You have to be more strategic," Pramilla would tell me, in general, about meeting the right kind of guy, about everything, but of course she had no idea that I had fallen for a woman. If this loving-a-woman thing became a real *thing*, I worried about what she would say. I could see her frown lines. Her skepticism. I would not have to go into the details. The details were for J. and me. For anonymous poems dropped into the trash. For the wind. I would not have some huge drama, some huge coming-out party. The world does not end when we transgress preconceived notions of ourselves; rather it becomes more of the world we want to live in. I was just human. A human who loved another human (yay?), but this human happened to have a soft face, not a stubbly one, a body that was like mine, but not like mine at all. My mother would come around; I knew it. Her disapproval could not be a part of the reasons not to—they were already piling up. Besides, I was not interested in labels.

I was more interested in figuring out *what I was doing*.

To clear my head, I booked a weekend at the Zen Mountain Monastery in the Catskill Mountains three hours away from the city. Just as the bus was pulling out of the musty darkness of Port Authority, my phone vibrated: in came a text from J. asking me if I wanted to come over for dinner that night. I leaped out of my seat, startling the other passengers, and told the driver to stop the bus right then and let me off into the roaring Eighth Avenue traffic. So much for zen. He grumbled at the inconvenience, but I told him that I didn't have a choice, *that it was for love after all, that love was hard to find, and when you had it you should do everything in your power not to lose it*, and he looked at me with a grimace I still can't erase from my memory.

J. was not a good receiver, of compliments, of anything. When I would ask her what it felt like to be so beautiful, genuinely asked her, she smiled a wry smile. She did not think of herself as beautiful, which made her even more beautiful to me. She wasn't good at receiving gifts, either, and never had time to buy things for herself. I, on the other hand, could not keep myself from buying her presents: Rumi books she never cracked open, a fancy pizza stone to make pizza for the girls (which I'd attempted to make for them though the inside turned out raw), and a silver charm bracelet that, to my relief, she did wear.

I once spent an entire hour in a packed Sephora in midtown just picking out a lipstick for her: the perfect shade for her skin tone—rosy with a plum undertone. She hadn't been wearing the right color on the rare days she put on any makeup. She preferred a more natural look. People would be apt to describe her as very attractive, but to me, she was stunning, with high cheekbones and full lips—she didn't need anything, but I wanted to get her a lipstick anyway. I endured being elbowed by frenzied shoppers, focusing on the vast selection with laser-like attention, striping the back of my hand in a rainbow of deep pinks. At home, I enveloped the small box of Christian Dior lipstick in pink tissue paper, spritzed my perfume on it, and snuggled it in the little Sephora bag. When I gave it to her, her girls were excited, but she seemed totally indifferent. She didn't smile or even say thank you. I wanted to cry— that was how pathetic I was—but I would never dare cry in front of her because then I would lose her, so I cried in the bathroom and then tidied up my mascara like nothing had happened. Everything had to be contained around her.

The last thing she needed was drama. The last thing she wanted was to feel anything, because if she let herself feel something, she would feel everything, and she couldn't afford to lose control of herself. She would never lay down her armor.

I could not say that I felt like an afterthought. I could not ask her what it meant when I slipped my hand in hers in a taxi and she squeezed it. Did it mean "I love you too"? Did it mean "There, there," as if I were a child who required soothing? Did it mean "I don't know what to do with you. You've fallen too deep, and I want to keep things light, and I don't know how to get rid of you"? I felt all alone in this kind of internal wonder about our secret relationship that we didn't call anything. I had one magnanimous friend in whom I confided, who listened and uttered reassurances over carafes of rosé after work. "She loves you, but she is scared," she would say. "You have to remember she's really fucked up." Her eyes watered at the sight of mine watering. "Just show her uncondi-tional love. Don't ask for anything," she ordained.

I followed this advice to a tee. This friend had gone through years of psychotherapy. This was a friend who really knew things. I did not know these kinds of things. I did not know about deep-seated emo-tional trauma that stemmed from childhood. Did not know that people coping with that were unpredictable by nature, possessed by an inner terror. Explosive. So I didn't ask for anything. I didn't express these asks of mine that came from my soul-bottom. I knew that there was a delicate balance to maintain: it could not be big and wild and deep. It had to be fun and light and unthreatening. I put a stopper on my emotions, my needs, forced them back down into the pit. I could do pleasantries, or so I thought.

Once, though, I felt her guard peel down, as if she was really going to share herself with me, merge her vulnerabilities with mine. I felt nervous and pulled back. She quickly clammed up. There is the exter-nal person, the one who is put forth, and then the internal person, the real person, the unguarded person caught in glimpses. What is it about total intimacy with someone else that is so terrifying? She told me that I should go marry a rich man and have a baby and that she and I could be together later. In a way, now she was the one telling me to be strategic, the way she had been or thought she had been. But I couldn't be; it wasn't in my nature, and I wanted her. I wanted her babies, whom I'd already fallen in love with. When you love someone who has kids, and you spend time with those kids, you love them too. It is dangerous. You fall in love with *the package*. I wanted to wake up next to her. To make plans with her. To snuggle her babies, who loved me in a way that made me love myself more. To make her smile so wide that her eyes crinkled. But she did not want that. Sometimes she seemed happy and lighthearted, but other times, miserable, bitter, exhausted, and like she had been dealt the short end of the stick. "I want to do right by you," she would say. She felt like she was keeping me from something.

She eventually ended things between us, explaining that she was an emotionally and logistically unavailable woman. We were on the sofa in her living room, and she was very matter-of-fact, tired.

But worse, way worse, she said that she did not love me in the way that I loved her. It felt like getting stabbed in the stomach five hundred million times. The power of one sentence.

I didn't even react. I think I may have just nodded my head and left, without making a scene, and then stumbled into St. Patrick's Cathedral where I let it go. I cried so hard and told god, the universe, whomever or whatever was out there, that I just needed her in my life. Maybe I didn't have to have her; maybe all my friends were right—that she had too much fear in her heart to have space for love, that she was bad for me, that she was a bitch, that I deserved a bigger love or whatever. I made a pact with the universe that I wouldn't ask for more if I could still have her and her girls in my ether, maybe not right away, but eventually when I no longer longed for her. I could not accept loving people like that and losing them forever. It did not seem natural.

My friend Camila comforted me, made me feel less rejected by saying that J. was walking away because she was terrified, that I was shining light on her darkness and she wasn't ready to work through it all.

I could not change her.

I could not save her from herself.

So I cried for her—all that could have been, all that was—and I cried for myself. I cried in my apartment, I cried in the subway, I cried in a restaurant, I cried in a bar. When I cried over her, I was also crying over my father, I think.

When I cry, I cry over everything.

Grief: it is an untidy, circuitous thing. It is hard to know when it's grief or when it's something else.

There were so many unknowns.

———

Yet I was becoming more and more about the unknown, grateful for it. Even floating in a part of the Arabian Sea I'd never swum in, in a mental state I'd never experienced before. Raku had left me alone with my thoughts, and I rocked in the water. I needed the space. Some part of me hoped that this time away from my regular life, away from the cult of busyness, away from a heaving, breathless mass of collective human pathologies, would help clear the way to something or somewhere that felt less empty. It was a possibility, I acknowledged, but as with most quiet, soul-driven things, the change would happen gradually, almost imperceptibly, as if it hadn't even happened because you didn't see it, and only a part of you really felt the shift. But it was possible that there would be nothing to show for it.

After three weeks of living by the principles of Ayurveda and being close to water, my mind started to slow down from the usual overdrive. Not completely—I'd probably have to live on a mountaintop somewhere for a very, very long time for that—but I noticed a shift. The act of slowing down made me aware of a terrible habit of mine: I was nearly constantly chasing, reaching, and yearning, forever looking at what was next. By noticing this, I was able to mindfully break the habit of driving forward and backward and instead stay gratefully rooted exactly where I was. The ambrosial scenery and the water, no doubt, added to my sense of well-being—after all, that is why people vacation in places like Maui.

Weirdly, I would give most of the credit to something completely ordinary: *breathing*. By that, I mean I'd started to breathe properly. Like most humans, I never consciously thought about breathing, except in yoga class where we're reminded to breathe so often it's almost annoying. Generally, though, on my own, I inhaled shallowly, scantily, an obligatory reflex as opposed to giant, juicy, deep breaths that can thoroughly nourish the body with oxygen. Yet the more air I took in, the more my thoughts stopped sticking to me. Even in the sea: I didn't want to go over and over the same things. I had to breathe myself away from the sadness, or at least some of it, picture it rolling off me, looking like a cloud in the sea where sand could have been kicked up.

In a sense, breathing is a form of freedom. It's a miracle I've survived all these years, given that I've been so cavalier about my life, not bothering to pay attention to my breath. Breathing is deceptively simple and soulful, within reach at any moment. Not only is it the link between body and mind, not only does it clear out physical debris and emotional blockages, but it has a deeply spiritual dimension. In Ayurveda, the breath is thought to have curative properties and is used as a means of increasing awareness. Even modern science has jumped on this centuries-old bandwagon, with advocates popping up everywhere from TED Talks to corporate wellness programs, all touting the meaningful impact breathing can have on our lives.

The more breathing I did, the deeper I was able to go into myself, the freer I felt, as if I were pushing back some thick, dusty drapes and letting in a stream of light.

Put simply: breathing is the first thing we do when we are born and the last thing we do before we die. I didn't want to take it for granted anymore.

I was alone with my father when he took his last breath—a soft, peaceful surrendering. His lungs gave out, and he couldn't breathe anymore. Even though he desperately wanted to stay with us, he couldn't exist without air. He knew when it was his time—he knew when he was going to go, he waited for me, and I came to say goodbye. There is something mystical in this universe, and no one can deny it. Denying that truth is like denying breath.

Breath was probably the most sacred thing I had.

With that in mind, I took the biggest breath I could muster—so deep it pinched my sternum—and paddled, gliding, not stopping until my board started to slide down one soft, velvety wave, the foam at its peak bubbling and spreading behind me. I sprang onto the board, my arms out like I was about to fly, exhaling wildly as I looked ahead at the wide stretch of ginger-colored beach in all of its shambolic beauty, and surrendered to the moment, to the weightlessness of it all.

Surrendered to the journey.

Surrendered to this pilgrimage I was on, where the farther I traveled, the closer to home I felt I was getting.

———

Almost reluctantly, before heading back to Mumbai, I left the fertile greenery of Kerala to take a jaunt inland to the brick-oven embrace of Madurai, the spiritual epicenter of Tamil Nadu, as I wanted to feel the unique energy of being in a city of worshippers encircled by towering temples, intricate structures that were testaments to the fact that something larger than us existed, that we were a part of that larger thing, and that it was a part of us. I knew as a non-Muslim I would never do a hajj to Mecca, and this seemed like one small stop along my own larger pilgrimage. Part of me felt like I'd entered what could easily become an endless stage of wandering, anchorless and with no definitive game plan, but part of me identified as a pilgrim in search of something sacred, something immaterial and transcending. In a way, I was traveling across the world to meet myself. This *was* holy work. I had no handbook. It was the work of a spiritual warrior, deeply entrenched in all of us but often squashed under everything material and external to us.

I hopped on a train toward the City of Temples, chugging through a landscape of rice paddies and shoddy villages just like any other pilgrim. I'd long been curious about an Indian train journey, and it lived up to its reputation as an exasperating experience. Normally, when I traveled in India with Pramilla—to the Golden Triangle up north, for example, or just within Mumbai—we always had a car and driver. When I was younger, Aunt Devi used to secretly take me places on buses teeming with other passengers, where I'd be standing pressed up against people's armpits. She would giggle at my expression.

"You need to see the real India!" she'd scold, in her pseudo-British accent. "You can't go around being such an American softy like your mother"—who by that point had been living in the US for more than half her life.

I would get quietly defensive, as I never spoke back to my aunt out of respect. It's true that Pramilla had a softer demeanor, the result of being the baby of the family, coddled by her older brothers. I suppose if I compared the two sisters, Pramilla came across as more princess-like, usually moving at a glacial pace as if she were singlehandedly tasked with balancing a crown of jewels on her head and everyone around her just had to wait for her to do her thing. "Why would I rush, when I have this lovely sway?" she responded when I asked her if she had ever thought about walking at a normal speed. Not to mention her tastes—her penchant for sparkly, borderline-gaudy clothing and extravagant, impractical cars (two Mercedes-Benzes, both of which she crashed, before finally moving on to the sturdy Toyota). Aunt Devi, on the other hand, was much more frugal, conservative, and minimalist about everything, from her jewelry choices to her apparel to her home furnishings, yet she was a woman of extreme elegance, regal in her own way. She wasn't in possession of that same American openness that Pramilla had, even though she had lived in the US for several years in the 1950s, in Washington, DC, where she worked at the Indian embassy, and in New York where she worked in advertising at J. Walter Thompson. To be honest, Aunt Devi could come across as distant and formal with people outside the family, and maybe even a touch snobby, displaying a sense of superiority at times. Around family, she was an adept and captivating conversationalist, opinionated about all earthly and nonearthly matters, and often highly comical without even trying. In some ways, however, life had sculpted her into a harder person; she had vivid recall of the trauma she experienced during the Partition of India, as she was twelve years old when she was a refugee. She had a hardy sense of adventure without carrying too much sentimentality about material possessions.

As far as I could tell, she had only been in love once, with a man named Jim from J. Walter Thompson. "Well, what happened?" I would inquire. She was coy, but I doubt anything physical had transpired, even though she made him out to be some sort of handsome cowboy gallivanting around Manhattan. I could picture her version of flirting back then, which was probably more on the restrained side. Even though she was a beautiful woman, I got the sense that American men found her untouchable, as she insisted on wearing the traditional Indian sari to the office every day.

"Didn't you want to blend in?" I asked.

"Nothing is more elegant than a well-draped sari," she insisted.

She once asked me to look for Jim when I was back in New York, and while I scoured social media and the internet, I didn't have a real handle on how to track this mystery man down nearly fifty years after they had worked together. Was he even alive? And if he was, wouldn't he be married with grandchildren by now? I felt terrible about not being able to find him, to help her close the loop on that love story, but she had resigned herself to being alone, not in a pathetic way but in an empowered way: her philosophy was that if she wasn't going to have her ideal man, then she'd rather be left to her spaciousness and her privacy, to her memories and her contemplations—her closest relationships were with her siblings and me, whom she often introduced as the daughter she never had.

I thought of her in my third-class train car—she would have been proud to see me wedged in the sticky close quarters, not flummoxed by the unrelenting parade of panhandlers. I was no longer a "softy," though a lot about India is hard—the day-to-day reality of the poor, the brutal class structure, the cruelty with which people treat their help, the often savage discrimination against women. This is why tourists tend to disappear into the crisply cool, safe confines of five-star hotels and never leave them. But I knew I couldn't just acknowledge the good parts of India—the rich history, the colorful religious mythology, the music and architecture and culture, the yoga and Ayurveda—and disregard the rest. The squalor, the injustice, the stark absence of a social safety net—they were right there in front of me at every turn.

For example, one woman on the train, a Christian convert named Mary who didn't look like she'd been faring too well, came begging for money. She handed each passenger a battered yellow card with a note explaining in English that her husband was a mason who had died from falling off a building and she was partially paralyzed:

> I have four femail children and no way to arrange there marryage. Therefore I earnestly request you to lend me a helping hand. Thanking you. Mary

I cringed. If what she wrote was true, her life could be only wretched. While self-immolation, or sati, on a husband's funeral pyre—a Hindu practice—is now banned in India, life for many widows in India is still daunting, and it is not entirely uncommon for their communities to shun them as they are perceived as unlucky. They are often forced to live in solitary confinement, practice abstinence, and renounce their inheritances. Despite sati being outlawed, the controversial ritual could be seen as part of a wider canvas of social attitudes that denigrate women on the lower rungs of the socioeconomic ladder in India. Sometimes the widows, who have never had to work and often have no skills, must turn to prostitution for mere survival. Many of them are simply abandoned by their families and forced to live in deplorable conditions or seek solace in ashrams.

As I watched Mary make her way through the carriage, I thought about Pramilla. *She is a widow too. My mother is a widow.* It did not seem real to me at all, any of it. It had a sickening element to it. I wanted to contest it. She was still relatively young; her hair still dark (thanks to L'Oréal). She was supposed to be in her golden years, touring Italy, or maybe the world, with my father, but no. While she would never be subjected to the same horrors—the discrimination, the economic injustice—if she moved back to India, her experience of being a widow, of being alone after being partnered most of her life, has been wholly catastrophic from an emotional standpoint. I feel it without needing to talk to her about it. We are synced up, connected by an invisible blood vessel, even when I travel thousands of miles away. Her pain is my pain. We are part of each other's oneness.

In so many ways, she has been my constant source of strength and support. Being a shy child, my entire adolescence was fraught with insecurity as girls were often unkind or competitive with me, and she would insist that I learn to toughen up.

"You have to get a thicker skin!" she'd scold. "They're just jealous, Tashie!"

Even now, when I complain about a colleague at work or a friend I've had a misunderstanding with, she invariably takes my side without even knowing all the facts. I cannot imagine anyone else loving me so thoroughly and unconditionally, but also with an almost religious respect for space. After my father died, I noticed we both liked to be by ourselves, finding comfort in knowing that we were both alone, but together in our aloneness, maybe not physically but on some deeper energetic level. "You'll never be alone," I always assure her. In spite of my fussing over her, she has told me she is scared of growing old partnerless, yet she would never consider a new companion. It would not be in the cards for her. I would not dare suggest it. Sacrilege.

I had wondered why she was fixated on me partnering. My experience of being on my own had, in large part, been joyful, allowed me to open up my life to many unusual things, wild, pressing things, continents. Dozens of small, impassioned love stories, some of the connections possibly more potent than a marriage. My aloneness was, subconsciously, chosen. I had deep friendships. Pramilla was never single as long as my friends and I had been, through our thirties, which meant she never cultivated those kinds of friendships, those close-knit communities, the kind that most single women in their thirties and forties and fifties have in this era.

When you don't marry young, if you stay largely single most of your adult life, your friends can become your bedrock, your lifeline, your only oasis of support and comfort outside of blood relatives. Women naturally give something to each other that perhaps they don't get, or seek, from male partners. This female bond surpasses logic, but perhaps can best be described as understanding each other more effortlessly by way of being part of the same gender, by sharing the experience of being in the world as a woman, which is very different from the way a man experiences the world. My friends, both male and female, feel like a crew of angels who really want me to thrive as much as I want them to thrive, because spiritually, psychologically, we are all intertwined in some way. Having this support system means that I am not lonely, generally, and if I ever become lonely I could always join some polyamorous community or alternative communal living situation, a trend that is on the rise (though I would not be inclined to jump on the cult bandwagon à la *Wild Wild Country*). I could be a convention shirker, like my mother in her own unplanned way. No doubt, I could come up with countless diversions that I've put on the backburner for years, such as wheel throwing, gemology, and learning Sanskrit. These things would definitely keep me occupied.

I often wonder if there is some other subversive force at play when it comes to the pressure to settle down into a monogamous, heterosexual relationship and get married. Though controversial, sometimes I believe a single, childless woman—especially one with an education and within a certain means—is perceived as a threat to the patriarchal norm. She has all this power and autonomy and freedom and fearlessness, and she can't be controlled or subjugated in any way by anybody or any institution—at least not in the West—and that makes way for a huge shift in power dynamics. I think we are starting to see the beginnings of that change now, and it's incredible.

But it still leaves us with one question: What happens at age sixty or seventy? Without the safety net of a spouse or children to take care of me in old age, would I be doomed? Would I be able to find a community to absorb into, to care for me if I developed some rare tropical disease that forced me to amputate my arms and legs?

I tried to rein in my imagination. Fear-based decisions are rarely good ones. I'd decided to let my soul lead the way for now, not my head, and I'd found my way onto a spiritual path. They were not mutually exclusive, but that seemed to be how it was unfolding at the moment, and I couldn't bring myself to fight it.

There was a deep comfort in surrendering.

————

The main destination in Madurai, India, is the gigantic festive shrine dedicated to the triple-breasted warrior goddess Meenakshi and her consort, Lord Sundareswarar. According to legend, the beautiful Meenakshi, an avatar of the Hindu goddess Parvati, was born with three breasts and a charming prophecy: her superfluous breast would melt away when she met her husband. It didn't say why or how. Most Hindu mythology is creative, not meant to be interrogated. How else does an elephant ride a rat? Or a man have sixteen heads?

That was all I was able to find out from the scrappy pamphlet I purchased on arrival from one of the dozens of souvenir wallahs lined up among the temple's large connecting areas. I roamed the mammoth temple alone in silence, traversing the entire six-hectare complex. While I wanted to know more about the edifice itself, I was curious to know whether or not Meenakshi met a nice guy in the end, and if so, what happened to her third breast? If it didn't melt away, did the guy stay with her anyway, or did he end up chickening out and going for some simple, two-breasted woman?

As I was thinking through these important questions and pondering the dating dynamics of the sixth century, I noticed a small mound of ash atop a slab of marble and walked toward it. Indians of all backgrounds sifted their fingers through the white ash, or *vibhuti*, that surrounded a small Ganesh statue like a pristine beach. I gave myself permission to join the delicate flurry of hands.

In all his glory, Ganesh was, as usual, sitting on a rat, which is considered the greediest of animals and is supposed to represent our senses, which are apparently never satisfied. The symbolism here is that wise people ride on their senses and by doing so, keep them under control—*Don't let your desires take you for a ride.* For many, Ganesh is the most powerful icon, a reminder of the deep wisdom that allows us to see ourselves as an integral part of the whole. I'd been keeping the small Ganesh from the jeweler with me, and when I pulled him out and looked at him, I saw no distinction between us. Physically, yes (he was a chubby, elephant-headed man), but he seemed to be mirroring me at my most regal moments, fleeting as they were: grounded, balanced, present, and knowing the whole of the universe was contained inside me.

Hands, all different shades of brown, grazed the surface of the soft powder, which was produced from a special kind of wood burned in a sacred fire. Each person pressed a thimbleful into their third-eye chakra, leaving a mark at the lower center of the forehead. The ash is supposed to make people more receptive, and the place where you apply it on your body becomes more sensitive and attuned.

I watched and followed suit, carefully pressing the sacred powder in between my eyebrows. Some of it tumbled onto my Vaseline-coated lips (and I quickly pushed the thought of a bad omen away). I then saw a woman press some powder onto her throat, and I did the same, knowing that I most likely had issues to work on related to my *vishud-dhi*, or throat chakra—the one of the seven chakras, or energy centers, that deals with communication and expression of feelings. I could be expressive in my journal, in a poem. In these safe spaces, it all oozed out—the thrill and relief of exorcising such private thoughts. Stacks and stacks of lumpy, tear-soaked journals and dirty-paged notebooks from my field missions were stored in long rectangular plastic containers under my bed in my childhood bedroom in Chevy Chase; they would never see the light of day. I wanted to burn them, but it would feel too much like burning old pieces of me.

Emotion expressed face-to-face: that was hard. Impossible, even. I could not talk about my grief over my father to anyone. Could not do it. I could write it out, but I could not give the words voice. I had done so only once, at his funeral.

In yoga and Ayurveda, however, everything should flow freely. Chakras denote wheels of energy swirling throughout the body, and the goal is to keep the energy flowing freely. Blocked energy in a chakra can lead to illness. I wondered if I would get some disease from all this repression. Even Western doctors have recognized this in varying degrees. In the revered tome on women's health, *Women's Bodies, Women's Wisdom*, Dr. Christiane Northrup writes about how all emotions and thoughts are linked to our bodies and have physical effects across our immune, endocrine, and central nervous systems: "Unexpressed emotions tend to stay in the body like small ticking time bombs—they are illnesses in incubation," she says. I also read somewhere that suppressed grief will express itself as anxiety, which I experienced firsthand. I realized I had some work to do on the free-flowing-feelings front. It is exhausting to not feel what you feel.

Seeing the world as a manifestation of energy, seeing people as energetic entities, appealed to my developing mystical sensibilities. Life is considered a vibrational energy phenomenon across much of Asia and in many ancient cultures around the world, each with their own terms for the life force, or soul, or spirit, or energy that animates living creatures: Indians call it *prana*; the Chinese call it *chi*, or *ki* in Japan; Native Americans call it the Great Spirit. "At the center of the universe dwells the Great Spirit," said Black Elk, a holy medicine man from the Sioux tribe in South Dakota. "And that center is really everywhere. It is within each of us."

As I pressed the powder into my skin, I felt imbued by the sacred. The contemplative pause of the ritual allowed for the recognition of the deepest truth: the universe was inside me. And in those flashes of heightened awareness, I wasn't brown or white. I wasn't Indian or American, Eastern or Western, rich or poor. I wasn't married or unmarried. I was only *everything*.

I was just one person, one of billions. On a bus. On a train. In a temple.

I was alone, but I was actually not alone at all.

———

Madurai at midday is like hanging out in a frying pan with the burner on high. The compact Indian city heaves with dilapidated bungalows, mammoth Hindu temples, and vegetable vendors selling fat purple eggplants and chunks of ginger shaped like camels doing yoga. Feeling woozy from the heat, I took a tuk-tuk back to my cheap hotel, blasted the air-conditioning, and ordered samosas with ketchup, my childhood comfort food (hardly Ayurveda-approved, but Dr. Jossy was far away, and I was too hot to care). I sprawled on the bed like a starfish, wishing that I'd stayed in Kerala. I shuddered at the possibility that I really was one of those people: always looking for the next best thing, not only in love but in life. Would it never end?

It was a real psychological issue: having too much choice. Every time I return to the US after being in an African country, for example, I am shocked by the range of choices to the point that I'm paralyzed. It usually hits me in the grocery store. I stand there in a daze looking at all the milk options as the air-conditioning slowly freezes my flesh. There used to be three choices—skim, whole, or low fat. Cow's milk. Now there's soy, cashew, almond, oat, flax, rice, hazelnut, coconut, even quinoa—each with their own range of brands and sweeteners and vanilla and chocolate flavorings. In one part of the world, people are starving to death, and in another, we have thirty different kinds of milk to choose from. These choices don't even make us happier. I should not complain about choice and freedom in general—these are supposed to be good things, hard-won gains for women especially, and I am grateful—but I was starting to feel I didn't want to have quite so much to *choose from* anymore, even when it came to love. There were too many dating apps, too many possible dates, too many potential soul mates, yet no one. No one who felt right, no one who made sense, no one who made me feel like I was *coming home*. Worse, I was no longer confident in my choices.

Even choosing a temple to visit the next day felt overwhelming, as Madurai is stuffed with them. But I had come precisely to see the temples, so I vowed to visit at least one other before heading back to Mumbai the day after. By late afternoon, the debilitating heat had subsided, and I went outside to flag down a tuk-tuk. A kind-looking old man was parked in front of the hotel as if he had been waiting just for me to shuffle through the automatic glass doors of the two-star hotel in my worn chappals. We agreed on a fare to the lesser-known Koodal Alagar temple, dedicated to Lord Vishnu, the blue-colored god with four arms considered to be the all-pervading power that preserves the universe and maintains the cosmic order (definitely a big deal in Hindu mythology). I was drawn to the Vishnu temple because they say he resides in the sun, that light is his immutable essence. It was smaller, too, less of a tourist attraction and more of an everyday temple, which was part of its appeal.

I told the driver not to wait for me. Handfuls of Hindus glided in, quietly orbiting the ancient monument and prostrating themselves on the temple grounds. Their bodies stretched out on the dark marble, their hands in prayer position. It made me think of bhakti yoga, a form of devotional worship in Hinduism centered on an intense personal love for and attachment to god. Also known as the "path of devotion," it is considered to be the superior spiritual path to moksha, or enlightenment, in the *Bhagavad Gita*, the holiest of Hindu scriptures. The other two paths are the "path of action," or selfless action (karma yoga) and the "path of knowledge," or understanding and meditating on the difference between what is real and what is unreal (jnana yoga). I had no clue what path I was on, probably the last one, as that seemed to be the figuring-stuff-out path. I was the only so-called tourist there and, clothed in Indian garments, passed relatively unremarked, not because I blended in—certainly I did not with my lighter, sun-fried hair—but perhaps because Hindu temples are meant to dissolve the boundaries between man and the divine.

I didn't know what was happening to me, but I felt my heart unclenching, that box of stuff deep inside of me unlatching, as I circled the monument along with the gentle swarm of devout Hindus, fellow beings on their own cosmic journeys performing their daily puja after a long day's work. Their unquestioning faith was infectious, profoundly touching, and it opened up something in me. Grief breaks us open and gets to the core of us: in that way, it is a gift.

I'd been so insular with my grief. I'd tried to regulate my darker emotions by distracting myself instead of facing them head-on. It was just too hard to feel the pain. I could not have a proper conversation with my mother or my brother about what we had all lost. I could not visit my father's tombstone in upstate New York, even though I felt I should. It beckoned me, but I was afraid of the sadness, of sinking into it and not being able to climb out. I told myself, *Maybe I will go in November, around his birthday. Maybe I will be ready by then.* I had said this the last four Novembers. I knew something magical would happen when I went. That there would be signs: the crunchy autumn leaves would eddy in my presence. There would be a rainbow or a sudden reassuring hush of the wind, birds swirling around, a chipmunk hopping in front of me. My father would know I'd like these things. He still sent me signs sometimes. It did not seem plausible that he was gone. Where did he go? Did he go? I clung to the words in Walt Whitman's *Leaves of Grass*: "Nothing is ever really lost, or can be lost."

At his funeral, everyone was in pain but stoic. That was his side of the family. An Irish quality. I was not made that way. I wrote a poem and read it to the large circle of family in black. From above, maybe we looked like a flock of crows. I don't know how I did not buckle when I read this thing; I think he was there with me, invisible (an energetic presence maybe?), making sure that I got through it. He always liked my poems, said I had a way with words. Afterward the obese guy from the funeral home squeezed me hard, from behind, around the shoulders. "He will never leave you," he said, over and over into my ear. His breath smelled like Chex Mix. It did not seem appropriate, this hug, the fact that Chex Mix had been eaten that day. That anything had been eaten at all (but what *was* appropriate anymore?). I could not escape him and became limp. I didn't care that this enormous stranger was possibly squeezing me to death. I didn't know how to move forward anyway. I had lost one leg and one arm, half of me.

But in that temple in Madurai, I was alone but not alone, acknowledging grief's existence. It was cathartic. I bought a candle for my father, lit it, and added it to the rows of flickering candles, pools of glowing light that looked like small spoonfuls of setting suns. I allowed my grief to rise before I pushed it down again. I feared that I could only grieve in spurts, that my heart wouldn't be able to take it all in one go—it would shatter. Yet there, then, alone but surrounded by—something—it was okay to cry. It was okay to feel devastated. *It was a relief to feel.*

I left the temple in unanticipated emotion, only to find the tuk-tuk driver waiting for me. I didn't tell him where to go next, but sensing my sadness, he took control. I needed to feel the warm wind drying my cheeks and the comforting chaos of the city, of lives being lived around me, of other people who had lost other people yet continued to breathe. Strange that I had to go across the world to feel safe enough to open myself up.

Yet strength isn't always about fighting and being resilient; sometimes it's about *letting go* and splitting yourself open. India was allowing me to split myself open and rebuild myself again.

India was teaching me that life is a delicate balance of surrender and control. That we have a deep knowing of the things we need to surrender to and the things we cannot control. That the hard part is actually *listening* to that knowing.

India had shown me that there was a mass of heavy liquid grief that had no place to go and was constantly floating inside the monastery of myself. My soul was suffocating in the wrack and had been calling out for me to let the dammed-up waters flow.

My sojourn was teaching me that like *agni*, the fire inside us, the soul needs tending. Like everything in life, cultivating the soul is a balancing act. We can only cultivate the soul when we honor what it has been through, when we give a voice and a space to the thoughts, emotions, and grief percolating inside, waiting to be acknowledged so that transformation can take place. This part, the hard part—the grieving—is the prerequisite. The threshold for everything ahead. The opening.

Maybe it was being inside temples that gave me a sudden, unusual tenderness toward myself regarding my devotion to this pilgrimage, if that was really what it was. Maybe it was the spaciousness I'd allowed myself, but something was breaking me open, even more than I'd broken before, and I was discovering a powerful energy inside. The singer-songwriter Leonard Cohen wrote that there's a crack in everything and that's how the light gets in.[8] That's where the healing happens: in the surrendering.

When we let the light in, slowly, over time, the light eats up the dark, surpasses the dark, and all that is left is love.

This love is the immutable essence that carries us forward.

Chapter 3

TRANSCENDING

Life shrinks or expands in proportion to one's courage.

—Anaïs Nin

By April, after spending three months in India, I found myself in a sprawling eighteenth-century farmhouse in a part of Sicily I couldn't even find on a map, surrounded by endless rows of olive trees, lime-green artichoke fields, and rolling vineyards. The weather was a wild change from the humid clutches of Mumbai. In this southeastern corner of the island, the salty wind from North Africa whipped at my skin, and ruddy-cheeked farmers, weathered by decades under the unapologetic sun, drove battered old Fiats.

My adventurous and entrepreneurial Italian friend Chiara had been increasingly unhappy living in London and after eighteen years had finally quit her job to move to Sicily, where she was renting a massive farmhouse near the famous wine-producing region of Nero D'Avola. Fulfilling a long-held dream, she had converted a former wheat mill into a space to host health and wellness retreats, and she invited me to be a guest at her first retreat, which happened to have a kundalini yoga theme. She wanted feedback from select friends as she got things off the ground.

Of course I said yes—this was integral to me committing to my path of self-discovery, to saving myself through saying yes to anything that served my well-being and transported me to beautiful and healing landscapes where I could be wildly true to the energy that was ready to rise up and through me. This retreat would help further awaken what I could only imagine had been my long-neglected kundalini, the female energy often visualized as a serpent coiled up at the base of our spines, inside the triangular bone known as the sacrum, and usually in a dormant state. The signs of a *kundalini rising* were already there—a dissatisfaction with the status quo and a longing for inner development, a heightened interest in metaphysics and anything esoteric, and a sense that something holy was happening inside me, though it was all mysterious and unnamed.

As intrigued as I was to tap more into my kundalini side, I had to skip half of the ten-day retreat because of a trip back home. After leaving India, I'd spent a couple of weeks in DC visiting the family, followed by a couple of weeks in New York for a work-related conference, before turning around and heading back across the Atlantic. I had been half dreading going back to New York, but I'd been given a long lead, so to speak, and didn't want to appear ungrateful by disowning my hardly crucial role in the latest bilateral brouhaha on Forty-Second Street. I'd been looking forward to seeing friends and familiar faces, eating a bagel and catching up on non-Bollywood cinema, but by no means did I want to get sucked back into the vortex. "New York is like an abusive boyfriend you keep coming back to," my friend Cornelia once remarked. Part of me still felt anchored there (it is cloying—once NYC is in you, does it ever leave?), but I was afraid I'd be pulled back to the office for administrative reasons. That was the first thought that entered my mind when I made my way down the carpeted hallway of my office building.

While I was there, I worked in the communal kitchen area, the depot for the deskless, project-based consultants who roamed in and out, many of them more comfortable working in a container in South Sudan or in a remote suboffice in Zambia than in HQ itself. On a positive note, the fact that there was literally no physical space for me in the office reinforced my case that I should continue working remotely through the summer as planned. Mads had to concede that my productivity hadn't faltered. I had worked hard the last few months.

"You've been doing a good job," he said, grudgingly. "Finish whatever personal development crap you're doing and get back here by September."

He had given me more time, the universe had given me more time, though I feared that at any moment he would rescind our agreement. If he did, I would have had to decline, no matter the consequences. I was in sync with something, and abandoning it now would have been like jumping off a moving walkway before I reached the end.

Yes, I wanted to leave New York before it seduced me back into it (that's our little game), but I also wanted to run off before I bumped into J. I wanted to see her, but I didn't want to see her. I felt I'd grown so much in the last few months, yet I wasn't convinced that I'd outgrown my feelings. I didn't want the emotions that would arise in her presence to derail me and make me feel like I hadn't evolved in any way, because I had. I had to have changed. Relief swept over me when I checked in at JFK without having had to confront her or any of the residual emotions I had about her.

———

I'd never set foot in Sicily, even though I had lived close to the island for more than two years. While I was technically based in Rome starting in 2008, a fair share of my time was spent outside of the country on UN missions, or on an extended posting in Bangkok, or in the prisonlike office near Fiumicino Airport working on communications related to natural disasters, wars, and other humanitarian crises. So my travel within Italy had been mostly limited to weekend trips to Abruzzi or lower Tuscany with Alessandro.

But Sicily. That was *un'altra cosa*—a whole other thing. It is the land of wild vegetation, rustic beaches, and the lava-strewn slopes of Mount Etna and Stromboli. Something pulled me toward it, so I made a beeline to its rugged shores as soon as Chiara gave me a reason to.

I would also have the chance to do something I'd been wanting to do for a while: work on a farm. While I was still working remotely, I was clocking only three days a week, which gave me four days to do whatever I wanted. To that end, I'd joined World Wide Opportunities on Organic Farms (WWOOF) as a member and was waiting to hear back from various farmers. The organization links volunteers, usually travelers with wanderlust on a budget, with organic farmers and growers. The volunteer works on the land in some capacity for four to six hours each day—making compost, gardening, planting, chopping wood, weeding, harvesting, and making wine, among other things—in exchange for meals and a place to sleep. The whole thing is based on trust, and there is no money involved. I'd met WWOOFers around the world, and they spoke of the experience the way Burners speak about the annual Burning Man festival in Nevada: it was a game changer.

Nature was something that had become unfamiliar to me in recent years, with my existence being entrenched in, even marred by, city living. Nature is what the shaman Sandra Ingerman describes as our "spiritual ally." There was no one to blame but myself—while nature was within reach, I hadn't made enough of an effort to steep myself in it in New York, beyond the sporadic bike ride in Central Park or jaunt to the Hamptons on summer weekends. Yet I'd been feeling a growing, inexplicable, almost primal longing to return to nature, and I'd felt that in Kerala. My job had become entirely cerebral, mostly computer based, and I wanted to get my hands dirty, to feel the earth, to have her chalky, brown flesh under my fingernails by the end of the day, to experience her healing powers firsthand. I was not alone in this hunger. In the spiritual circles I retreated in and out of, Gaia—the primordial Earth or mother goddess in Greek mythology, one of the deities who governed the universe—was regularly invoked as a source of spiritual nourishment in rituals and chants to heighten awareness and enhance our connection with the earth. Kooky as it sounds, unlike our ancestors who lived off the earth, many of us have lifestyles that deprive us of that close union to the planet. We have closer relationships with our technologies.

A last-ditch trip to Tulum on Mexico's Yucatan Peninsula the year before—the very spot where I'd befriended Chiara, in fact, at a yoga retreat—had made me realize that sand, green things, water, mountains, and air carrying the scent of sun instead of taxi fumes were lacking in my life in a grave way. A reading with a no-nonsense Mayan astrologer on that trip surfaced what at the time I'd known only subconsciously: I desperately needed nature. This was no shocker. "If you don't get nature in your life somehow, you will wilt," warned Luce, looking at me with her lucid brown eyes as we sat in her stuffy, sage-scented tent at Uno, a hippie-filled *astrolodge* on a stretch of white-sand beach popular with kite surfers.

I knew she was right, but I hadn't heeded her advice until a whole year later. In the meantime, until I'd set foot in Kerala, I'd been visibly wilting. I looked like I was. I felt like I was. I was pretty blasé about my well-being. There was no luster to me; a once-youthful glow had been sandblasted off by all the hustling, stress, and lack of sleep that came with the modern way of living and the vestiges of grief—my *ojas* were all but depleted. After India, however, my skin and hair were golden; I was also energetically different. *I was carrying a lighter load.* Confronting some of my grief must have siphoned off some of the heaviness I'd been hauling around. I also felt like a heightened awareness that I didn't really have before had been awakened in me, and I didn't want to lose whatever that thing was, but explore it more. I'd made space for it—*yutori*. My life was no longer crunched up but stretching out like an accordion, and so was I. I wasn't clamping down on everything, but rather allowing things—my emotions, my breath—to flow in and out in whatever way they wanted.

———

The morning after I arrived at Chiara's *masseria*, or farmhouse, I found myself sitting on a yoga mat in lotus position, quivering under the red fleece blanket draped across my lap, and engaging in "breaths of fire." Kundalini yoga, brought to the US from India in the late 1960s by the late Yogi Bhajan (born Harbhajan Singh Puri, a controversial figure among followers of the ancient Sikh religion), can seem quirky at times, but there was something profoundly compelling in the phrase largely attributed to Yogi Bhajan: "If you can't see God in all, you can't see God at all." The main breathing technique practiced in kundalini yoga, *Kapalabhati Pranayama*, is supposed to awaken the white-hot kundalini energy that purportedly exists in every body, coiled at the spine, that can be jolted awake by engaging in various spiritual disciplines, such as abdominal breathing exercises that force the stomach to jut in and out and involve quick, forceful exhalations followed by passive inhalations. Despite the tedium, the breathing technique is said to wipe away toxic buildup from the blood and lungs and to energize practitioners, even after only three minutes of doing it. Another benefit: stimulating this type of energy in the lower part of the body (the second chakra) is supposed to work wonders for reproductive health and fertility.

As I breathed in, I thought about the subtle plane where kundalini operates and how the female physical anatomy—its ability to be a conduit for new life—renders us more powerful than men, though current power structures would suggest otherwise. Everyone in spiritual circles is saying that the consciousness of the planet is shifting into the feminine; that we're moving into the Age of Aquarius, which is about no longer denying the feminine energy but reintegrating it with the male in an equal partnership; that women from all walks of life are emerging and coming into their power; that we will be a collective force to reckon with; and that much of that power will help heal the planet. Yogi Bhajan recognized the power of the female in his teachings, remarking that a woman's intuition is sixteen times stronger than a man's. I liken this intuition to a playful and powerful goddess inside me who knows everything but is largely left sleeping and ignored unless I awaken her through dedicated interior work, the engagement of spiritual practices, such as meditation, yoga, and chanting.

"Now open your heart by pushing your breast bone away from you," the Italian teacher said, guiding the class along with her raspy voice.

Extending my chest back and upward, I looked at the skylight in the dome-shaped ceiling that was cracked from age. Sunlight beamed into the unseasonably chilly room. It was exquisite, the stretching. My heart was open, more open than it had been, but I knew it could be *more* open, maybe not like a child's but less like someone who had loved and lost, as if loving and losing weren't a natural part of life. While the Ayurveda I'd started practicing in India had been cleansing and balancing to a degree, I thought being in nature and working on a farm would take it to the next level, offer its own form of therapy by opening me up to myself even more. I'd only just scratched the surface of the long journey into the wilderness of the self, and I wanted to continue while I was on a roll instead of bailing after a couple of months and possibly losing that heightened awareness that had been switched on by darkness, my teacher, the thing that I'd been afraid of that turned out to be revelatory. I was committed to this journey of saving myself, even if I wasn't sure exactly how I was going to do it. A good start, I figured, was finding new ways of being alive.

The retreat itself was about transcending the human ego and connecting with our true nature. Given the surroundings, there was an element of actual nature infused organically within the retreat. I arrived in time to enjoy a handful of eclectic group activities, such as a breathwalk, a silent form of walking meditation. It reminded me of an insight meditation retreat I attended at Spirit Rock, a meditation center in Northern California, where we practiced *Vipassana*, continuous close attention to sensation—of walking, of breathing, of eating, all in silence—a process of self-purification through an almost piercing self-observation that can kind of drive you bonkers. At that retreat, a large group of (mostly white) folks was instructed to do things like walk around outside in an extremely slow, crazy-looking manner, basically like zombies, ignoring each other but paying attention to each step: the crushing sound of the dried grass when stepped on, the gravelly feel of the road. One of the exercises involved taste awareness. We were given small paper cups containing three raisins, but we couldn't eat them straight away. We had to first look at them, taking in their shriveled-up-ness; then we felt the texture of a single raisin with our fingers and put the raisin on our tongue, rolling it around to see what that felt like, before biting into it. Only once we had fully appreciated the small explosion of sweet tartness on our taste buds were we slowly to chew the raisin for five minutes before swallowing. Most people can't eat that way all the time, for time-management, starvation, and sanity-preservation reasons, but it was a thought-provoking exercise: *the art of noticing*.

On Chiara's property, a more diverse group of us—a mishmash from London, Brussels, Barcelona, Sicily, and New York, both men and women, yoga aficionados and regular people—meandered similarly through open artichoke and wheat fields at dawn in our yoga attire, wholly focused on listening to the sounds of nature while trying not to step on any vipers. "Do not speak or make eye contact with others," commanded the yoga teacher, and we all giggled like schoolchildren while I sneezed in a frightful bout of hay fever. The morning wind brushed across the long stalks of wheat and through the olive trees, sounding like a million tiny hands clapping. I'd read about *Shinrin-yoku*, a term that translates to "forest bathing" in English. It was a practice developed in Japan during the 1980s after researchers discovered the healing benefits of spending time under the canopy of a living forest. I didn't need a lot of scientific references to be convinced.

Sensory-wise, my hankering to work with the land—to hear those sounds every day and to feel like I was doing something productive, something tangible, instead of spending my life on endless conference calls, in meetings, and reading emails—was further reinforced. There was something life-affirming about it. I knew shamefully little about agriculture. My paternal grandfather had run a nursery in upstate New York, but when it came to growing anything, keeping something herbal alive, I was clueless. Even the basil plants and orchids I splurged on from Whole Foods seemed to perish in my apartment within hours, but it had to be in my blood, buried somewhere.

The Sicilians at the retreat all poked fun at my desire to "reconnect with nature," because it was such a part of their daily lives. But I was over the moon when the artichokes or zucchini I'd plucked with my own hands from the surrounding land ended up in the frittata or made their way into the evening's risotto. Food gathering was so raw and primal. *"Sei molto americana,"* they'd say, but I didn't mind. I didn't think wanting to have a farm experience was so American, rather more human and carnal. Generally, though, if you had nature in your life, then you would not know what it felt like to be imbalanced by the lack of it being there and to want it so badly. If, on a daily basis, you went from your apartment to the inside of a subway car to Grand Central Terminal, and then passed concrete building after concrete building, with a smattering of stark trees sagging from pollution, on the way to your own concrete building, and the reverse on the way home, only then would you know how empty and thirsty you could feel for it. Maybe, like me, you wouldn't understand how powerful that thirst was, how dry and crackly and vacant you were feeling inside, for quite some time.

Or how that thirst could diminish your wholeness in a way you never thought possible and propel you to step way outside of your comfort zone in order to fill your reserves back up again.

———

After everyone left, I stayed on, waiting to hear back from the WWOOF farms. I enjoyed the rugged scenery and waking up in the *masseria*, which was surrounded by cacti, grapevines, lemon and olive trees, and other vegetation indigenous to the area. Afternoons I'd work on the terrace in the gentle, gradually deepening sunshine broken up by gusts of sea-chilled wind. In the mornings, Chiara, who was a passionate and life-loving force of nature, would show me around the land she'd fallen in love with that was at her fingertips every day. She took me on hardy walks through blood orange groves and to the Vendicari Nature Reserve, which was dotted with rusty-rose flamingos, where milky-blue waves crashed against the rocky coastline with abandon. I was in awe of the life she had manifested. She made the whole thing look effort-less, though I knew it took major guts and extreme logistical patience seeing that it was Italy, where bureaucracy is the norm. I was living my dream of having some freedom and spaciousness; she was definitely living her dream of dumping a job she'd grown out of to start her own retreat center. We had progressed from the stuck places we'd both been in when we met in Tulum, though I still had a way to go toward what I wanted, which was not entirely clear. It was a subtle but tangible feeling of moving forward, of moving through and beyond something.

When I realized just how untethered I was without a home of my own, for example, it was a bit frightening. In a way, I was grateful for my UN contract. Even though I was annoyed that I had to tote a laptop to Sicily and work when I wanted to do other things, the work not only paid me and enabled me to travel but also anchored me to something, kept me from floating away into the ether. They say that if you love what's in your way, it will transform. I decided to look at my assignments as reminders of what had drawn me into this line of work all those years ago: the opportunity to witness the world, to experience a deep human connection, and maybe, subconsciously, to bring darkness into my world in order to have the complete human experience. Strangely, it paralleled exactly what I was going through during these months—what drove me was what I was receiving. I'd never heard myself say, "I just want to be happy." It was always more complex than that. Even if my mind was exploring different avenues, in my heart I was still aligned with my career. Being face-to-face with grief and loss in emergency settings through my work had been transformational for me; it had helped me prepare for my own losses, and I was grateful for it. While I could not glorify all humanitarian-aid or disaster-relief work—there were plenty of valid questions around the effectiveness and sustainability of some of the more common approaches—I still trusted the instincts that pushed me in that direction in the first place, even though it was taking a back seat temporarily so I could put myself and my spiritual development first. There was a shift, an evening-out period.

As a housewarming gift, I decided to plant Chiara an herb garden on her new plot of land. I'd become a little obsessed with the idea of creating through connecting with the earth. I went to a nearby store where I purchased *rosmarino, timo, basilico, salvia, menta,* and various seeds from a large Sicilian man who helped me carry the heaving trays of herbs into Chiara's car after she put down a tarp so that the soil wouldn't grind into the back seat. There was something about bringing life forth through planting that appealed to me because it gave me a teeny role in nature's biological process, as arguably I wasn't heeding my own. Another thing: I'd seen and written about death, a lot of it, through my humanitarian work and then, of course, in my own world; but I also wanted or needed to focus on life, for my own self-preservation.

There had to be light to balance out the dark. The world is an expression of dualities. It's in mythology. It's present across cultures. In Chinese medicine, the feminine and masculine energies of yin and yang are opposite yet complementary forces that cannot exist without the other, and together they form a whole. In Hinduism, Shakti and Shiva are different sides of the same coin—these feminine and masculine energies need each other to create life. If, ultimately, I was striving for a sense of wholeness, whatever that felt like, I had to tend to both sides. I had to even things out.

A woman wouldn't feel pleasure if she didn't know pain.

Life could not exist without death.

In opposition, there is balance. There is the right amount of gravity keeping everything together.

I could think about death, know it deeply in my bones, but I needed to think about life, too, and be active and engaged in its unfolding. Nature felt like the most welcoming way to step into that.

But when I got down to it, I couldn't find a shovel, a small detail I'd overlooked. I started digging with a large spoon from the kitchen as Stella, the mutt who lived on the property, looked on with amusement. Clearing out a patch of grass with a spoon is harder and more time-consuming than it would seem, or *should* seem, but physics was not my strong suit. I'd initially been too shy to go to the property next door to ask the men who were constructing some sort of addition to the *masseria* for a shovel. There are many words I simply didn't know in Italian because I had never needed to use them in Rome—*shovel*, for example. (In my defense, neither did Chiara, and she is a native Italian speaker.) But when my patience thinned, I ventured next door and bumped into a hunky workman who introduced himself as Marcello. I pointed toward a cluster of disparate shovels leaning upright against a thick stack of chopped wood and explained I needed one of those things for a *giardino* I was planting. He handed me one with a glint in his turquoise eyes. I felt an instant physical attraction to his almost corrosive hotness, his fitted shirt charred with cigarette burns, mottled with coffee stains or dirt. I hadn't thought about being with a man *in months.* My fast from men had been liberating in that sense, with any kind of sexual hunger siphoned into more esoteric pursuits.

The Sanskrit word *Brahmacharya,* which is often translated as "going after god, or Brahma," is widely used in relation to celibacy. The idea is that by moderating our sexual or sensory pleasures, by keeping our lives clean and simple, we save our vital energy for spiritual pursuits and self-realization, which brings us closer to god. I had been celibate, and didn't really miss sex, especially as sex without an emotional or spiritual connection was no longer of interest to me, though in this instance I was reminded of that carnal, animalistic desire inside all of us.

I dragged the heavy shovel back to the other side of the house with little grace and struggled to get it to break the ground. Marcello came by to check on me several minutes later, and when he saw the mess I was making, he took the shovel from my hands. *"Fai cosi,"* he said as he stepped on the back of it with his big boot, breaking the earth without exerting much effort. *"Facile,"* he said. It was *facile*—easy—with a bit of gunpower. I weighed less than his bicep. Obviously, I was not a natural at this kind of thing.

As I got into the rhythm of planting, I felt the velvety-soft soil between my fingers, cool like glass, and didn't even flinch at the squirming worms, simply brushed them aside as I sneezed my way through the sowing of each herb, occasionally tumbling over from my squat, my dust-caked calves numb from holding the position. It was a small project, but when I was done, when I saw Chiara's genuine smile later that afternoon as I unveiled my modest masterpiece, I noticed how good it felt to create something with my hands. To be dirty and merged with the earth, surrounded by endless landscape and wind and silence, which heightens kundalini energy and enhances spiritual intuition. Maybe if I created enough small things, individual, self-sustaining, imperfect masterpieces, I could eventually create something much bigger, something important that would leave some sort of legacy.

Maybe that's exactly what life is: like Russian dolls, an accumulation of small creations, within a creation, within a creation. Shakti, the primordial feminine creative force that manifests, the Great Divine Mother, the evolutionary force of infinite wisdom, is always speaking through us, through our subtle bodies, and it is our most sacred job to listen.

———

I could have stayed with Chiara, lounging around the *masseria*, plucking oranges off trees and eating from the land, but it felt like time to move on, to feed my soul with whatever it was hungering for. Ultimately, I planned to make my way down to the island of Pantelleria, known as the black pearl of the Mediterranean—a rugged and sparsely populated volcanic outcrop off the southwest coast of Sicily, about sixty miles from Tunisia. I'd wanted to go there for years because it was *selvaggia*, or savage and wild, nature at its most extreme according to Alessandro, whose tastes were always in line with my own. The man managed to be sophisticated, cool, and unflappable all in an uncontrived way, refined to the point that he spoke and wrote in exquisite Italian, unusual in Rome even among Italians, while I butchered mine with my non-native grammar. While the difference in our ages and our mutual commitment issues drove us apart romantically, we were now friends. There was a real tenderness between us. I trusted this man's advice when I called him from Chiara's to say hello and he said, "Nathy, *vai lì*." I would go there, but I wanted to do the farming thing first.

Coordinating with the WWOOF farms, however, had taken longer than I'd hoped. Not only had I left it to the last minute, but most places weren't looking for help until early summer. The other challenge that I hadn't entirely thought through was transportation: without my own car, I was doomed to a logistical nightmare involving irregular Sicilian buses that would surely leave me stranded on the side of some dusty road for hours. I was being silly and bratty: I was stressed that I didn't have a place to farm at, that I'd decided to wing it as usual instead of thinking things through, leaving me feeling pitifully disorganized. I took several deep breaths and waited for guidance, a new practice I'd started. Asking, waiting. I recalled that one of the couples at the retreat, Maya and Filip, lived on a vineyard at the foothills of Mount Etna—the tallest active volcano in Europe at nearly eleven thousand feet. I got their number from Chiara and phoned them to see if they needed a helping hand. Turned out, they were part of WWOOF and frequently had WWOOFers working on their vineyard. *Kismet.* They told me to come on by, that they had plenty of work for me.

There was no way to avoid the buses, though. My only choice was to take one up to Linguaglossa, the main town on the northern side of Mount Etna, via Catania. It was confusing, and I missed a couple of transfers, but fortunately I'd left my rather large suitcase at the *masseria* and was traveling with nothing but a big tote bag, a tatty copy of *Walden*, and my laptop, which I'd have left behind had I not needed to work part of the time. As Yogi Bhajan said, "Travel light, live light, spread the light, be the light." It felt good to pare down, and I knew I was not alone in wanting to purge materially. A trend of minimalism was growing in the US, an almost fetishized simplicity, possibly a reaction to years of capitalist overindulgence. Since being in India, I'd started to realize that getting rid of things helped me *see* and understand myself more. The less I had externally, the more I had internally. Stuff—in the form of furniture, books, clothes, superfluous gadgets, and so on—had weight. Weight diminished presence. Presence was the hole through which light could be perceived.

I bounced out of the bus at the Europa Café stop as instructed and was picked up by the effervescent Maya, the owner of Terre di Maya, the vineyard where I would be WWOOFing. It was chilly and overcast as I slipped into her jeep with a pashmina swathed around my head, but I was happy to see her. I hadn't spoken to her much at the retreat on account of my being a few days late, but I could already tell she was one of those really cool women. Originally a real estate agent from New York, Maya had spent decades living in Belgium, Pakistan, and Japan in many incarnations—a nightclub manager in Tokyo, the wife of an Italian diplomat in Pakistan, an art agent in Belgium, and finally a wine producer in Sicily. In between those things, she was also a healer, a writer, a musician, and an artist. I couldn't tell how old she was; she was sort of ageless. She had a warm, inviting energy, childlike in her effervescence, but with three grown kids and three marriages, I estimated she was in her late fifties at the least. She had a svelte body and prominent rear, which her hair cascaded toward in long dreadlocks. Ethnically she was Afro-Caribbean, but she said she also had Nordic blood and described herself as "a multiethnic free spirit," a hybrid person who didn't really fit into a box—something I could identify with.

That question—"Where are you from?"—plagues a lot of nomadic types with composite identities, which would describe most, if not all, of my colleagues over the last decade. A typical profile would be the half-Japanese/half-Australian colleague who lived in Kigali, Rome, and Bangui, or the Canadian-Italian who lived in Colombo, Kabul, and Erbil. They probably studied in France or Switzerland or the UK, and spoke a minimum of three languages each. These folks have no real answer to questions about where they're from.

When you have lived everywhere, you become everything. You become a part of the universal fabric. You speak its language. In that sense, Maya and I were also kindred spirits. After all, according to Ayurveda, like attracts like. I wasn't really Indian, but I didn't feel entirely American either. I was somewhere in between. Today no one is purely one thing. Edward Said, who wrote extensively about imperialism and orientalism, described labels—Indian, woman, American—as mere jumping-off points, which if followed into an individual's actual experience are quickly left behind.[1] This was one of the many relics of imperialism—the merging of cultures and identities on a macro scale.

As for Maya, she had an unwillingness to limit herself to one ethnicity, one career, one geographical location, or even one man. She embodied the idea that you could be many things at the same time or many things at different times. She did not abide by any rules except for one: not to harm the planet. She was definitely not someone you could pigeonhole in any way—and to my mind, those are the most interesting people. She gave herself permission to live life on her own terms, to live the fullest life she could envision for herself, and that is exactly what she had done.

While I had tried to live that way, I experienced episodes of self-consciousness or guilt about going against convention, as if I were breaking a pact I'd made with some invisible oligarchy, or if I did anything else I would be a failure. Maya, on the other hand, was unapologetic about it all, and her home was a reflection of her heterogeneous ideals. It was like walking into a small, highly curated museum. Filip, her much younger (rugged and handsome) husband, who was out of the country on some sort of healing seminar, was also a former art dealer from Brussels, and the rooms were shrouded with the most eclectic mix of acrylic paintings, nude sculptures, African masks, handwoven Kashmiri throws, and hundreds of thick coffee-table books on art. Various instruments lined the walls, such as flutes and a set of djembe drums. A long, gorgeous sitar, a plucked stringed instrument from India, was enshrined in the corner near a huge Buddha statue. There was no prototype for her home, no ostensible theme, so anything or anyone could fit in. Etna, a snow-covered majesty, hovered in the backdrop of it all.

Another WWOOFer was there when I arrived, a young German who had been there for two weeks and was leaving the next morning. He was staying in a small guest room on the other side of the spacious kitchen. I slept on the couch in the living room that night, and Maya was in the master bedroom on the second level. He was in his early twenties, and I was instantly confronted with his lightness of being. He told me he had been WWOOFing his way across Europe for several months. Working in nature, I was convinced, had a salubrious effect on people. Through my own work, I'd spent time with countless farmers facing drought or flooded crops—in the Ethiopian highlands, in northern Bangladesh, and in the mountains of Pakistan—and in spite of the backbreaking work, in spite of the very real anxiety of not knowing if they would have enough food to last them through the season, somehow these people who lived such hard but honest and simple lives entirely dependent on nature, wholly affected by her fickle, indiscriminate ways, seemed less anxious, lighter than the people back home. They were generally more grounded and at peace with things; in some cases, they even seemed happier than my friends who appeared to have everything. No doubt, working on the land, in nature, was good for the soul. It made complete sense: we emerged from it. We came from its compost. To that end, each time we reconnect with it, *we are returning home.* When we are severed from it, we feel lost—at least that was how I'd been starting to feel in New York. It was my mental home, the place where I probably knew the most people, but not my spiritual home.

Farm work, unsurprisingly, was also good for physical fitness. In fact, I felt unnerved by the German's tall, lean, muscular body, his self-described penchant for manual work. He was leaving big shoes to fill, and I hoped Maya didn't expect me to lift anything heavy. I was old(ish), after all, just over a hundred pounds, and definitely unskilled in farm labor—not that I wasn't up for a challenge. To prepare myself for the farm experiment, I'd done what any upper-middle-class neophyte would do: I researched. On the plane over, I watched *Into the Wild,* Sean Penn's film about some guy's immersion in the Alaskan wilderness where he hunts wild animals with a .22 caliber rifle and basically lives off the land. In addition to that, I read the few nonboring chunks of *How to Stay Alive in the Woods: A Complete Guide to Food, Shelter, and Self-Preservation That Makes Starvation in the Wilderness Next to*

Impossible. I was also slowly making my way through Thoreau's *Walden* for the second time since high school. This time, though, I was actually *reading* it instead of just gleaning the highlights for a term paper. The reality, however, was that all of that was overkill—I doubted I would need to know how to extract birch syrup from the inner bark of a tree for survival.

"It won't be too bad," assured the young German, while I peppered him with questions. "You look tough enough," he said, smiling as he cast a curious eye over my sundress.

I already knew that I was—tough enough.

Life proves our resilience over and over.

We can either rise to the challenge or become meek and get swallowed up in the folds of our own sorrow. In every moment of every day, I felt I was making that choice over and over. Finding new ways of being alive was a huge part of it.

———

The evening before, Maya had summoned the man who lived on the property and tended the land out of his modest living quarters to introduce us. He was a chiseled, hardworking Romanian named Dumitru. His face was slick and hungry looking.

"She is going to help you farm tomorrow," she explained.

Dumitru looked me up and down. It seemed as if he was pretty sure that I wasn't going to be of much use to him. He barely said hello before retreating into his quarters.

The next morning confirmed that Dumitru was a man of few words, but he had a real presence about him, a quiet fortitude. A lean man with scars up and down his sun-crisped arms, he commanded respect through his quietude. Maya told me his whole family lived back in Bucharest, and he sent money home, sometimes taking the long bus journey with pocketfuls of cash. He'd once cut off his finger working, the blood gushing everywhere, and instead of going to the local hospital—where he ran the risk of revealing his then-illegal status in Italy—he wrapped his hand and detached finger in a T-shirt and took a bus to Romania to get treated. This was no wuss. I could see that. A cigarette stayed rooted in his mouth as he wielded his chainsaw and grunted at me to follow him. I trailed behind him up the terraces, intrepid. I really didn't *feel* like using a chainsaw, certain it would end in a bloodbath with all of my fingers gone. And that wouldn't help me with the whole dirt-under-my-nails thing. That was the whole point: to merge with the earth, not whack her apart.

"That looks heavy," I said, speaking to him in Italian since that would be our common language. When I received no response, I continued, of course. "So, what exactly am I going to be doing?"

He turned and stared at me with his blueberry eyes and then pointed his callused hands toward the ground. In almost indecipherable Romanian-Italian, he explained that I was to remove all the long sticks from the pathway—sticks that looked like long, bumpy gray fingers—and I could use them to prop the grapevines up, to keep them trellised. He also needed me to clear the pathway of any stones or rubbish so that when he passed through with the tractor, the machine wouldn't get stuck. This was easy. I was definitely overprepared mentally, if not physically, but I welcomed the simplicity of the task.

I was disappointed that I wouldn't actually be *picking grapes*—harvest season was several months away, in September, and I felt a twinge of embarrassment at my ignorance around that. At that moment, the grapes were just tiny green bubbles. In any case, I did what I was told, sloping off on my own to collect the sticks and tidy everything up around the vines. Running a vineyard, I soon learned, involves much more than planting grapes, waiting for them to ripen, squishing them into wine, and then gulping it all down—there are about a million boring steps in between. I noted the irony in abstaining from drinking while working on the vineyard.

When I climbed up the many terraces, I was met with the deafening sound of uncontaminated silence. No cars or voices. Just breathing insects, the sigh of the sirocco. The sunshine peeled down in lemony streaks, making the vineyards glow. Is this what Yogi Bhajan meant by seeing god in all? I felt like I was looking at god, or some expression of divinity. Maybe it was that easy, but just as I was getting lost in the splendor of it all, my thoughts stopped me.

No, the world wasn't perfect at all. For some reason, my mind drifted to my time in Haiti after the earthquake. It was my first on-the-ground emergency—one of the most physically and emotionally taxing things I'd ever gone through. I don't think anyone is ever prepared for the kind of shock, the kind of misery that can result from a natural disaster, or any kind of humanitarian disaster for that matter. I was dispatched as a spokesperson, doing TV interviews on news outlets like CNN to raise awareness of humanitarian needs and bringing convoys of journalists to earthquake-ravaged areas where the UN agency I represented was distributing aid. Like everyone else down there, I worked well past midnight each night, toiling away in a heat that grilled everything, sleeping in a tent or on top of a dumpster amid suffocating dust. My first night, I actually "slept" in the military compound in an abandoned tent, which collapsed in the middle of the night. My first week, I fled riots that had broken out at an aid-distribution site and was forced to run out on the street and jump into the back of a pickup truck for safety.

But it was the exposure to death and destruction—the sheer amount of need—that was the most draining, the most faith-shaking. To meet families that had lost their homes, lost their children, and were trapped in the direst of situations, destitute and heartbroken, their resilience tested on every front. How could I see god in that? Sometimes I felt like I carried a world of pain inside me that was not even mine. I had no right to that pain. I had witnessed it, but I wasn't allowed to own it or wallow in it. I absorbed it anyway just by nature of being exposed to it.

Then there was my own pain, still clawing. I thought of the envelope of baby teeth. I found it in my father's leather jewelry box where he kept precious things: letters from his father and a man's ring, gold with a creamy green gemstone, that his father-in-law had given him on my parents' wedding day. I didn't know that he had kept my baby teeth, but I discovered them after he died, when we were going through things slowly, quietly, with a stomach-wrenching sorrow. I could not bear to think of him keeping them all those years. To think about how much you have to love someone to keep their old teeth.

I was scared I would be sad forever. Yet I knew my father wouldn't want that. He would not have wanted the loss of him to be a shroud, to darken my whole life's path. I kept reading that the universe doesn't give you more than you can handle, a platitude that offers little comfort, but the universe is under no obligation to make sense to us. At Etna, I was steeped in beauty, in light, but I'd been steeped in the opposite for so long, and it was hard to align both of those things in my soul. Questioning things has a generative power, that much I understood, but I didn't understand exactly *what* it generated. There is a richness that can come from not knowing. It can lead us through a gateway.

I was willing to admit that I didn't know anything when it came to these pressing mystical questions. I was trying to find a thread in the chaos, but I hadn't yet. Somehow, though, I found a trace of comfort in reaching a place where I could admit to that bare unknowingness.

Mount Etna is several nested stratovolcanoes—conical volcanoes built up by many layers mostly consisting of hardened lava, pumice, and volcanic ash—and has not one but four distinct summit craters. Sicilians often refer to her as Mungibeddu.

On a clear day, I could feel Etna watching me—her almost deific presence towering in the background as I bent over, sneezing, making my tiny contribution to this vast stretch of undulating land that required constant care. She was the only company I had most days, as Dumitru was out of sight much of the time doing the heavy-duty work. Even if I was probably the least helpful farmhand he'd ever encountered, we shared a silent bond. It was the most I had ever communicated with someone without words or touching. Maya, too, spent most days toiling in the vegetation, gloves up to her elbows, with a determined look and a cherry-red handkerchief around her forehead. Yet Etna: I drenched myself in her copious, self-assured silence. There was something comforting about Etna's existence—if something as incredible as Etna could exist, anything was possible. At first I felt a little silly, *molto americana* about the whole thing, but then it felt as if my energy was aligning with the energy around me; it felt clean and creative and unstoppable. I wondered if it was part of the kundalini rising in me, or in Etna. There is a determination in nature; it is complex but not complicated. It is reliable: it will do what it was born to do, and I wondered, as a living organism myself, if I was doing what I was born to do.

Career-wise, I was uncertain: from journalist to bureaucrat to aid worker to consultant to free spirit, without much of a game plan or a burning desire to climb up the corporate ladder. I was still childless, and I wondered if I wanted a child because it was what was expected of me, or I was trying to fill a void, or I wanted something that would love me back unconditionally, at least for a little while, or if it was for irrational biological reasons that I had no control over. Or perhaps it had become about bringing back my father through me, re-creating him in some form. Or maybe I knew it was the purest form of love, and I wanted to have access to that feeling. Did I have to make sense to anyone, or could I simply be like the universe—mysterious and unfolding and nonsensical? There were no definitive answers except spreading light. If I could do just that, continue to do that, continue to find the light within and harness it instead of surrendering to darkness, I think I would be fulfilling some silent human prophecy. Maybe we can appreciate the light only when we have seen the dark.

That was Maya's general belief system: we all have light and dark within us, and it is a matter of beaming light. These were the types of discussions we had at night. On occasion, Maya would break out into slam poetry or tell me how she used to "hang out with Jimi Hendrix" or recount her near-death experience. Over the course of my time there, we would build fires, smoke pot, and discuss conspiracy theories. I would hold her sitar across my lap and strum, not knowing what I was doing but feeling drawn to the instrument.

During our conversations, Maya sporadically came out with penetrating statements, small shards of wisdom, such as "We have to live through the things we resist" and "If the universe gives you more time, you take it." Her gems would keep me thinking for days, especially about where I was in my life.

What I was feeling, perhaps, was simply a longing for wholeness in the presence of another, yet there was so much to do internally before I got there. I had resisted processing my grief, resisted exploring my fears around commitment, resisted my emotions for certain people, but I was starting to live through them now. They were bubbling up the way that lava does, hot and determined. I wondered if that was part of the kundalini stuff too. I'd been opening myself up to my grief three years later in a way that I hadn't allowed myself to earlier. In terms of my commitment issues, I realized that I'd sabotaged any viable relationships I'd had in my twenties and early thirties—with Niall, the soulful Irishman; with Alessandro, the Italian film director; with Jean-Claude, the young French biochemist. And the others, well, they were attractive precisely because of their unviability—J., the trysts in the field, the emotionally unavailable or married men whom I seemed to attract in throngs. Niall was the one person in all those years who made any sense, who felt right, whom my father had met and loved, who knew me completely and loved me completely anyway. He was safe and kind and lovely as hell, yet I pushed him away, toward another woman, whom he married even though he pledged his love to me up until the week before his marriage to her. The thing is, I hadn't needed him: I had the security and love of both my parents and big dreams, naive ones, ones that involved saving the world, and I didn't want him to stand in the way of what I, mistakenly or not, thought was my destiny.

And yes, the universe was giving me time, and I'd taken it to let my life catch up to me before I moved on to the next thing, whether it would be having a family or falling in love again or becoming an entrepreneur or writing a book or moving to a ranch and wearing cowboy boots and shorts every day or finding a source of income where I could get paid for being myself, whatever that would mean—all things that I fantasized about. Since Kerala, I'd been feeling strong, useful, balanced, present. There was a real equilibrium in my life that I wanted to preserve.

Even while moving between natural paradises, I'd kept up with my workflow, making myself available for conference calls that suited New York's schedule, writing scripts, producing and managing a heavy influx of videos from Zambia, Iraq, and Sierra Leone, among other places. I had no complaints from Mads besides a few snarky emails here and there about my stroke of luck at being able to work remotely. "I'm such a sucker," he would write. I imagined all the emails in his inbox, many with red exclamation marks next to them. If I had leaned into my career more instead of taking two steps back, I would have been in the same boat as Mads: financially secure but personally spent, in possession of a fancy title but trapped in what they call a golden cage, and eventually bogged down to the point where my life force felt squeezed out—my *agni* all but extinguished.

I thought of something I'd heard or read from the poet Diane Ackerman. She didn't want to get to the end of her life and find that she'd lived just the length of it. She wanted to have lived the width of it as well. I wanted to live widely, too, and Etna made me feel the width of me. Sometimes I chastised myself for always choosing the hard road or the wide road over the straight and narrow road. I don't know why I did it, even though the easier path was right there, right within reach. I was drawn off the beaten path more than ever, more interested in an ayahuasca ceremony in the jungle than in dinner-party small talk. Being boiled down to my essence in nature fed this hunger to be constantly cognizant of spirit. And now I was on a new kind of road, with brambles and whispers, with shadows and foamy flashes of golden light that came and went like lightning, and it was moving me away from masculine-mind wisdom and into feminine-body wisdom, something basic but yet entirely unfamiliar.

Sometimes, though, there was comfort, freedom, in the unknown. "Leave the door open for the unknown, the door into the dark. That's where the most important things come from, where you yourself came from, and where you will go," writes Rebecca Solnit in *A Field Guide to Getting Lost*. I had to go where the end of the road was unseen, get lost in the woods halfway there, in the labyrinth of life, and then lose myself some more. But each time I lost myself, I gained more of myself that I had not known before. The most interesting lives, it seemed, were not supposed to be linear. They were vast and confusing and meant to be lived across while living the questions around us, some of them like tiny buds on a vine, tight and mysterious, full of potential but completely understood only with time, and maybe, possibly, one day, with the right amount of courage, some of them might even be answered.

———

I had sort of fallen into Maya's world; I liked the way she lived. She was light yet contemplative. Worldly yet humble. Free-spirited yet productive. She and her husband had so much freedom, yet they were both committed to their spiritual lives and aligned. Sometimes they would head up to Norway in their camper for a couple of weeks to go to a tantric workshop or make their way over to Spain for a spiritual festival of sorts. They placed value on health, not only spiritual but physical. Their fastidious habits were probably the reason they looked much younger than they actually were, and I readily adopted those rituals during my stay. For example, instead of caffeine in the morning, we would have a large glass of homemade kombucha. We followed that with a filling smoothie, made with kefir. To them, food had a functional purpose as an energy source, because farming could be physically taxing and therefore the body needed to run optimally. Even the smallest-seeming tasks wiped me out, so I needed all the help I could get.

I spent one afternoon wrestling a row of overgrown rosemary bushes. I did not know this, but rosemary, an evergreen perennial herb, can easily grow up to five feet, which can be a force to reckon with, especially when you are barely over five feet yourself. I toiled around them, ripping out or cutting the dead branches, scraping myself in the process, leaving thin red lines embossed on my forearms. The sense of accomplishment I felt, though, as I glowered at the huge mound of dead rosemary branches next to me hours later when the task was completed made the physical abuse worth it. It was something I did. Not an email I sent that went into cyberspace, but something I did with my hands. Likewise with the weeding. Weeds protruded from all corners of the property, around the *noccioli* and lemon trees, near the rosebushes and grapevines, behind the numerous patches of cacti and unidentifiable plants. The work seemed endless, but as I yanked and yanked, slowly, I would see the progress I was making as the size of the piles morphed into small grassy mountains despite me having to stop and sneeze continuously. While weeding in itself was not interesting, there was something meditative about the work, cleansing even. Monotony can offer a certain sanctuary. I understood why people garden as a form of therapy: it halts that unrelenting stream of thoughts so that the mind, too, can breathe.

One morning, I overslept, waking up at the godforsaken hour of eight. I was committed to my vineyard/farming experiment, but I blamed the hay fever, which was draining me, making me sloppy and reckless; I didn't know it could get so bad, the itching eyes, the headaches, the sinus issues, but what else did I expect on a farm in April? Everything was so *alive*. I went outside to find Dumitru and noticed that he had taken all the herbs we'd purchased the day before and planted them without me. *I was fuming.* Planting herbs was the one thing I knew how to do relatively well, and he knew how excited I was about it. He did it to punish me for not waking up when the first bits of daylight flickered across the dewy terrain, still dark and cool from night. Farm people, annoyingly, are all about being superactive in the morning, but I was *tired*. I went to weed, sulking hugely (not that anyone noticed), and then at lunch, I skulked off into town, a thirty-minute walk down isolated, vineyard-lined roads, to get a cappuccino—my first in weeks—which made me feel like I'd snorted a line of cocaine. On my way back to the vineyard, I encountered a hundred goats. I had no clue where they were going, but their brass bells tinkled like wind chimes as they made their way down the empty road. I didn't see a shepherd, only a couple of dogs scurrying around. When the goats saw me, they all stopped and looked at me with their big, soft eyes. I looked back at them. At first I was a little scared. They were blocking the road, and there was no way around them. The question of whether goats bite popped into my head. The standoff lasted for several long minutes. Then, somehow, my fear melted away as I saw myself in them, or maybe I was seeing god in them. We came from the same limitless source; that much I felt—the light in them was the same light in me. I gingerly moved to the side of the road and the goats flooded by me, picking up speed as they passed, while eyeing me suspiciously.

There is nothing living that is not connected.

By that reasoning, when we give in to anger toward someone else, we are also punishing ourselves.

They say holding on to anger is like drinking poison and expecting the other person to die.

So I returned to Dumitru like nothing had happened. *I let it go.* My body had told me as much. After all, I was the one to blame—I had overslept. But I couldn't even go through the process of being angry at myself: what was the point? I returned to the vineyards, to the rich, allergen-laden tapestry of life that was enlivening me, stirring something deep in me that I'd been neglecting all these years, showing me my width, my very own expansiveness, awakening something that could not be contained even within my whole body.

———

A trek up Mount Etna was in order. I wanted to see her up close, feel her black lava flesh crunch under my boots. Maya and I decided to do the trek in the late afternoon, and we drove up an empty coiling road to an abandoned ski lift area where we would begin our ascent. She drove like a seventy-year-old woman, slowly and in the middle of the road (I started to suspect that she was, in fact, seventy). After we parked, she rolled a fat joint with her shellacked nails, and we smoked it at the base of the mountain. Maya closed her eyes, feigning sobriety and grabbing my hand hard, and recited a prayer: "Mother Etna, thank you for welcoming us onto your sacred soil. Namaste."

We were the only ones in sight on the mountain, and every single rock looked like a piece of divinity. I'll never know whether it was the pot or the divine coming through nature, or both, but it didn't matter. Maya started speaking to her, to Etna, expressing her gratitude, invoking continued guidance. It was completely crazy, but not crazy at all. Maya lived on Etna's land, and she had a deep respect for the mountain. There was a *sisterhood* of sorts. I was passing through, a stranger, a city dweller. Etna demanded a certain respect from me too. I needed to urinate, though, and felt guilty about it, but Maya told me it was an honor. In the spirit of this sisterhood, she squatted down near me, and we both peed long, hot streams on Etna. "Oh my god," screamed Maya, laughing. Peeing in the wild: liberating, carnal.

My father, who grew up on a farm, was the first person to show me to honor, respect, and *listen* to nature, even if it was just in our little green front yard. Nature was his religion. Every morning for as far back as I can remember, he went outside and stood on the front step, sometimes smoking a Marlboro Light, sometimes not. If I asked him what he was doing, he would inevitably say, "I'm just saying good morning to Mother Nature." I think this is why, a few months after he died, I disappeared into an ashram in the middle of a forest in upstate New York. I would walk deep into the woods and sink down under a canopy of leaves. I wanted the forest to swallow me with its cool, wet, autumn mouth. I'd sit with my back against a tree and then wait to connect with him through the silence. Those windows of silence. If I could get to the silence, I could get to him again.

Everything I needed to know I could learn from nature. Nature is a part of god, and god is holy; therefore, nature is holy. Einstein famously said, "Look deep, deep into nature, and then you will understand everything better."[2] According to Navajo tradition, the elements of the world are equipped to provide guidance and instruction to people, most notably wind. In Ayurveda, wind is air, which is ether in action. Ether was what we had at the very beginning, before any of the other elements. All matter was born through ether, which developed out of the very, very faint cosmic vibration of om. This is what the ancient rishis, or enlightened sages, believed: The beginning of the world was an unmanifested state of consciousness, and everything was eventually born out of that first vibration; the universe was born out of the womb of Prakruti, the Divine Mother, the feminine principle, the activating power and energy of Shakti.[3]

Etna was offering me some of that comforting wisdom and that silence. I wanted to take it with me when I left, but I wasn't sure how.

Now that my ears and soul had fully tasted it, they could no longer do without it. I wanted quiet, not noise. No loud bars, no screeching subway cars, no restaurants with people's voices climbing over each other but not really saying anything of significance.

After our trek, Maya and I made our way back to the parking lot. The sun was setting over Etna, smoke was rising out of her, a long spiral slowly carving its way through the sunset-streaked sky, the clouds like carrot and plum pillows. There was no one around. "We can't leave her now," Maya said. I wholeheartedly agreed. She put the radio on, and Italian pop music careened out of the car. Maya started dancing, a wine glass in one hand and a bottle in the other, whipping around in circles like a Sufi dervish, her red thong peeking out of her tight black pants. She had this huge smile, like a child discovering dance for the first time. For the sake of communion, even though I was still abstaining from alcohol, I had a sip of the earthy Syrah that came from Etna's flesh, made with her grapes, and it was hands down the most palatable thing I'd ever drunk.

Maya's improvised dancing made me think of something she'd said the previous night: "The hardest part about the inner child is birthing her." She must have been working on just that. Her happiness was contagious. I started dancing too. If anyone had passed by, they would have thought we were lunatics. But we were birthing our inner children, and that required a certain degree of lunacy. Maya showed that you could be old in years but still maintain that inner innocence, keep a piece of yourself untainted, wild and free, no matter what struggles you'd been through. You didn't have to be one or the other, lived in and lived through or innocent; you could be both. Maybe as we grew older, we started making our way inward, toward that little child within us who thankfully, staunchly, resolutely refused to become adultlike. Maybe that little girl was Shakti energy, waiting to come out and play, to conquer the joylessness around us. There is a term for it—*anhedonia*: a lack of pleasure or of the capacity to experience it. Adults are good at suffering from this. Yet you can always return to that place. The invitation is there, always. For me, I'd been invited over and over these last few years and finally accepted. Teresa of Ávila, the sixteenth-century Spanish mystic, famously said, "It is foolish to think that we will enter heaven without entering into ourselves."

Well, I had entered. But I still wasn't quite sure what I would find, or what it would lead to.

———

My time here ended as quickly as it began, but it felt like time to move on from Etna, from Maya, from Dumitru. Maya had shown me a way to live that defied conventions. Even Dumitru turned out to be a muse of sorts—hardworking, honest, serious, humble, simple, kind, pure. The kind of guy who'd had a rough life, but stayed solid and good by staunch resolution. I was surprised that he had any parting words for me, but he did, and it was the most I'd heard him speak.

"Don't get lost in the noise," he forewarned. "Or forget where you've been." I wondered if he meant the noise in my head, or the noise in the world.

The thing is, I hadn't been alone in weeks, and even if I had time by myself on the vineyard or in the garden during the day, the social evenings at Maya's, the piles of people passing through, the impromptu community dinner parties with wild Sicilian food cooked by Maya herself—grilled local fennel, velvety pasta with mushrooms woven in, a spongy eggplant dish called caponata—were beginning to take a toll.

In the last few years, I craved space like oxygen; I had to consistently move into solitude in order to remember my center. Yet I never feel alone in my solitude, which I know is mostly a good thing. But sometimes when you get so used to being alone, it becomes difficult to imagine being with other people, or even one other person, all the time. In *Walden*, Thoreau writes, "I find it wholesome to be alone the greater part of the time. To be in company, even with the best, is soon wearisome and dissipating." It was a bit unnerving, that a passage like that could resonate with me, and I started to wonder if I was secretly becoming a crabby old man inside, or maybe I was just owning up to being an introvert at heart. Since my father had died, I found myself craving quiet, avoiding crowds. I found people exhausting on some level, all their projections. Even though humans are tribal, I was on the brink of internal anarchy when I didn't have that downtime, that re-centering time, and I know I am not the only woman who feels that way. The next few weeks would be about isolating myself, if possible, and wrestling with some of the fears around what was happening to me, where I was going with my life, where I would end up, and whether I'd reached a point beyond normalcy, a point of no return. This had surfaced after being away from the familiar. Working in nature was restorative in some respects, but not healing in the way I thought it would be. Rather, it loosened everything up inside, or maybe that emotional and physical discomfort was *part of* the healing. When a wound heals, it scabs and itches.

The plan was to go to Stromboli, one of the seven Aeolian Islands—a volcanic archipelago north of Sicily—to hike its famously active volcano and get a wide perspective of everything from high up and over, to feel the comforting width of the world, to breathe widely. But *l'aqua agitata* meant that the ferryboat might not be able to dock. "We can go, but we're not sure if we'll get there," was the rough translation of what the disheveled guy in the *biglietteria* had communicated to me while two thin streams of smoke exited his nostrils. That didn't sound like much fun, so instead I made my way to the nearby island of Vulcano, named after the Roman god of fire. There were volcanoes on the island, as well, though they'd been dormant for centuries except for a steady stream of sulfurous gases that fed the thermal pools at Fanghi di Vulcano at the island's port.

On the ferry over, I'd booked a cheap homestay on my phone. My remote-working situation felt unsustainable—too good to be true—so I forced myself to be frugal, even though I wanted to treat myself to a nice hotel after all the work on the vineyard. My body was bruised like a rotten banana, my sinuses were incensed at what I'd exposed them to, my skin looked like a rabid cat scratched it, but still I decided not to splurge. When I arrived at the port, dizzy from the noxious smell of rotten egg emanating from the nearby hot springs, I called the *albergo*, and a sixtysomething man named Gaetano came to scoop me up. He was originally Roman and had a warm, welcoming vibe about him, especially when he found out I had lived in the Eternal City and had a soft spot for all things Italian. He introduced me to his wife, Domenica, a stocky, muscular woman with oily, cropped black hair and a big smile. She was wearing cut-off jean shorts and cowboy boots like mine (I'd accidentally left my sneakers on the bus to Etna, so that was all I'd had to wear the previous few weeks). They immediately invited me to lunch that afternoon—a traditional Sicilian dish, *pasta alla norma* (pasta with eggplant, tomatoes, and *ricotta salata*)—after which they rolled an electric bike toward me and sent me on my way with a small, vague map of the island, insisting that I couldn't get lost.

I biked straight to the base of Fossa di Vulcano and did the steep, slippery climb up to see the volcanic crater, which is about 2 miles wide and stands at around nearly 1,300 feet above sea level. Fissures under huge amounts of pressure, or fumaroles, located throughout the crater, expelled hot sulfurous gases. These long curls of toxic smoke unnerved me as I peered into the gigantic crater, feeling vertigo. I preferred the breathtaking view across the archipelago, the sapphire sea, when I turned around.

The scenery reminded me of a family trip to Maui the four of us had taken when my brother and I were in middle school, ages twelve and ten respectively. I can picture us clearly: my brother, with his jacked-up shorts, black bowl cut, and glasses, which were soon to be replaced with contacts, on the cusp of transitioning from nerd to cool prep school kid; my mother with a big red flower in her long dark hair, tucked behind her ear, a floral strapless dress that flared to her knees, some sort of tropical 1980s design; my father with a pale-pink cotton polo shirt, short-sleeved, tucked into khaki pants; me in a monokini and a skort, my hair in a high ponytail, my pre-braces teeth in disarray but smiling anyway. Three of us were brown from a blend of sun and ethnicity, and then there was my father, with his rosy skin.

My brother tanned the darkest, and I was always a little jealous of him for "looking more Indian" than I did, that he was the "more exotic" one, even though I think he was self-conscious about it. I accused my mother of loving my brother more because he was browner, closer to her skin tone. It sounds totally nuts, but that was how I felt, especially when we fought. She was more protective of him, conscious that his experience in this place that we all lived in would still be that of the *other*. Brown people were others, and they didn't always have it as easy, even in a country buzzing with immigrants. Meanwhile, I desperately wanted to be the other. I dyed my hair black and pierced my nose to look more Indian, but it didn't work. I was a composite by-product of East and West, a mongrel. I was unidentifiable that way, not one or the other—I just was.

There is a photograph of my parents from this trip leaning into each other, smiling widely, leis draped around their necks, the Pacific Ocean as the backdrop. They look like they could be on the cover of a glossy magazine for Hawaiian honeymooners.

I knew that the kind of deep, loving companionship my parents had shared for forty years was rare. My standards were impossibly high from the get-go, but nothing less would do. Why else merge my life with another—all my imperfections with another person's imperfections? Now I wasn't even sure if I could really connect with someone who hadn't grieved or had some sort of major transformation involving trauma. We wouldn't be able to speak the soul-throttling language of loss. I wanted a partner who'd been to the depths and back, who could even reach those depths. Most people stay on the surface, gliding along, navigating petty problems until some kind of tragedy forces them to descend; when they come back out, they are so much richer and layered and wise. Survival does that: it sends us back with more than we had.

When my father was really sick, I watched the way my mother took care of him. There were nurses, but she wanted to do it. She wanted to wash his hair, make him grilled cheese sandwiches on sliced Italian bread—without the sesame seeds so they wouldn't get stuck in his teeth. While our little house was full of fear and worry and dread, stronger, way more powerful than all of that, was this pure, palpable energy of love. I basked in it, enveloped myself in it as if I were going to lose it, even if I did not need to. All that love was already inside me.

People spend their whole lives looking for love, approval, and acceptance. I'd had it from the start. Not from the start and then gradually whittled away owing to some dire and neglected childhood, which I was fortunate *not* to have experienced (but sadly, many people *do* experience abandonment wounds of radical proportions). I'd had it from birth, and then my parents reinforced it. It was precisely the security of that fortified love that enabled me to drift, travel, experiment, and have, for whatever they were worth, my own encounters with love. Though in retrospect some of them were risky and unconventional—none had materialized into a marriage like my parents'—I never felt I was lacking love.

My whole life, I'd mistakenly prized romantic love over so many other kinds of love. In fact, the ancient Greeks were so attuned to the different types of love (beyond eros) that they had special names for all of them. Among them were *storge*, the natural, familiar love that flows between parents and children or brother and sister, such as the kind I have mentioned; *philea*, the affectionate, platonic love between friends (what they considered a love between equals); *philautia*, or self-love (what Buddhists call self-compassion or self-acceptance), which can also be negative when one becomes excessively self-involved (think Narcissus, who, according to Greek mythology, was so handsome that he fell in love with his own reflection in a pool of water); and *agape*, the most rare and powerful type of love, unconditional, forgiving, and spiritual in nature, based on total acceptance (and to that end, is mentioned extensively in the Greek New Testament, where it is often used to describe God's love). After all this time, I was starting to realize that the deductive narrative society had fed me—that romantic love is the ultimate love—was not only wrong, but limiting. Within this realization of all the love I'd received or given over the years that fell inside *and* outside the scope of eros, I was almost spellbound by the fullness I suddenly felt.

Besides, I'd realized that *true love* was never about finding the right person. It was much larger than that, and I would know when I'd found it because all of that unnecessary waiting, or the illusion of waiting, would quietly dissipate, leaving behind nothing but a faint and steady shimmer.

It was psychoanalyst Erich Fromm who discovered that love is not a relationship to a single person but an "orientation of character" that determines the connection of a person to the world as a whole. If you can love one person, you can love the world through that person, and that love will also be toward the self.[4] So maybe it's not something to fall in and out of. That's too flippant. I thought of a swirly, colorful drawing my five-year-old niece made for me, of a tall green flower with large red hearts with a peace sign as the bud, and next to it she wrote, "Love is love."

The truth is, love is always there in some form, always accessible when the body is open and receptive and not defensive out of fear. It is right there, disguised in millions of ways, yet not disguised at all. "Love is the whole thing," wrote Rumi. "We are only pieces."

In this expansive view, in the giant color-swathed landscape before me that seemed not to be of this world, was the love that I thought I didn't have that I did have, that we all have. It's the underlying force in our lives. Even as gabbing tourists poked their walking sticks into the ground and crowded near me, as the toxic fumaroles churned ominously just behind my shoulders—even with all those distractions, all those threats to my peaceful existence—there it was, more than anything else: love.

When someone you love dies, does that love go anywhere?

No, it doesn't ever go away, because you can't ever lose love once it exists.

Love.

It is not an affront to freedom; it is freedom itself.

———

Gaetano adored Domenica. You could see it in his eyes, which twinkled when he looked at her. They had one of *those* stories: she walked into his *albergo*, and they knew. A whimsical visit to Vulcano on her part lent itself to unexpected romance, culminating in a planned lifelong coupling through the contract of marriage. Seventeen years and counting. Gaetano was a kindhearted man, earthy, with a palatable sense of humor. In his sixties, the bulk of his jokes were tinged with the harmless callousness embedded in all things Roman. He was very affectionate with Domenica as he prodded her with his relentless teasing. There was clearly a deep bond between them. However, as they inadvertently blew the smoke from their filterless cigarettes in my face, I could sense something stirring in Domenica as I spoke of the time I was taking to step away from my "normal life" to dig deep into things.

"I need to do that," she said, half joking.

When she asked what it entailed, I told her I was designing my little self-help project as I went along (which is why half the time I felt like I was just drifting around aimlessly), but that I'd kicked off the whole thing with a couple of months of Ayurveda, yoga, and meditation. Then I'd worked on a farm, or more accurately, *un vigneto*.

She grabbed Gaetano's arm. "We need this," she urged.

He kept turning it into a joke. "I meditate every day when you're in the kitchen. I pray that you won't make the pasta too al dente."

She laughed it off, but I could sense there was a hunger inside her. She was ready to go beyond where she was. Maybe she was also experiencing some sort of kundalini awakening.

The three of us went for a drive around the island. The plan was to pull over somewhere beautiful and for me to show them "how to meditate," even though I told them I was hardly an expert, but I knew the basics. After a rich lunch, however, being in the back seat of a jeep that careened down twisty roads, my stomach was lurching. About to vomit, I rolled down the window. I had eaten too much, been served way more than two fistfuls of pasta, and eaten faster than comfortable to keep pace with their table of friends. Then I ate fruit, which was breaking a sacred Ayurvedic rule (*eat fresh fruit separately from other foods, especially heavy foods like dairy products and grains*), but one of their friends, a fruit seller from Catania, had brought over special boxes of colorful fruit that morning and *insisted* that I try some. Sicilians were *even worse* than Indians when it came to insistence around food consumption, probably because they were rightfully proud of their food. He had been dull and aloof all through lunch but watched me with such intensity and anticipation as I bit into his oranges and melons, as they squirted across the table, and he nodded enthusiastically in approval.

When we finally stopped the car and pulled over, relief washed over me. The three of us ambled toward an abandoned lighthouse and took in the panoramic view from the southern part of the island. Then Domenica tossed her puffy pink jacket on the gravel and collapsed on top of it. Yes, a nap seemed in order. I was in no state to meditate and was glad they didn't seem too bothered about it.

Domenica and I were both lying on our backs in the succulent sunshine. Out of the blue, she told me that she had tried to have a baby, but she had been unsuccessful. She had gone to Barcelona to use a sperm donor in her thirties. "Don't wait for a man," she scolded me when I told her I'd been entertaining the same thought, but wasn't sure. I wanted to cry when I heard her story. There were plenty of women who were childless-by-choice and absolutely fine or childless-*not*-by-choice and absolutely fine, but Domenica seemed to have a void in her. *I could feel it.*

Why was the universe doing this to me? We stopped talking, lost in thoughts. I started to feel the way I felt when Sita and I were talking in that little shop in Kerala: the abdomen ache. *If I really want to be a mom,* I thought, *shouldn't I be in Barcelona right now trying the very same thing instead of climbing volcanoes?* But I had to climb a volcano. I would be a better mom for it, maybe. Part of me believed the baby would come to me when it was time; I would just know, deep down, when I needed to be proactive. Another part of me felt that my father's soul was lingering around me, waiting for me to reincarnate him, and I wanted to do it before he got tired of waiting for me, or before some other "more ready" person *stole* him, but like the universe, none of that made any sense at all. I thought of the ancient wisdom of Lao Tzu, who once said, "Nature does not hurry, yet everything is accomplished." It was the spirit of the Tao, the notion of going with the flow, wu wei, and trusting that the river of life would take you toward your goal, maybe in a winding way, if you kept that destination loosely in your mind. My astrologer-cum-therapist Bob, a grumpy but insightful guy from Jersey City who works at the back of a small witchcraft shop in the East Village, once told me he believes in the law of attraction, but not in *obsession*.

"I think you think about something once. If the voice inside you says, 'That's where you're going,' then you just live your life moment to moment," he said. "If you're in a physical landscape and you want to get to the top of Mount Fuji, if you keep looking at Mount Fuji you're eventually going to trip over something. Just know where Mount Fuji is. Know you're heading in the right direction, and make sure you know where you're stepping so that you don't step in any horse pies."

It was probably impossible to go through life without stepping in any horse pies. But I *was* nature, an extension of it: *we came from it.* I didn't want to worry or hurry. Dr. Anjali had told me not to, and she was a licensed medical professional on Wall Street. *I will not hurry. I will not worry,* I repeated to myself like a mantra. I was ready to drift into a carbohydrate-induced coma, when Domenica suddenly flipped her body toward me.

"Have you ever been with a woman?" she asked, sotto voce but with an intensity that startled me out of my daze.

I hesitated before answering. "Yes."

Then she started stroking my bare arm.

I thought about J. Thought about her neck. About how her hair was thick and silky, how she smelled so good naturally, even when she had been sweating. How she never bought herself perfume, only wore the bottle of Poison by Dior that her mother gave her at Christmas every year until it ran out, until it faded on her skin and there was just her natural smell, kind of like cake icing mixed with sunlight.

I thought about how the lighter she wanted to keep it, the deeper I was drawn in. About how people who want to keep things light are afraid of going deep because they are afraid of what they will find there. J. was terrified of stillness, of what would catch up with her if she stopped, if she went inward. She was mistaken in her fear—the excavation into the wells of ourselves is how we return to our truths.

J. and I had stopped communicating, but I felt like our souls still communicated—even with me being so far away—without us even knowing. We could go on living our distracting human lives, but all this work was still being done below the surface. Even after a break-up, or when someone dies, when intense relationships end, there is a continuing communication underneath and between the souls involved, a healing of sorts. Something continues to be worked out. I don't know how I know this, but I just do, in the deepest way one can know anything. That love? It stays. All the men I'd loved, I still love, and will always love. I will always love J. There is something profoundly comforting in that—that the love that was released into the world out of my deepest being cannot be taken away by anyone or anything, not even time.

"Can I kiss you?" Domenica's grainy voice drew me back into the present, and I opened my eyes. She was sitting up and leaning over me, her head and neck precariously close. On her arm, she had tattooed passages from Kahlil Gibran's *The Prophet*. She had been reciting them in the car. I had to translate it in my head into English: "The deeper that sorrow carves into your being, the more joy you can contain." She told me she got that tattoo after her parents died.

I didn't want to kiss her, and I felt really bad about that. Kundalini amplifies everything, good or bad. I still felt nauseous from the food, from the bite of fried sardines that was all but forced into my mouth. Besides, the only woman I had ever wanted to kiss was J.

I turned my head a little bit, directly into the wind. My eyebrows felt like they'd be blown off.

"Non ti piaccio?" she said, looking down with an exquisite sorrow, as her husband napped a few yards away on the wide step of the lighthouse entrance, his large stomach heaving in the sunshine.

"Of course I like you," I said. I paused. "But not that way," I explained.

She looked disconsolate. My rejection of her felt like a rejection of tenderness itself. Her desire felt so pure. She was seeking connection and intimacy, not anything vulgar. I didn't want her to feel rejected, but that did not change the fact that I did not feel like kissing her. I couldn't do anything I didn't feel like doing, especially when it came to love. I could do only what made sense to my interior.

Unexpectedly, she flipped up her shirt and her bare breasts popped out, and then she grabbed them with her hands and squeezed them together. Her short fingernails were painted different metallic colors. "I need to get them done," she said, about her breasts.

"No, they look good," I assured her, awkwardly, and she looked at me expectantly. Strangely, since my relationship with J., it seemed that more women were interested in me sexually, or maybe I was only starting to notice it and had been blind to it before. Maybe it had opened something up in me, another side of myself. Maybe I now liked women *and* men, or both, or neither. A dog seemed way less complicated.

Gaetano woke up and came over. "*Basta!* Enough of this lesbian stuff," he said.

Domenica let her shirt fall back down. They started arguing. I didn't want to come in between them. The tension in the car was thick on the way back. I slumped down in my seat, contrite even though it wasn't my fault. My presence had inadvertently ignited something that was already within Domenica, a restlessness or longing of sorts, bound to surface sooner or later. I happened to be some sort of catalyst, and of course she had unleashed some feelings in me that I'd had around J. We'd triggered something in each other, and now the work was done— our purpose for meeting fulfilled even though it wasn't clear what it was.

I leaped out of the car when we arrived at the house and tried to make myself scarce the rest of the afternoon, grabbing my laptop and heading straight to a café where I counted the hours until I could flee the island on the first ferry out.

I'd wanted to be alone, but life didn't seem to want that for me for some reason. All the strangers I'd met up until now were like vacuums wrenching things out of me that I'd pushed down into a quiet, dark space.

I was trying to shut other people out, thinking I needed solitude to get inside myself, but I would later realize they were helping me to reach deeper within.

I had been thinking about Pantelleria for years. It held this near-mystical allure. A volcanic isle lodged between Sicily and Tunisia, it was far from anyone I knew and offered a chance to really be free, to be antisocial, quiet, and insular without apology. The island dished up an experience of nature at its most savage, raw, and unfamiliar. The island's unusual landscape is punctuated with terraced slopes alternating between arid planes of lava rock and wild vegetation, bone-dry from no rain. Grisly rock formations sculpted by the pounding of two unrelenting Mediterranean winds, the mistral and the sirocco, which have unleashed their destructive powers unapologetically for centuries, give the island its signature look. Even the olive trees and vineyards are forced to stay low to the ground, as if trying to stay out of the way. I planned to do the same.

While technically a part of Sicily, locals consider it to be a separate entity, referring to the mainland as *Sicilia*. I'd quickly learn that while these locals are a bit rough around the edges, they are beyond generous. I'd booked a couple nights in one of the dilapidated hotels snuggled around the port so that I could get my bearings and find a house I could *affittare*, or rent, for ten days. The only way to be alone was to sequester myself somewhere, with regular access to a car so that I could explore the island. Rumor had it that there was only one automatic car on the island. To my luck, the owner of a restaurant I'd eaten at managed to track it down, and I ended up getting *free* accommodation through a restaurant waiter in an empty *dammuso*, a traditional dwelling typical of Pantelleria. The small shallow-domed structure, originally designed to keep occupants cool, was comfortable enough. The religious trinkets that adorned every wall spooked me at first and then comforted me as I got used to their presence. I slept under a small icon of the Madonna herself, which was secured against the headboard.

The convenience of having my own set of wheels was welcome after weeks of being dependent on the erratic schedules of Sicilian buses and ferries, or on the kindness of strangers trucking me around, or on the few instances when I'd hitchhiked in somebody's dusty old car. With the windows down, I jacked up the radio volume, which belched out songs with no predictability, alternating between Italian pop songs and American classics like "Hotel California." The tiny white car hugged the narrow road as I looped around the island, which was encircled by a choppy blue sea.

I drove to a lookout point where I could actually see Africa in the distance, Tunisia specifically, which happened to be the last place I'd been to on the continent. It was during the Libyan war, which caused more than seven hundred thousand people—many of them migrant workers and their families from sub-Saharan Africa—to flee the chaos and the carnage in Libya and seek refuge in neighboring countries.[5] Large numbers crossed the border into Tunisia where a massive refugee camp had been swelling. I was in that camp trying to communicate what was happening in real time to raise awareness of pressing humanitarian needs and, in turn, donations, alongside spokespeople from other UN agencies and NGOs. The media latched on, until the noise was drowned out by other crises in the world—that was the cycle. There was always a crucial window at the beginning of a humanitarian crisis when people were all ears. They took it all in, were rightfully horrified, but then moved on.

I, too, had moved on and felt guilty about it. Through my work, I got more than I gave, even though it was supposed to be the other way around, and I felt a deep guilt about that. I loved my work but often wondered if I had made a tangible difference. What I knew: helping others had helped me, had taught me about human nature, about resilience. I hadn't moved on from caring about people; I had done a ton of collective engagement, for *years*, but I was rejiggering the way that I thought I could be most useful to the world. It was within this newfound freedom, this distance, I'd hoped that answer would surface. I wanted to find the deepest gift I had and bring it out to the world.

Besides, saving the world meant saving myself little by little. That's everyone's sole task, to save themselves, to love themselves.

This is how I would really begin to transcend.

———

The next day I made my way over to the Specchio di Venere, or Mirror of Venus—a heart-shaped lake slapped in the middle of a volcanic crater bubbling with hot springs. Beyond doubt, it is one of the most striking natural formations I have seen. The lake color shifts from emerald green to turquoise to light blue to marine blue over the course of the day, like a mood ring. As with the hot springs on Vulcano, the lake has therapeutic properties, with mineral-rich mud and hot sulfur springs off to one side. A mineral found primarily near hot springs and volcanic craters, sulfur is a natural treatment for skin diseases, such as eczema, and wading in the nutrient-rich hot water is a form of balneotherapy that can supposedly work wonders on aches and pains and be good for blood pressure and a slew of other things. Some say the waters even have healing powers, which is why soaking in sulfur can be traced back as far as ancient Egyptian and Roman times. As I stood in the lake, my heels sank in slowly, and I dug my hand deep into the soft bottom, scooped out a large chunk of chocolate-colored mud, and spread it up and down my legs and arms into a full body mask. Technically you're supposed to walk around the entire lake until the mud dries, but I stood there in the sun and the wind talking to a gay couple from Milan who thought my little experiment was "fascinating" (it appeared I was great at marketing what to me still felt very esoteric). The dark mask eventually turned ashy gray, tightening my skin until it felt like my flesh would crack. I swam to the center of the lake as instructed and slowly let the caked mud slide off. The residue was stubborn, but I sloughed off most of it, emerging from the water with rosy brown skin, with a light dust of sulfur that would wash away after a couple of hot showers. I was getting rid of my old skin and stepping into the new.

On the way back, I saw a sign for Arco dell'Elefante, and I followed the road that led me to a view of a bizarre rock formation resembling an elephant drinking from the sea. On this whole journey, I realized that Ganesh, remover of obstacles, god of wisdom, was following me. He'd managed to pop up everywhere in different forms over the last few months. In India, that was unsurprising, but in Sicily, he turned up in frames or as hanging fixtures on the walls of the bed-and-breakfasts I'd stayed in, as a statue in Maya's house, even as a land mass.

At the risk of seeming insane, I began to think that Ganesh had been removing obstacles in my life at every turn, right from the start of my journey, as if it were all part of some cosmic arrangement. The notion seemed too benign for a world in which there is no shortage of suffering, where certain spots become a wasteland of unrealized dreams. And yet there was a generosity to my experience: I didn't have the money to travel for an extended period and do all the things I wanted to do as part of my self-actualization. I set the intention and welcomed my remote-work situation. I didn't know anyone with a farm in Sicily but wanted to farm in Sicily. *Boom*: I met Maya at a kundalini yoga retreat. I didn't have a car or a house in Pantelleria. I got the word out, and within twenty-four hours, *done*. Delivery upon request. I'd made a pact from the start not to worry about the details, expecting the universe, or Ganesh, or who- or whatever was cheering me on, to deliver. But I now realized it was not any one thing. It was this notion of *let go and let god*, a refrain often associated with alcoholics turning their problems over to a higher power, but a notion that is rooted in providence. It was wu wei. It was that mysterious flow that I had somehow stepped into while wandering on my own, because my awareness was heightened. An intelligence was at work conspiring to make me realize that there is nothing that is not a possibility. It was as if everything was talking to me, enchanted in some way. That heightened awareness was literally a godsend; it was actually the very essence of *living in the now*. I was afraid this would slip away when I returned to my normal life, to my legal-pad lists of things to do, to my clusters of troubles, all of which have a way of shaking me out of the flow.

But Ganesh—he was always there, a reminder of my own wisdom, that deep well of knowing we all have, waiting to be tapped, that ever-present inner voice—benevolent, and *alive*. A temple of wisdom inside.

As the sirocco dried my skin, a pleasant chill went down my spine, and I realized I was *awake*. Not only was I awake, but I really had been having an awakening. I had no doubts about that now. And I also realized that the point of awakening was not to transcend my material life—to sell everything I owned, shave my head, and move to a mountaintop or into a temple—but to *bring the divine into my life* as it was, every day. It would take work, I knew. Every day I would have to choose the divine over the mundane, joy over bitterness, an abundance mindset over scarcity. Every decision in life, it seemed, was one where I could choose either fear or love. When love chose me and I chose it back, I became a better person for it; the world became better for it, even though it was not something I could measure with my own eyes or my own hands. With J., it showed me—even though I didn't want to be shown—how deeply I could love, my capacity for loving another person, someone imperfect. And it showed me how to fall in love with those imperfections. It was so deep and wide that the lines between loving her and loving myself were skewed and eventually blotted out. Through loving her, I was sending love to myself. That is when everything becomes everything: a glimpse of oneness, however fleeting.

Tolstoy said that the key to happiness lies in our ability to love others. The truth is, the more love you put into the world, the more love you fill up with, even if you don't know where that love is coming from—that part doesn't matter.

Like the universe, love is under no obligation to make sense to us.

———

A few days later, I returned to Cala Gadir on the east side of the island where there was another hot spring. It was crowded on the weekend but deserted during the week, which meant the several tiny pools of warm, hot, and boiling hot water underneath a huge sheath of volcanic rock were all for my sole dunking pleasure. As there was no one around, I tossed aside the cotton sundress I bought from Sita in Kerala and climbed into the second-hottest pool naked, slipping on the slimy algae before laying my head against a huge volcanic rock. I swallowed the sunrays with deep breaths. The wind whipped by, and the waves licked the rocks. Mounds of volcanic rock extended above me, but between the sun and the volcano-heated water, I was all alone, and through that aloneness, that nakedness, I experienced a tremendous feeling of immense freedom.

When was I ever naked in New York? The answer, unfortunately, was *rarely*. That afternoon, moved by the feelings I'd experienced at Cala Gadir, I decided I wanted to get more comfortable with the idea of nakedness. With it being a *natural* thing and all, I did what any ordinary person would do: I practiced. This was entirely feasible because signs of life at my *dammuso* were scarce, barring geckos, a perpetual circus of bumblebees, and invisible insects that left throbbing, itchy bumps on my ankles. And two bony cats. Over the course of ten days, I saw the next-door neighbor only once—a swarthy middle-aged man who came to tell me that all my underwear, which I'd carefully placed on the dry-ing line, had blown into his yard. "I could tell it wasn't my wife's," he explained, his brow weathered from wind and life, as he handed over a wad of black lace panties. Mortified yet grateful, I accepted them back.

To be alone and naked on a remote island was something. In New York, I was usually rushing out the door in the morning, jamming myself onto the subway to work, clobbering down the pavement to get to the office, which had an open-plan setup, attending a packed yoga class after work or going out to a bar, or an event, or a dinner. There were always *people, people, people* everywhere I turned. But naked, like an animal, wild—that was something else.

The *dammuso* had an adjoining stone brick oven that was large and mountable, with a rough but flat cement surface that was good for sunbathing. I took to lying on top of it naked, with only my sarong underneath me, and relished the prospect of no tan lines as my exposed skin drank in the sun—a literal sunbath, or *atapa snana* in yogic terms, regarded as cleansing in moderation, as the skin releases toxins through its sweat. I started doing sun salutations naked as part of my yoga practice, knowing that there was no one behind me, just disinterested plants, and the wind-jerked sea in front of me in the distance, visible across scattered shrubs and cacti buzzing with insects. Often, I would sit at my computer naked outside in the sun, with nothing but a pair of sunglasses on, elbows perched on a wooden picnic table, my skin darkening in the near-African sun, and respond to the endless stream of work emails. Normally, Mads and I would FaceTime, but I told him the connection was bad (which it was), and I was pretty sure my gay boss had zero desire to see me naked.

I wanted to see how long I could do the naked thing, slowly getting comfortable with my perfectly imperfect body. I thought about how, in the past, I was overly critical of my body—sadly, like every woman—and I had an unquellable urge to cry. It was this sacred and sturdy shell that had carried me around the world, been abused by lack of food and sleep, survived on a diet of Pringles and shots of bourbon for days at a time, and yet it did not abandon me. It did not even cause me any physical pain. I should have been worshipping it. I should have been worshipping my womb, the source of human life. We pay attention only to the body's defects and rarely the miracle of it until it starts to decline, and then we want it all back, everything, all the way it was. By allowing myself to be naked longer, I accepted my body more—its curves and mushy bits. Instead of denying it, I spoiled it with sunshine and wind and freedom.

After all, skin is a live organ. It has a soul too.

When I left the *dammuso,* though, I was clothed. I had become friendly with the restaurant owner who helped me find the lone automatic-transmission car on the island. Tommaso was a local, a born-and-bred Pantellerian. Something about him screamed sex. Still on my fast from men, I was not looking for sex. While I came to the island to spend time alone—to write, to meditate, to regenerate, to process, to simply be in raw, unrefined nature—Tommaso frequently invited me to join him for interesting-sounding mini-adventures. A jaunt to the natural-built sauna in the middle of the island or a sunset *aperitivo* at such-and-such hotel built on volcanic rock, which I knew I would not be able to find without a local. I would say, "No, I shouldn't. I should [fill in the blank]," but then he would say, *"Dai, vieni per solo un goccino"* ("Come for just a sip"), which would turn into a glass of *passito,* sweet white wine native to the island made from Zibibbo grapes dried in the sun to raise the sugar levels. I'd been pretty good about abstaining, but I fell off the wagon once or twice on this island.

Though duly warned since birth, I didn't fully realize it at the time—Sicilian men are in possession of a sneaky and subtle persistence. They miraculously coax you into doing things that you didn't plan on doing by making you think you are overreacting or are insane in some way if you don't agree to do them.

I came to Pantelleria *to be alone* and connect with nature. I'd also started writing quite a bit, finding it healing, and wanted the space to do it. I'd made myself submissive to everything, open and listening—to advice on writing dished out by Jack Kerouac or spirituality dished out by almost every seeker. There was a new receptivity, a *porousness.* Like other writers, I realized that I could only really make sense of the world when I put my thoughts and feelings down on paper. Writing was where I encountered myself most, where I could document the waking up that was happening within me in case I went home and decided it was all a mirage. I didn't want to go back to where I was, but beyond. That is the definition of transcendence: the act of rising above something to a superior state. When I wrote, I felt like a layer of me was being pulled off. There was a cleansing quality to the purging.

And while I rarely felt lonely on my own, having a local show me the island's hidden rocky alcoves or a natural sauna was hard to pass up. Also, while I could chalk it up to all the time I'd spent in nature, I was feeling *scarily* sexual. There was something about Tommaso himself, but the slow, ripe unfolding of nature had triggered something in me. "It's the biggest orgasm there is," said Luce, the Mayan astrologer in Tulum. The weeks I had spent living inside nature, on volcanoes, near lakes and oceans, in forests, and on farms, proved her right.

Whenever Tommaso was near me, I felt a surge of heat climb over my body. Sometimes I was afraid of the wild sexuality within me and tried to temper it. Yet it was his smell—a sultry bouquet of espresso, clove cigars, and sweat. It was the scent of man mixed with a heavy, sensual animal odor. Something about our cocktail of pheromones was intoxicating. He had *nero di seppia*—black squid ink—under his nails, which he said he had cooked a few nights before with pasta, but apparently it wouldn't wash off. There was something so sexy about a man with dirt under his nails, especially after years of dealing with a zillion metrosexuals hosed down with Diptyque in New York, smelling of Bloomingdale's instead of something primitive and earthy.

Like a dumb American tourist, I said yes when he insisted on taking me to the lake to see the full moon, which was apparently *meraviglioso* when reflected in the water.

I told myself it was research.

La luna was indeed marvelous. Potent and overbearing the way a beautiful woman like J. was, sucking up all the attention, but also omniscient, stern, clever, enigmatic—humorous even. Under that full moon, I wanted to be alone. Alone with my divine feminine energy, which was being reflected back to me through the moon. I couldn't even remember the last time that I'd looked into space or thought about space. It's kind of a big deal—that three-dimensional expanse of dark and light that begins where the Earth's atmosphere ends, stuffed with planets and stars. It is the place that is completely silent—without atmosphere, there's no medium for sound to travel. It's so easy to forget that we are made up of stardust. The moon was reminding me of that, and I felt a little guilty not just reveling in her light. I felt her speaking to me as Tommaso slithered his hands up and down my supple body. No, I was no victim—I was obviously sending out major *come hither* signals from my armpits or wherever. *It was not my fault, just biology doing its thing.* I thought about something the kundalini yoga teacher had said at Chiara's retreat: "If the energy in the lower chakras is not balanced and transformed into higher energy frequencies, a person can be a total slave to her sexuality." Apparently, the way to address all that is to sit in camel pose for two minutes and do breaths of fire.

Sometimes, though, camel pose just isn't enough.

———

I wouldn't say that I totally fell off my man fast. I still wasn't making the search for a man, or a woman I suppose, a central focus in my life—I'd dropped all of that like dead weight in the hope of regenerating myself. I'd already been feeling the high that comes with any kind of detox (eventually). While I'd had a little nibble of fleshy masculinity, I was ready to continue my pilgrimage without the distraction of it all; it had been freeing to embody the idea that nothing was missing, that I was complete on my own, and that there were other kinds of love out there that were just as real and filling.

The problem was, as it often is, the man involved and I had different expectations after our full-moon night. Tommaso wanted possession and togetherness. I wasn't looking for any of that. His presence felt all-consuming even though he wasn't near me most of the time, but the island was small enough and the air pure enough that with my sharpened intuition, I could almost hear his thoughts. When he called, he would insist on meeting and then sulk if I declined an invitation.

"What are you doing?" he'd ask.

"Working," I'd say, naked legs outstretched, laptop on thighs.

"Do you want to have dinner tonight?"

"I can't tonight, sorry."

"Do you want to meet for *aperitivo*?"

"I can't, sorry. Let's do it another night."

"*Dai*, it's just dinner—you have to eat."

"I had a big lunch," I would say, even if it wasn't true (though usually it was).

He would hang up in a huff, and I would hide at home at night, nibbling on a baguette I'd picked up that morning that had already gone stale. Should I have gone out, and been spotted anywhere, trouble would have ensued. I wasn't trying to be *molto americana*, but I had inner work, and actual paid work, to do—I wasn't doing a study-abroad program, but he had no understanding of the thousands of things I was tending to in my head and soul.

Even if I *had* been looking for a relationship, I did not feel that we were compatible. I didn't know much about Tommaso except that he loved Tunisia, Louis Vuitton travel gear, cigars, Apple products, and arguing (though I'm normally not a fan, I found it fun in Italian, which has such an expressive quality to it). I had my doubts on all fronts: he didn't have the so-called five melons, and I wasn't convinced he was kind. As the days went by, his unrelenting texting of various emoticons of a flirtatious nature became both unnerving and irritating. I shut off my phone for hours on end, only to turn it on to find a dozen text messages and missed calls from him grilling me as to my whereabouts. I wrote to him:

I came here to write and be alone.
I'm not looking for a relationship.
I'm good on my own.
I just want space.
I can't breathe.
Per favore.

His response:

You'll be alone forever.

I was livid. Then, after a few hours, the anger melted away. I sat with the thought. It seemed extreme, impossible even. When I'd sat in stillness long enough, I realized that if I were to be alone forever, it would be because I'd wanted exactly that.

There was something transcendental about owning that.

We come into this world alone and we leave alone. I wasn't going to fool myself into thinking otherwise.

Chapter 4

Connecting

The one who asks questions doesn't lose his way.

—*African proverb*

By July, my job was sending me to Tanzania on a photography assignment, and I made my way from Catania to Rome to Dar es Salaam. While I'd been to eastern Africa for food security work before, I was mostly familiar with Ethiopia. I'd spent time in the northern part of the country and the capital, Addis Ababa; and during the summer of 2011, I traveled to a refugee camp in Dolo Ado, a border town where refugees were flooding in from Somalia because of drought and violent conflict that had caused massive displacement, forcing unprecedented numbers of Somalis to cross its borders into neighboring countries in search of food and safety.[1] In Tanzania, while there was no drought, conflict, or famine making headlines, other serious health threats were affecting people: malaria, tuberculosis, HIV, and what are awkwardly referred to in medical lingo as "neglected tropical diseases," such as schistosomiasis, or snail fever, a parasitic disease carried by freshwater snails. The UN agency I was working for sent me on a storytelling mission to document our efforts to help reduce the transmission and occurrence of these diseases and to investigate progress on some of the treatments, including the development of vaccines at labs and hospitals and their distribution. As part of my work, I spent hours in crowded hospitals photographing tuberculosis and malaria patients, some of them in abject conditions, as well as interviewing doctors and medical experts. One of my site visits included a school on the outskirts of Dar es Salaam where, as a part of a government-led parasite-prevention program, a mass drug distribution was taking place at a small school at the end of a dirt road.

By some miracle, every time I felt my work pushing me to my limit emotionally—even if there was a certain desensitization involved to get the job done—I always seemed to get a snippet of something uplifting. It usually had to do with kids. No matter where I traveled, children were always curious and ready to engage, especially when they spotted a camera (yes, it's the cliché image of a Western aid worker). Yet after the previous sites, I was relieved to be around healthy, boisterous children eating rice and beans and running around without a care in the world. This was what the work was about: moments of being in another world encircled by beings I would have never otherwise met, the *connection* that was not based on anything but our shared humanity.

Yet it can be hard to leave the people you love, the people you know, for people you don't know. I was conflicted about it every single time. Leaving the safety, comfort, and familiarity of home, or any of my bases—New York, Rome, Mumbai, or DC—was harder than I wanted it to be and became more difficult as my parents got older. While I hated putting them through the worry, I was also addicted to my job. At that time, I was focused almost exclusively on career advancement and external adventure. Sometimes, though, I did still feel that longing for intimate connection, companionship, and the safety of someone who would know me at my deepest, brightest, and worst moments, and choose to stick by me. Most women know what I am talking about— no matter how self-governing and strong you are, no matter that you don't need anyone ever for anything because you are a self-sufficient, economically independent, multitasking powerhouse, there is still that annoying, undeniable, irrepressible, instinctive human craving for companionship and acceptance by another in the form of a relationship. Another person to witness your life as it unfolds, to be invested in your success just as much as you are. Someone to do things like plan out your fortieth or fiftieth birthday and be along for the ride, in the front seat with you. In this longing for intimacy and companionship (or in the relationship itself), we sometimes lose ourselves, even though it's an integral part of being a social animal. "Connection is why we are here," says Brené Brown. "It's what gives purpose and meaning to our lives . . . Neurobiologically, that's how we're hardwired."[2]

Deploying to a humanitarian crisis, a refugee camp, or simply a corner of the world staggering under the weight of poverty was on the extreme end of things, but deep down I was drawn to that type of work, not just because it was interesting and felt important—though that was certainly part of it—but because of the connection it made me feel to something larger (humankind?). In a way, instead of pursuing a single relationship, I went after one with the entire world. I didn't want to brush against disaster and grief because I was masochistic; rather, I was chasing that sense of being connected to people, which you experience deepest in desperate circumstances, like in the aftermath of a natural disaster, where rawness and vulnerability and authenticity are expansively present, in a way I didn't feel in magazine publishing or in a TV control room. And for some reason I wanted this connection more than anything.

Beyond that, there was something poignant, almost mystical, about my encounters with the women I met in these places—something humbling about their jaw-dropping resilience. In spite of their circumstances, these survivors of earthquakes, floods, and wars exemplified a huge-heartedness that was unfathomable. For example, when I was thirty-three and working in a sprawling refugee camp near Zarzis in southeastern Tunisia, overrun by countless refugees who had fled from

Libya—where the heat was almost unbearable, parching our insides, and where, like a virus, the metallic poison of war had been carried over to the camp itself in the form of volatile outbursts among the men—I found some sort of spiritual solace in the presence of the refugee women with whom I spent time. A life-affirming human connection. Even when a makeshift school in the camp was set on fire or an outbreak of violence spurred a "security incident," forcing all of us aid workers to pile into Land Rovers and careen toward a "secure base," I would go back to these women because it was my job to hear their stories and share them with the world. They needed to be *heard*, and I needed to listen.

When I spent all that time working in Mumbai's red-light district, meeting women who had been trafficked into prostitution and sexually exploited, I worried that speaking to them would open up their wounds, but the NGO workers encouraged talking; they knew that getting the women to share their stories was part of their healing, a form of talk therapy, even though some of them seemed dead inside. Being listened to, being truly heard by someone else, having their suffering acknowledged even though there was no way to eradicate the past or "fix things," seemed to reduce the loneliness, the scars, and the destitution that ballooned inside and consumed them.

"The single thing all women need in the world is inspiration, and inspiration comes from storytelling," said Zainab Salbi, the Iraqi-born founder of Women for Women International who has dedicated her life to helping women in war-torn regions rebuild their lives. Storytelling enlarges our humanity, and we all crave truth-telling. The stories I heard firsthand during those weeks on the Libya-Tunisia border inspired me— they were lumpy, unedited offerings, testaments to raw human endurance. There was Fatmah, the fifteen-year-old mother of two originally from Niger, who left her home of more than five years in Sabha, Libya, because of the war. She squeezed her ten-month-old against her small frame and looked distressed as she recalled the relentless shelling that kept her up at night. I won't forget meeting Awatef, a refugee originally from Darfur in Sudan, who had fled Tripoli by bus at the end of March with her seven children after living in Libya for twenty-eight years. "I fled one war and now another. I just want to live somewhere in peace where my kids can study and find good jobs," she told me.

These stories made me feel awe at the power of the human spirit, especially in the strength and resilience of womankind. They made me think of my mother, though her situation had been more fortunate. She was not left to fend for herself. She never had to live in a refugee camp. I felt a connection to these women, as if I was giving back through her. It was a full-circle thing.

Some people are inspired by the notion of humanitarian or development aid work; others are skeptical or critical. Do some aid workers or development professionals perceive things from a position of white privilege? Perhaps, inadvertently, yes. That is impossible to control even with self-awareness of how to occupy a position of privilege in a poor place. Sure, there are issues there, also with some development models, approaches, and the gospel of aid work when it has a missionary-style approach. Yet while some people argue that aid workers draw a salary from disaster, this isn't the way I see it. Admittedly, it is difficult to measure the actual impact one individual has in a fast-unfolding humanitarian crisis—it is easy to sometimes feel like a useless speck in the chaos—yet my firsthand experience has always dictated this: in every place I have ever been for work, the response I've received has been one of deep gratitude. This is what I mean by feeling like I got more than I gave—to be acknowledged in that way, even for just listening to someone's story. It validates what I've long known: if empathy is the foundation of emotional intelligence, and compassion is the bridge that connects us to other people, then it is the deepest way to live (working in development aid is one way to exercise empathy and live out humanitarian ideals, but of course there are countless other ways to do so).

Even these women, swathed in garments from head to toe, who'd fled Libya and been forced to leave so much behind, wanted to connect, share their stories, share their truths. They would, for example, extend the warmest hospitality, inviting me into their tents, insisting that I drink their sugary tea or eat their fruit. I knew they felt bad for me: a young-looking aid worker who probably appeared tired and dirty in my T-shirt and jeans, which is ironic given what they'd gone through. Between women, we didn't always need words; they were, at times, superfluous. Everything was already *understood*.

Human connection. What I'd lacked in a singular long-term relationship, I'd found tenfold through my work, not with one person, but with an entire universe of people, transcending geographical divides, ethnicities, and religions. Women mainly—teachers, mothers, survivors, and *witnesses*—and children. We were all witnesses together, without even wanting to be, but there we were—witnessing, sharing, *connecting*.

When we don't feel connected to anything, inside of us, outside of us, that is when it can become dangerous.

I say this because in 2014, one of my oldest, most precious friends hanged himself out of loneliness. It was a loneliness that fed off of a severe, long-term clinical depression that had become all-consuming. It grew and grew until it enveloped him completely.

I met Kenny in college. He was smart, hardworking, creative, and gay. He giggled at my jokes. In spite of my unibrow, questionable sense of style, and bagel-induced chub, he thought I was pretty and followed me around with a Nikon taking photographs. We became fast friends. At the time, the plan was for me to be a famous magazine editor and for him to be a famous interior designer. I don't know why fame was so important to us back then, but that's what we talked about while eating salads with carrot-ginger dressing at Dojo, a budget-friendly Japanese diner in Greenwich Village. We even had a baby plan: if we didn't meet our partners by thirty-five, we would have a baby together. We were the same age—Kenny's birthday was just a month before mine. But we kind of assumed that we would have found the loves of our lives by then.

The years went by, I left the US and came back, left and came back, and each time, Kenny would have just started or ended a relationship with someone.

"It's exhausting," he would say, when it didn't work out with one of his boyfriends.

"I know," I would wholeheartedly agree.

In the last several months before he committed suicide, he had been going through a tough time. Financially, he'd opened up his own lifestyle and design store in Chelsea and was drowning in debt. He'd had a falling out with his mother and his brother, and they were not on speaking terms. His father was not in his life. After Kenny's funeral, his cousin told me that he was on antidepressants and that she had driven him to a psychiatric hospital on more than one occasion so that he could voluntarily check himself in for suicide watch, though he always changed his mind about going in at the last minute out of fear that he would get stuck there. I didn't know he was on medication or that he was suicidal—he kept those parts private.

The last time I saw him, we had pad thai at a little Thai restaurant in my old neighborhood, NoLIta. It was a blustery March evening; we were both wearing puffer jackets. I was flying to a TED conference in Canada the next day, and I remember being a little distracted. He was talking about how he was tired of waiting to meet someone, of how much he wanted love. I commiserated with him. It was some of our usual banter, but I later realized he was much more intense, talking at a rapid pace about how he wished he would be successful and didn't understand why everything was taking so long. His words were singed with hopelessness. My efforts to cheer him up fell flat. I tried every-thing, dipping deep into my well of self-help knowledge, all the stuff that was supposed to be helping me with my own grief, as my father had passed away less than a year before, but nothing seemed to resonate with him. A few days later, after watching a TED Talk by San Franciscan Sergeant Kevin Briggs on suicide on the Golden Gate Bridge, I thought to myself, *I've got to sit down with Kenny when I get back to New York*. In his talk, Briggs recommends asking the "Have you thought about taking your life?" question head-on to a friend who seems especially down, saying that it can possibly save a person. Sometimes people just need to be listened to. That was what I was going to do: be a better listener, be a better friend.

But it was too late. The night before I flew back, Kenny's mother called my cell phone while I was in my hotel in Vancouver. In his suicide note, he had left her with a short list of friends to tell of his passing. When I went to the small funeral that week, she handed me an album of photographs he had taken of me when we were students, all black and white. "He really loved you," she cried.

I felt like I was imploding. I wonder what actually happens inside in these horrible, horrible moments—a silent explosion. Do things fragment, break apart, unravel like braids? Do cells pop in the chaos of emotion, a snapping that no one can hear? All I could think was, *Contain, contain, contain*. It may sound like stoicism, but it was actually stifling. I learned how to do this in my work; I wanted to unlearn it because it didn't seem healthy, but it was difficult. I felt heavy with guilt, but I am sure it was nothing compared to hers. I had nothing on his brother's guilt either. Kenny had left behind two little nieces who adored him, who looked anxious and confused in the dark parlor in their small black dresses. They didn't understand what had happened to Uncle Kenny.

Could I have saved him? That is what we all wondered afterward, when a handful of his close friends gathered at a nearby restaurant after the service. We were all still in shock. We all felt like bad friends, like self-absorbed failures. We felt we should have paid more attention, seen the signs. We were so distracted by our own lives, our own demons.

"No," the cousin said, trying to comfort us. "You don't understand depression."

It was true—we did not. Only later would I read that depression-related mortality is very high, especially for men, and even more seriously for gay men. That mortality most commonly takes the form of suicide. Clinical depression can be entirely overwhelming and isolating, and it is not easy to treat. You can't meditate it away.

Even so, Kenny experienced such acute loneliness that he felt disconnected and isolated enough to take his own life. He was overwhelmed by the expectations of the world he lived in—expectations that he be successful, that he be rich, that he be coupled, that he be admired—layered with the horrible burden of clinical depression. I wish he had realized that we're all connected to each other, and if we are all connected to each other, then we are never alone. But you can't say it and have it mean anything; it just sounds like new-age bullshit. The person has to experience it on their own, in quietude, in order to understand it. Some of us don't even get there. And you can't feel that connection when you're being swallowed up by a devastating disorder like depression, an all-consuming beast that entrenches itself into the whole being of a person. It is incredibly hard to live with. I understand that only now, and now is too late. I don't even know how to scrape the meaning out of what happened.

"No one can pull anyone back from anywhere. You save yourself or you remain unsaved," wrote author Alice Sebold in her memoir, *Lucky*, which details her rape as an eighteen-year-old college freshman.

We save ourselves, or we remain unsaved.

———

As I happened to be in Tanzania already, a country known for its vast wilderness areas, I decided to go on a safari for the first time. With sixteen national parks, including the famed Serengeti National Park, and seventeen game reserves, this East African country has some of the continent's greatest concentrations of wild animals, making it a major destination for safaris.

I wanted a chance to see the country's beauty up close, experience the wide-open fresh air, especially after being in congested hospitals brimming with sick patients. My birthday had just passed, and I've always been a big believer in treating myself on my birthday. There is a certain symbolism there, a self-love thing, sort of like, *You've made it this far, so to celebrate your continued existence, here is something your heart wants.*

I decided to head to the lesser-known southern part of the country instead of the more popular Serengeti circuit in the north. The best thing about the south, aside from fewer tourists, was that I could get there by car, saving on the cost of flights and making it less logistically complicated. My friend's wife happened to run a safari company, and I signed up for a four-night, five-day package, as that was all my budget could handle. The days would be split across the Selous Game Reserve and Mikumi National Park, with two nights spent in mid-budget-level lodges, and two spent glamping (which suited my finances even though I didn't really know what glamping entailed). In a way, the whole thing felt rushed, like everything else I ended up doing, but I figured a little taste would be better than nothing, and I wasn't sure when I'd have another opportunity to go on a safari.

Besides, this safari felt like my last hurrah. In a few weeks I would have to return to my cubicle, if there was even one waiting for me, back at headquarters. I dreaded the idea of being back in full swing—the commuting, the distractions, the materialism. I feared that I'd again lose the centeredness I'd started to feel within, feared that I would stop being awake. It was too precious to lose. I didn't want to think of it, and hadn't, until I'd started planning for the safari and wanted more reasons to justify the expense. Mads had already sent me a flurry of emails around plans for the UN General Assembly, which takes place every September in New York. It is always a chaotic time at the UN, and these precious months away would soon feel like a different lifetime.

After Andrew, my safari guide, a forty-year-old Tanzanian, scooped me up from my hotel in Dar, I kept coming back to this idea that I was weird, going on a safari by myself. It was usually honeymooners or families who went on safaris, though I am sure other women have done solo safaris. Andrew had known there would be only one person—the safari company would have told him that—but still he asked, not with malice but more as a conversation starter. When I confirmed that yes, it would just be me and the unwieldy camera I was carrying, he paused.

"So, you're like the leopard."

"What do you mean?"

"The leopard likes her solitude."

Yes. Like the leopard. I didn't know much about the leopard (I was so animal-ignorant at the time), but I liked being compared to one. They are strong and beautiful and secretive and kind of mystical and fleeting. They probably don't feel weird about wanting to be alone, so why should I?

After hours of driving on a highway that turned into a bumpy dirt road, which sliced through miles and miles of leafy greenery, we landed in a nature reserve the size of Switzerland and Poland combined, and I found myself staring at a pile of rubbery-looking mammals against the backdrop of a flowing river.

"Their sweat is pink," said Andrew, after several minutes of silence. I stared at the hippos. They looked like giant gray pigs and did seem to have a pinkish undertone to their hairless skin. I could almost smell their heavy musk.

I quickly discovered that Andrew's talents were many: not only was he an excellent driver, but he basically doubled as a walking field guide with laser-like vision. His knowledge of wildlife and the mating patterns of mammals seemed infinite. He even explained the detailed chemical composition of this particular secretion, unique to hippos, though it still remained something of a biological mystery to me. For some inexplicable reason—perhaps heat-induced delirium or just because I like the color pink—I wanted to get closer to the hippos, to connect with them, maybe by petting them? When I asked if I could get out of the jeep to do just that, especially since the hippos looked like they were in what my niece calls a "cuddle pile," snoozing away, Andrew informed me that they would charge the vehicle the instant my hiking boots slapped the ground and basically crush me to smithereens. At an average weight of 3,300 pounds, I couldn't imagine them moving very quickly, and they looked so sweet and nonaggressive, but I decided to heed his advice and not tempt fate. This time.

"They are not like your dogs you have in the US," he said, amused at my naivete.

True, I *was* a naive animal lover (which is why I didn't even eat them). Every time we drove close to a dazzle of zebras, a tower of giraffes, or a herd of elephants, once the awe at actually seeing them in the flesh had subsided, my instinct was to leap out of the jeep, run across the uneven, shrub-tangled savanna, and touch them. Of course I did not; I'd been warned by Andrew that it would be "unwise," but that was what I *felt* like doing. I had to contain my restlessness, sit back, and watch, which was hard for me—not engaging, not moving. Connecting to the world around me in a different way, in a way that primarily involved observing, took some effort at first. I couldn't even make sounds at them to get them to look my way. That was another safari faux pas for which I'd been gently admonished. This is why, at least on day one, I filled the blanket of silence with a steady stream of arguably inane questions, which Andrew duly answered:

"Are elephants and lions friends?"

"If zebras are faster than lions, does that mean that they can never be caught by one?"

"How do giraffes sleep?"

"If you had to die by one animal here, which one would you choose?"

"Elephant," he said. "One kick and you are done."

That did not surprise me. Larger elephants can eat up to nearly seven hundred pounds of shrubs and grass a day (and poop twenty times a day).

"Not a lion then?" I asked. "I thought they were expert killers."

"No, not the lion." He paused, in thought. "The lion takes his time."

The lion takes his time. I liked that; it had a certain ring to it. I was all for taking time, conceptually at least, though in practice I found it more challenging. I had a reverent fear of the lion, nonetheless. While lions were symbols of strength and courage, of royalty and dignity, they were also downright terrifying.

Earlier that afternoon, we'd had to make a pit stop in the reserve itself, which was massive and with few facilities. Andrew, who seemed eternally relaxed, was not worried in the slightest when I asked about the likelihood of a lion lunging out of nowhere and biting his butt. "If the lion want to eat me, why not? I can feed the lion," he casually mused in response to my concerns, disappearing behind some sharp shrubs as I squeezed my legs together. He said it in a way that felt both cavalier and Darwinian—it was the natural order of things, for the strong to eat the weak; why couldn't I just accept that common truth? After all, nature did.

I definitely did not want to be eaten by a lion—that much I knew. It just didn't seem like the right ending for me. But I also *really* didn't want to soil my cargo pants. I cursed myself for drinking loads of water at lunch. Discomfort eventually swayed me into undertaking the risky endeavor of peeing in a lion's habitat. So much for my newfound love of urinating in nature. I did a careful 360 with my binoculars and then squatted down, nearly tipping over with fear, thinking, *This is what you wanted—to connect with yourself, to connect with the basics. What better*

way than to be solely responsible for your very own survival, to put yourself
in a life-or-death situation where the only thing you can count on are your
own senses?

Andrew was a teacher in this regard: he was grounded and connected to himself and to the world around him. There was a harmony
to him; he realized he was an individual within an ecosystem, self-
sustaining but also part of a much greater whole. A creation within a
creation within a creation. I wondered if, like Dumitru, his wisdom
came from being in nature, from being around basic yet miraculous
things all day long. He was very present and *awake*, qualities I aspired
to have that become more pronounced, it seems, the more connected
we are to ourselves, the more aligned we are with our various parts
(mind, body, spirit), and the more time we spend steeped in silence,
witnessing ourselves.

I also wondered if it was because he didn't have a cell phone.

This much I knew: becoming fully awake and connected takes practice and patience—there is no easy fix, only small steps in the direction of awareness, and they are rarely linear. It is like walking on a
tightrope—at any moment, you can fall out of awareness if the balance
isn't there, but then you regain your balance and try again. Self-work
is daily work. It is exhausting in that you're never done, but liberating
in that you know every moment presents a new opportunity to change
and grow.

———

By the third day of the safari, I'd learned how to settle more into the
passive experience. Instead of being active, instead of always being a par-
ticipant in the world, I tried to cultivate the art of observing. Sometimes
I would make eye contact with a curious giraffe or an impala, and I
would feel the same as when I ran into all those goats on Etna—a deep,

protective connection that made me want to cry with love, even though I had no clue why.

Andrew was the perfect companion—available for conversation if either of us felt chatty but respectful of the need for silence during the epic moments of witnessing such majestic creatures in their natural habitats. They were single entities, but also part of a pack. They did not—maybe could not—exist without each other, as they were a part of an interlinked ecosystem that included humans. They appeared content chewing on shrubs separately, but they also seemed comforted knowing that they were connected to a larger group in some way, an extension of themselves, even if they weren't actively interacting most of the time.

Sometimes I wished I had someone along with me on the journey, someone to share in the amazingness of the experience. It was hardly new for Andrew. It was his everyday job. I thought a lot about my father—he would have loved a safari, and I told myself that he was living it through me. *When someone dies, the connection stays; the love continues to exist.* That is what I'd felt in the most profound way at the top of that volcano, and that is what I choose to believe. I don't care if science can prove it or not. Sometimes you just know what you know, and you have to leave it at that.

I also thought a bit about Niall, who had been more regularly in touch. His divorce was finalized, and he had moved to Madrid. We had spoken on the phone a few times over the past year; he had a deep, calming voice, his Irish accent still detectable after all these years away from Dublin. He used to be careful with his words, sparse, so I was surprised at how open he'd become. "I've been in love with you my whole life," he told me. "You've always been the one."

It was a deeply comforting thought: the idea of returning to an old flame who knew me before I'd become a woman, who knew me before I'd experienced any suffering, and who not only knew me before I lost my father, but who also knew my father. Had shaken hands with him. Had looked into his eyes. Had read his memoir. I imagined that if anything were to transpire between us now, it would be welcoming, like stepping into a warm bath. It would probably be the easiest, safest thing in the world. It would not be breathless, but more *breathful*. I'd read that when a woman is released from the all-consuming passion of new romantic love, she can love her partner in more comfortable ways (because most people know that being wildly in love is exhausting and hardly sustainable).

But I couldn't be certain of what the future held. Rather than get lost in fantasy, I forced myself to stay in the present, before it, too, was gone. I found myself relishing the wilderness, harboring a real openness toward it and all of its fleeting creatures.

Andrew and I kept a lookout for leopards, as I wanted to see what Andrew believed was the animal version of me, but she remained elusive. It was perhaps more flattering than being likened to the elephant, at least in terms of size and grace, and appetite (they spend all day eating), though I was personally humbled by the sheer presence of these wild African elephants. Again, Ganesh incarnated? These beasts are considered to be some of the most intelligent animals on Earth.

As part of my wildlife education, Andrew made me hold elephant poop with my bare hands. "It's just grass," he said, tossing the poop in the air like a small basketball with grass spiking out of it. He handed it to me and, reluctantly, I held it, feeling the weight of it in my palms. If I wanted to bridge the gaps not only within myself, but between myself and everything around me, maybe I also had to connect with something as elemental as elephant dung.

Andrew explained that elephants have a matriarchal system, with adult females traveling in groups of other females and their young. During mating season, or rainy season, when the female is in heat, she sends out a come-hither vibe through her urine, which has, to use Andrew's words, "a nice fragrance." Next, male elephants follow the pee trail, and the female in heat chooses the most impressive male to make sweet love to her. They mate two to three times a day during her receptive period, and then the male elephant leaves, sauntering off into the wild, never looking back—the elephant version of a one-night stand. The female will be pregnant for twenty-two months and then deliver her baby lying on her side, like it's no big deal. Newborns, which weigh an average of 220 pounds, can stand and walk within a few hours. She raises the baby with the help of the herd.

The female elephant was a force to be reckoned with: she was independent, took what she wanted from the male, sent him on his merry way, and hung out in her harem of women raising her little elephant baby. She was a no-nonsense powerhouse within her ecosystem. Being a leopard was cool. Being a female elephant might be cooler.

They were connected. We are all connected. Our ecology has relied on interdependence for centuries and centuries. The idea that we are independent of each other is almost solipsistic. The separateness and singularity is an illusion. The loss of one species affects others. For example, during the dry season, elephants dig for water with their tusks, trunks, and powerful feet, and the resulting pools not only keep them alive but also provide water for other animals. Even the dung I held is crucial to the ecosystem: it is full of seeds from all the plants the elephants eat. When the dung is dropped, the seeds germinate, and new grasses, bushes, and trees grow. Everything is interconnected. Everything has a purpose, a reason for being—there is no waste in nature. There is no waste in the universe. Everything feeds everything and gets recycled back into the universe. The universe feeds on itself. Everything feeds the journey of life, the soul, even if we are not aware that we are hungry.

In Ayurveda, everything is energy behaving with cosmic intelligence, the same energy recognized by quantum physics as being the building blocks of the universe. To that end, our bodies are energetic entities dancing in the cosmic soup of the universe, not separate from it but deeply connected to it. Neil deGrasse Tyson supports this idea of connectivity, vouching that we are not only biologically connected to each other, and chemically to the earth, but also atomically connected to the rest of the universe.³ To boot, this scientist is part of a rare breed who gets the whole occult side of things: "Not only are we in the universe, the universe is in us. I don't know of any deeper spiritual feeling than what that brings upon me."⁴

All of it made me realize there is no waste in life, really. Any heartache or disappointment I've had has evolved into something else, grown into something else. Just by way of existing, we are fertile ground, an infinite palette for creativity. It is who we are in the most organic sense. The sadness that burrows itself into us always becomes something; something comes out of it—like every plant or tree or shrub that sprouts out across an African savanna from a seedling. It may take time to see what it amounts to, but grief, sorrow, pain—they are seeds. Heartache, hopelessness, dejection—they are seeds. In their own twisted way, they are invitations.

If I had not loved hard and lost hard, I would not have become more, grown into the person I continue to become. I would have stopped somewhere way back. I would not have amounted to more than I was. That is why we have to take those emotional risks—our very evolution depends on it.

If I had not lost my father, I would not have started asking questions. I would not have swung from one question to the next, seeking. I would not have lived inside those questions with my eyes open, seeing and being in a way I'd never seen and been before. That seed, watered with tears, became the odyssey that I was on. It was teaching me to live differently, in a more sacred way.

Loss can show you what is sacred and what is not.

———

As observing keenly is an integral part of the safari experience, I took it seriously, which was easier with no technology to distract me, no schedule to restrict me. There was something meditative about watching animals in their natural habitat. I was not even a bird person, yet there were so many iridescent birds, unlike anything I'd seen before. I spent at least half an hour one morning watching an African jacana—a graceful bird with a rich chestnut belly and long, dainty toes—as it walked delicately across floating vegetation and hunted for insects, small crabs, and snails. In an era of tweets and Instagram, being attentive and patient felt almost like a homecoming for my mind. After a few days on a safari, away from the internet, away from interactions with anyone other than Andrew (who was tremendously easy on the nerves), after I'd stopped feeling weird and owned up to my leopard-like ways, after I recognized that I was the opposite of alone and was probably in some universal way connected to the very elephant dung I'd held, I grew a Buddha mind—at times experiencing almost pure emptiness.

There was a lot about my father that I found Buddha-like. He was calm, peaceful, and free of angst—a safe place to come back to over and over. With him gone, there was no place for me to retreat to, only inside, only into silence, into the place where I felt him the most. That stillness, that quiet, allowed me to recognize how life is a constant and total unfolding of miracles. When you slow yourself into stillness, the whole world comes to you, whatever is inside. The universe? In a way, I had to disconnect from everything else to really connect with that knowingness. Slowing down is the key to unlocking this magic. I'd come across this feeling on Etna and in India. "Attention is the beginning of devotion," the poet Mary Oliver wrote. I was learning what she meant.

While *noticing*, I was enchanted by nature's unrestrained beauty and intelligence. I learned that the white circle on a water buck's rear helps others to recognize its identity, that elephants have a specific alarm call that means "human," and that impalas, giraffes, and zebras all face different directions while grazing as a form of protection. If a threat arises, they have different signals that they give to each other, such as making a particular noise or kicking the ground.

Even the trees seemed to have *purpose* or some kind of botanical intelligence. The reserve was quintessential rolling savanna punctuated by grassy plains, woodlands, and all sorts of trees—tamarind, acacia, and toothbrush trees, to name a few. The whistling thorn, a type of acacia tree, is equipped with sharp thorns that surround hollow pods. Inside these pods live violent little ants drawn to the tree because of its sweet nectar. In exchange, the ants help protect the tree from grazing animals by swarming and stinging whatever touches it. The slow-growing tamarind trees, which can sprout from seeds in the waste of baboons, often grow at the base of giant baobab trees, which Andrew explained is because they like shade from the sun and the baobab trees act like shields. "They are very needy trees," he told me. But that was just it—everything seemed to need everything else. In New York, everyone operated in their own silos. We were probably too independent for our own good.

The baobab tree is called the tree of life. Native to the African savanna (as well as Australia and Madagascar, and also found in southern Asia and the Caribbean), it can be a source of pretty much all necessities—a one-stop shop for food, shelter, and water. Resilient, thriving in hot, dry conditions where most trees would perish, it stores vast quantities of fresh water in its trunk, produces fruit chock-full of nutrients, vitamin- and protein-rich seeds used like coffee, and leaves with high quantities of vitamin C, which can be eaten as a salad. Its cork-like bark, which is fire-resistant and regenerates easily after stripping, serves as food for elephants in times of drought *and* can be made into rope, roofing material, and other handy things. Identifiable by its massive trunk and slender, twisting branches, the baobab tree seems otherworldly. The oldest dated tree has been growing for more than a thousand years. Like a leopard, I climbed a baobab tree we came across and leaned against it, absorbing its energy, quietly worshipping its wholeness, the entire universe inside it.

———

I never spotted the leopard. But just knowing that she existed in the world—in all her strength and beauty, solitary but not lonely—reassured me, just like Etna's presence had. I felt inspired, so after my safari, I decided to put wisdom into practice by doing something unusual and perfect: I decided to marry myself.

Obviously, this was highly symbolic, but not as bizarre as some might suppose. In China, as in India, there is huge pressure to get married. "Leftover woman" is the term used for women over twenty-five who are still single in China. The notorious one-child policy (enforced from 1979 to 2015) and the strong cultural preference for sons mean that there are about twenty million more men than women of prime marriage age in China. If a woman reaches thirty and has not found a partner, she can kiss her marriage plans goodbye. So some women have chosen to marry themselves, sometimes in elaborate ceremonies with all the accoutrements: the white dress, the diamond ring, wedding guests, and a professional photographer. These are more social statements than pathetic delusions—a reaction to the way that society makes single women of a certain age feel like abysmal failures. It can be seen as a way of maintaining self-worth when we do not fit into society's preferred mold but rather into more of a wild woman archetype, the soulful, creative woman that psychologist Clarissa Pinkola Estés describes in her juicy tome *Women Who Run with the Wolves*. The courageous and strong woman who is full of ageless knowing, coursing with kundalini energy, in touch with her innate wildness, an "endangered species" that is often at odds with civilized society. It is happening in the US and Europe as well, as part of a burgeoning self-empowerment trend, behaviors through which women celebrate their singleness and lifelong commitment to themselves, which includes for some single women the wearing of wedding bands on either their left or right ring fingers. Known by a hodgepodge of terms, including *sologamy* and *self-marriage*, these rituals form part of a growing self-worth movement, part of the "quirkyalone"[5] culture, and are considered by many to form a new class of feminist coming-of-age rituals.

While critics of the movement call it self-absorbed and narcissistic (the idea of throwing a lavish party for yourself and pretty much celebrating your existence), I find that viewpoint shortsighted and a bit reductive. The real marriage is between me and myself; you and yourself. All of this deep work is about committing to yourself anyway; about prizing yourself, your life, your friends, your community, your family over a single relationship—we all know the whole spiel. Radical self-love is the main thing, but marrying yourself is also about rejecting patriarchal norms—like the negative stereotype of the spinster—while celebrating the independent woman. Being uncoupled doesn't mean you're alone. That insecurity is fraught with inaccuracy, and capitalism and society feed off it.

You have to love yourself before you can love others or be loved. It is women saying yes to themselves, saying we are enough, even without a partner. Interestingly, sociologists like Eric Klinenberg have discovered that people today live alone whenever they can afford to, a symptom of a society's growing wealth. In his book *Going Solo: The Extraordinary Rise and Surprising Appeal of Living Alone*, a seven-year research project, Klinenberg discovered single urbanites are happy to live alone (and are even a bit smug about it) and don't fulfill the stereotype of being sad, lonely, and friendless. Whatever one's reasons for sologamy, making a ceremonial commitment to one's self can be powerful and spiritual— and it felt like the right thing for me to do as I neared the end of my man fast.

The thing is, for me, it was more of an elopement, as I'd decided to marry myself only on my safari. It was the baobab tree; it made me realize that I was whole, that I was everything I needed, and that while other people would come and go, I had to stay resilient and rooted into myself.

Like most of my decisions, it was last-minute, so I had to do without the company of close friends and family. I already knew *where* I was getting married: Zanzibar. After the safari, when I returned to Dar, I took the two-hour ferry to Stone Town, the old part of Zanzibar City. At home in the city's peppery blend of Arab, Indian, and African influences, I wandered side alleys and paused in contemplation at the regular call to prayer that pulsed throughout the Muslim city. Hearing the call to prayer broadcasted over loudspeakers in a Muslim country always reminds me to stop, listen, and be present. Prayer, independent of religion, can be very powerful. When we've fallen off that tightrope, prayer is a chance to start again, to whisper our dreams to the universe, to connect with that hidden higher intelligence, to honor the space we are in.

As for the ring, while I am not a huge gemstone consumer, apparently I *had* to buy tanzanite while in Tanzania. A friend of my mother's instructed me not to come home without one of these velvety-blue rocks. Discovered in commercial quantities in the late 1960s, tanzanite is a thousand times rarer than diamond. The gem variety of the mineral zoisite, it is found in only one place on Earth—in the hills of Merelani in northern Tanzania near the base of Mount Kilimanjaro, the highest mountain in Africa.

I'd read that occultists consider tanzanite to be a highly metaphysical stone, ideal for spiritual exploration, with the ability to heighten psychic powers with its vibrational energy and summon a meditative state. I figured that even if I purchased a small lighter-hued lavender stone—which was much cheaper than the expensive dark-blue ones, and all I could afford—it would still have these magical aspects to it. A friend who had lived in Zanzibar vouched for an ethical jewelry place with funky designs, and there I found a chunky band of textured silver with a small piece of uncut tanzanite, a wispy violet color, in the center. It was beautiful, affordable, and unusual enough to be a conversation piece.

In deciding what to wear, I wanted to honor what captivated me most about Tanzania: the color. Women there wear bright, saturated colors either in a traditional cloth wrap locally known as a *khanga*, which is used alternatively as a sarong, shawl, baby-carrier, and toga-style dress, or kaftans also known as *diras*, which are voluminous and flowing and have this regal quality to them. I wanted regal—it was my wedding after all, maybe the only one I would ever have. I walked by the window of a little shack on one of the dusty side streets, and dangling off a small wire hanger was a long pomegranate-red kaftan made from supersoft cotton with a zigzagging pattern of blue puddles and moon-yellow tulip-like shapes. It was bold and cheerful, vibrant and unapologetic—it was exactly what I wanted and set me back only ten dollars. None of the white virgin crap. I had lived life, and I was not ashamed of it.

Without realizing it, I got into a conversation about marriage with the married Tanzanian taxi driver who was taking me across the island. Amused by my self-marriage plans, he said something that sort of stuck with me: "Here, we don't really think too much about whom we marry."

It sounded nuts and refreshing at the same time. Maybe, like Sita had said, one just needed to find someone good. I was good, and good enough. I flung my hand near the taxi driver to show him the small glistening rock on my hand.

"I see," he said. "You're doing it to show everyone you're married." He laughed.

No, I assured him, on the contrary, I was doing it to free myself *from* that.

As for the venue, it was exactly the kind of place I envisioned for the ceremony. I'd chosen a room in an eco-friendly six-bedroom villa run by an Italian couple. Located in a tiny fishing village called Jambiani, right on the turquoise waters of the Indian ocean, the design of the place was beautiful—stylish, earthy, and minimalist, with light wooden furniture, giant clay vases, a simple plunge pool, and spacious, dreamy rooms, all interspersed with pops of African color and topped with a thatched roof.

Quarters at the villa were tight, and the dining area intimate, so the guests had become acquainted with each other over the weekend. Most were couples, and everyone seemed curious about the single woman wearing a kaftan and dining while reading Isak Dinesen's memoir, as if I were part of some exotic species they had only read about. *There are many of us back in New York!* I wanted to declare, but on the other hand, I'd always enjoyed being unconventional. Maybe I *was* like the leopard. There was the elegant couple from South Africa with whom I discussed the tireless charades of American politicians; the lovely but discombobulated sisters from Argentina with their small children in tow, who were plainly coveting my freedom; the sturdy, blue-eyed German couple from Arusha and their three-year-old with bouncy blond curls; and the harried thirtysomething Italian couple from Venice who managed the place, which had opened only a month before. I got used to hearing the voices of these people over the course of forty-eight hours and thought, for a moment, that I could invite them to my self-marriage ceremony. When it came to the moment, though, I felt too shy about the whole thing, so I just invited the universe.

I invited the universe to my wedding to myself.

I never really thought I would write those words.

I decided to do it at sunrise on the day I was leaving, as a kind of morning meditation. I didn't need anyone around to witness it—the universe was enough. The sun, the ocean, the sky—they were enough. The whole thing was sort of a nonevent, but also special in its own way: I woke up, brushed my teeth, threw on my kaftan, and then glided across the sand, sleepy-eyed and yawning, plopping under a bamboo huppah leftover from a different sort of wedding on the property the week before. As the sun lifted through the haze, flooding the sky with dewy pink, and disinterested cows ambled down the beach, I silently read the vows I'd written the night before:

I, Natasha, give myself permission to pursue happiness and meaning in nontraditional ways and will continue to carve out my own authentic life path (and stop caring what others think).

I, Natasha, promise to enjoy inhabiting my own life and will no longer take for granted all the love and abundance I already have.

I, Natasha, will allow my life the space it needs to be healthy, continue to focus on my overall well-being, and live in a slower, more mindful way.

I, Natasha, promise to tap into my own inner wisdom and know that there is an infinite reserve within me at all times that I can harness for guidance.

I, Natasha, am whole and will never again doubt my own wholeness.

Chapter 5

Becoming

I am the divine seed within all beings.

—*Lord Krishna, Bhagavad Gita*[1]

After Tanzania, as I neared the end of what had turned out to be a nine-month pilgrimage of sorts, I looked for ways to continue on my spiritual journey. I decided to deeply study the *Bhagavad Gita*,[2] as well as some lesser-known Sufi mystical poetry, all while deepening my meditation practice. I used my mother's house in Chevy Chase as a base for a few weeks as August lingered with its muggy, enveloping presence.

They say that Einstein died with the *Bhagavad Gita* on his heart. Now I don't know if this is true, and I can't even remember where I read it, but he was certainly not the only clever person who appreciated the wisdom encapsulated in this ancient Hindu text. The *Gita* (as it is known for short) is considered by Eastern and Western scholars alike to be among the greatest spiritual books ever written. Ralph Waldo Emerson, Henry David Thoreau, Hermann Hesse, Mahatma Gandhi, and Carl Jung all had colossal respect for it, referencing it in their own philosophical works and teachings. Aldous Huxley called it "the most systematic statement of spiritual evolution of endowing value to mankind."

The *Gita* is a Sanskrit poem full of drama and "honey-sweet words," embedded as a small but critical part in the *Mahabharata*,[3] the epic narrative of the eighteen-day Kurukshetra War, where millions of warriors fought and very few survived. By epic, I mean at about 1.8 million words, it is crazy-long, estimated to be at least seven times the length of the *Iliad* and the *Odyssey* combined. I'm not a *Gita* scholar, but here's my take on it. In a nutshell, it explains a war fought between two clans of a dynastic family in northern India—the Pandavas (the good guys) and the Kauravas (the bad guys)—for the throne of Hastinapura. The leader of the good guys is a distinguished warrior named Prince Arjuna who, as he charges out into the open field between the two armies, is paralyzed by a moral dilemma while on the brink of battle—to fight, or not to fight.[4] He doesn't want to fight, for understandable reasons. Overwhelmed with despair at the thought of killing fathers, teachers, grandfathers, uncles, brothers, and friends, he turns to his wise friend Krishna,[5] his chariot driver (who turns out to be Lord Krishna as god incarnate),[6] and pleads with him to tell him "where his duty lies." What follows is a conversation between Lord Krishna and Prince Arjuna— seven hundred verses covering everything from meditation to nonattachment to the nature of the self to yoga, and, significantly, teachings on reincarnation and karma, the basic tenets of Hinduism—many of the ideas I'd been exploring on my man fast, that had become critical to my understanding of what, in many ways, felt like an existential crisis.

They say the entire knowledge of the cosmos is packed into the *Gita*, that it presents the principles of complex metaphysical science in the most basic form—a poem. However, esoteric by nature, it is definitely not something that you can unpack in one go. You have to contend with it, reread it, ingest and digest it. Every time I make my way through it, I take away something that makes me richer and wiser, going deeper into myself. The late Indian spiritual teacher Sri

Swami Satchidananda once said, "That is the greatness of the holy scriptures . . . Each time we read these works we elevate ourselves to see a little more."[7]

The last time I'd grappled with the *Gita* was years ago on a two-month trip to Mumbai. I'd started going to a weekly study group with an older cousin of mine and realized this was a body of work that—even for Indians who have grown up with regular exposure to it—warranted proper, careful study and analysis, especially in its original Sanskrit verse. I remember the stark room being filled with middle-aged Indians pressing down the pages of their worn, dog-eared *Gita*s as the verses were studied one by one by one. I was lost. There was never an end in sight. Like the self as outlined in the *Gita*, its teachings were infinite. Now I knew that somewhere in this text, the answers I was seeking would rise up to meet me because I was ready for them, whereas before I was blocked, not open and inquisitive. These answers would parallel the truths that I had already excavated over the last several months. Their anatomy might be different, but the essence of them would be identical, the truest of truths transcending all language, all religious dogma.

The *Gita*, of course, is a Hindu scripture. I used to be hugely, vastly, resolutely anti-religion—for all the ways religion has been used to oppress and control women or justify the oppression of minorities, for all the ways it discourages people from thinking for themselves, for all the ways it's been used to manipulate, divide, and deceive people into thinking that we don't all share the same god or mystical source (whatever you want to call it)—but I can't ignore the value of religion in this world when it is used in an *intelligent* way. History should be read with conditional respect. Religious or spiritual texts should be interpreted with a real understanding of the historical contexts in which they were written, as moral frameworks of sorts that add wholesome fodder to individual belief systems, not to be taken literally, but as *inspiration*—helping us to see the bigger picture and the ultimate truth: there is no separation between us. Some religious texts, patriarchal to the core, are built around the notion of one male supreme being external to us, but everything about my authentic quest to unearth the truth suggested otherwise. Everything is one, formless. If I wanted to experience god, all I had to do was shut my eyes and go inside. Eventually, with practice and time and patience, I would be able to see god in everything, including in other people. Not believe in god, but *know* god, which is a whole other thing, and much more profound.

Religion, generally, is too restrictive to allow for deep spiritual knowing; there are too many tenets to transcend to get there. Something so ineffable cannot be so prescribed, reduced to a canon. Religion is manmade, dogmatic, and exclusionary. In my opinion, religions as they stand, or cultural practices and ideologies spawned as an offshoot of religion, rarely allow for the full flowering of the female; instead, they often empower religious leaders to sanctify existing social structures that oppress women and force them to defer to male leadership. Part of my stepping away from the notion of coupledom and the so-called sanctity of traditional marriage—analyzing it from a distance—was to try to understand whether I would be drawn into a relationship out of conditioning or out of an authentic craving for it. It is important to at least try to understand *why* we pursue the things we pursue or why we want the things we want. The late Indian philosopher Jiddu Krishnamurti said, "All ideologies are idiotic, whether religious or political, for it is conceptual thinking, the conceptual word, which so unfortunately divided man." He believed that part of the awakening of intelligence is not listening to anyone but oneself.

While my own interspiritual perspective does allow for, or rather appeal to, the full flowering of the feminine self, it is challenging for me to uphold my beliefs while having complete awareness of the countless manmade cruelties of the world—human trafficking and the forced sexual enslavement of women and children; the brutality of war, torture, and imprisonment; the sustained ravaging of the planet's resources; corruption and political deceit; and discrimination, racism, and misogyny, to name just a few. My only feasible answer to myself is that these people who exemplify no regard for other people are so disconnected from themselves, from the god inside them (or *God*), that they have totally lost the plot. They are disturbed, seized by a vengeful darkness that flourishes in people in the absence of any trace of light or love or self-awareness. Their *agni* is completely burned out, and only darkness remains inside.

———

While I knew that Pramilla had gone to an upscale Protestant school in Mumbai called Cathedral, I was surprised to discover that, even as a (lapsed) Hindu who ate the occasional steak, she had never read or studied the *Gita* of her own volition, even eschewing it in her later years in favor of John Grisham novels.

"Why not?" I asked her. "You're not interested?"

"I don't want to become too engrossed."

"Why not?"

"I don't want to become a religious nut."

Needless to say, I did not grow up in a religious household. Pramilla self-identified as Hindu, but was hardly a practicing one; my father's "religion" was nature. I will be forever grateful because that loose agnosticism allowed me to freely explore various belief systems without feeling like I was going against any faith that had been pressed upon me from an early age. I was free to think and believe and decide what I wanted. What I'd realized during my theology studies at NYU was that people who were powerful and knowledgeable in spiritual issues used to matter, then they really didn't matter, but now they were starting to be relevant again. It is cyclical, but that kind of wisdom is crucial to the fertility of a civilization. According to a religious landscape study conducted by the Pew Research Center, there is a striking trend among American adults: a growing percentage of them no longer identifies with a religious group. The new fashion is to describe oneself as "spiritual but not religious" (there is even an acronym for it: SBNR), meaning that one is open to experiences beyond institutional religion, and there is a growing number of these unaffiliated swaths of the population. It is not because Richard Dawkins and Christopher Hitchens unfurled a New Atheism movement that successfully evangelized people *away* from religion through fundamentalist atheism and a cutthroat denunciation of literalist religious beliefs. Many people are more attracted to an unstructured, arguably more empowering landscape that takes the "middleman" out of believing in another entity that in turn believes in you. They opt to circumvent the trappings of religious dogma and go straight to the source inside themselves, where it has been all along.

Comparably, with marriage, couples are essentially allowing the government to get involved in their personal affairs, intertwining their coupledom legally and financially with an outside authority. Of course there are financial perks to being married, not to mention health-care benefits, especially for the unemployed, both of which serve as major incentives for couples to tie the knot. But by doing so, are we not just perpetuating a neoliberal system that compels people to marry and take on the burden for their own health care, instead of demanding a more humane system that provides lifesaving benefits to everyone, irrespective of marital status? That is what the writer and activist Yasmin Nair contemplates, and she further asks, "How is a system that systematically denies those same benefits to single people ever anything but fundamentally unequal?"[8]

Again, that is the problem with any ideology, such as a marriage ideology that posits marriage as the most important and sacred of relationships (though that actually can't be true because it's all purely subjective). That's why Krishnamurti is right about conceptual thinking; why divide ourselves into pieces and categories instead of seeing ourselves as part of the whole of humanity?

What's exceptional about the *Gita* is that it does not put forward any specific religious ideology or secular view.[9] While reincarnation is one of its core themes, there is no dogma attached to it that severs us from each other. It simply calls on readers to realize "the true nature of the divine."

While the *Gita* explores these concepts—how to live a spiritually meaningful life without withdrawing from society, the importance of letting go and of acting out of love with no attachment to the outcome or expectations, and the impermanence of everything (except for the soul)—the most central theme in the *Gita* is self-realization.

Lord Krishna says,

> The truly wise, Arjuna
>
> who dive deep into themselves
>
> fearless, one-pointed, know me
>
> as the inexhaustible source.

Basically, the universe or god is within us, and it is infinite. Naturally, this is difficult for the human mind to grasp, because some spiritual stuff doesn't make sense when we try to contain it with words or when we look at any of it through a scientific lens. This is why seekers, or those living the questions, are sometimes drawn to psychedelic drugs or medicine to deepen or stir up this consciousness—especially as hallucinogens tend to heighten this *awareness* visually, making it a little easier to understand. Famously, the Mazatec shaman María Sabina started tripping at the age of eight after discovering small mushrooms, *teonanácatl*,[10] the sacred mushroom of Mesoamerican folklore, near her home village. When she ingested the psychedelic mushrooms (which made her vomit), she purportedly received mystical insights into the causes of people's sicknesses. She became a saintlike figure, a healer, exorcising people of their fevers and illnesses. The late George Harrison of the Beatles said taking LSD made him more insightful.[11] Huxley also experimented with psychedelic drugs. In 1963, when Huxley was dying of cancer, he famously asked his wife to inject him with LSD on his deathbed. In his 1954 book, *The Doors of Perception and Heaven and Hell*, he documents his experiences taking mescaline, which is a hallucinogenic substance found within the peyote cactus, a small, round cactus that grows in the Chihuahuan Desert and is considered by many to be sacred. Given its location, it has a long history of use among the natives of northern Mexico and the southwestern US.

I tried peyote once, kind of by accident. A couple of summers ago, I ended up at an Israeli ashram in the middle of a Costa Rican jungle. I had no clue that where I was going for a two-week vacation, where I thought I'd be doing a juice cleanse, was a place where people specifically go to "take medicine"[12] to *enlighten* themselves and connect with their higher power—or in other words, *take drugs to experience god*. All I could tell from the website was that it was cheerful (that should have been a clue) and hippie-style affordable (another clue). When I arrived, a lethargic Israeli woman brought me to my tree house and, strangely, asked me about my psychological disposition. I would have been suspicious, but I was too petrified by the bats perched under the little roof where I'd be sleeping.

"They won't bite you," she assured me with a sultry smile when she saw my ashen face.

"I don't think I can do this," I told her. "I think I'll be needing a refund."

She shrugged her shoulders and said fine, but that I had to stay until the following morning as, being in the middle of the jungle, it was too late to arrange transportation. That night, at the communal meal area, I met a very handsome tree surgeon named Jake who lived in Brighton. As I poked at my tempeh, I told him I was probably going to leave the next day—that is, if I survived the night, as I was pretty sure bats were going to bite my neck and suck all my blood out in the next twelve hours.

"And miss psychedelic rock night?" He almost sprayed a mouthful of quinoa into my hair in disbelief. "It's like going to Paris and not seeing the Eiffel Tower."

Obviously, I stayed and survived the bats. He and I had a very steamy time together. For a moment I thought, *Could he be the one?* I got carried away with my fantasies about us, though I barely knew the guy. I even emailed Pramilla to let her know I'd met a cute Brit, a yoga-practicing surgeon (I left out the tree part). It turned out it could not be a long-term thing based on our different trajectories—Jake's entire life consisted of roaming around the world participating in ayahuasca ceremonies and other spiritual adventures involving "medicine." In his spare time, he chopped down trees for cash.

I now realize I was more in love with the *idea of love* and the possibility of what could be—that space between not-knowing and knowing—rather than what actually was. Fasting from men had helped me realize that—how much I preferred my illusions and the realm of possibilities to what was in my actual ether. How much I relished the novelty of the new until the fear kicked in, the fear of having to surrender parts of myself to make a relationship work, of being in a situation where there wasn't enough room for *all* of me, the dismemberment inevitable. What I realized: I liked being on the cusp of something rather than being *in that something.*

But they do say things come to us when they are supposed to help us on our path toward self-actualization. At my spiritual core, I also believe *people* come into our lives when they are supposed to, in order to show us something, shape us in some way, painful or not, or bring us somewhere. The American spiritual teacher Ram Dass once wrote, "We're all just walking each other home."

Jake was walking me home. After all, had it not been for him, I would not have seen the universe inside me.

On psychedelic rock night, in the middle of a rainforest, under a heaving white moon, next to the gyrating flames of a mammoth bonfire, against the cadenced thunder of music coming from the all-night DJ, I swallowed several teaspoons of powdered peyote given to me by a very serious-looking shaman during a group ceremony. It was like swallowing dirt. I washed the bitter powder down with ginger tea. As the nausea rose inside me, I dutifully sipped on the tea, at Jake's urging, to keep myself from vomiting and waited (though apparently, vomiting means you are releasing darkness and negative emotions from your past). I'd always been wary of mind-altering substances, especially the chemical ones, but even with this natural medicine, I had a maelstrom of fears and doubts. I figured, though, that I'd ended up where I was for this exact reason—I was destined to try it. A powerful hallucinogen, mescaline puts peyote in the same category as heroin. Its effects are similar to that of LSD, but less edgy, and taking it could put someone at risk if they have a history of psychosis. And I was told that if I *thought* I was going to have a bad trip, I would have one. The *Gita* says, "A man consists of his faith, and as his faith is, so is he."[13] I interpret that loosely as what you believe you become, or that thoughts become things, as my friend Camila always reminds me. So I pictured myself mushing anything negative into a ball and lobbing it into the flames, surrendering to the experience without judgment. I really didn't want to have a bad trip. I bathed in the moonlight and waited.

Half an hour had passed. I closed my eyes. What happened next was sort of like a rollercoaster ride within a moving landscape that kept folding into itself. It was thrilling and mind-bending. I felt like I was flying through another plane of existence, through time and space. The tapestry of color changed continuously as I glided along weightlessly—some of it was bright and light, and some seemed darker. I would open my eyes, stare into the fire, and be safe again. I would close them, and

I was back in the game. I had this feeling that the universe was putting on a show for me; it was showing off, coaxing me to follow it, but it also seemed to want me to merge with it. It was playing with me, or *wanted* to play with me. In Hinduism, there is a concept called *leela*—a word that refers to the dance of life, the path of the playful. The idea behind it is that the entire cosmos is the outcome of some divine creative play. That's what my trip felt like:

the universe was inside me,

infinite,

and it wanted to play with me.

If a dark thought popped into my head, it took me somewhere frightening; if I stayed calm and positive, the colors stayed light and unthreatening. It made me realize how important our thoughts are—how we can literally think things into being. Our thoughts affect our physical realities. This is well-documented in a fascinating study on water by the Japanese scientist Masaru Emoto,[14] who discovered that crystals formed in frozen water show specific changes when concentrated negative or positive thoughts are directed toward them. The German poet Goethe said, "The way we see people is the way we treat them, and the way we treat them is what they become." Proponents of the Law of Attraction, popularized by books such as *Think and Grow Rich*, *E-Squared: Nine Do-It-Yourself Energy Experiments That Prove Your Thoughts*, and *The Secret*, harp on about the importance of talking, visualizing, and thinking about what we want in our lives, rather than the reverse. The idea is that if you think the universe adores you, then it will; whatever we have around us is a manifestation of what is inside our heads. "If you think the world is your oyster, then the world will be falling at your feet," a psychic from California once told me over Skype. This is why meditation, a state of thoughtless awareness, is so important—it cleanses us, recalibrates us. Not only that, but studies show that it causes the brain's fight or flight (or fear) center, the amygdala, to shrink. As that part of the brain shrinks, the prefrontal cortex—associated with awareness and concentration—becomes larger. In the *Gita*, the wandering mind, untamed, "drives away wisdom, like the wind blowing a ship off course."[15]

The next morning, after the requisite slices of watermelon, the coconut water, and the small goblet of chocolate magic mushroom tonic, I absorbed what I'd long known to be the truth:

the divine is inside us,

we are all expressions of the divine,

and we are all connected to each other by that divinity.

The namaste or namaskar greeting in Hindu culture, now almost mandatory at the end of every Western yoga class, is the very expression of this sentiment. The Sanskrit word *namaste* literally means "bow me you" or "I bow to you," signaling the divine spark in each of us located in the heart chakra. In the *Gita*, Lord Krishna says, "I am the Self, Arjuna, seated in the heart of all beings."[16] That's why with namaste you often see people with their hands clasped in prayer position, bowing slightly. They're saying, "The light in me sees the light in you. The divine in me recognizes the divine in you."

God is everywhere—on the inside and outside of us. In a flower. In a shark. In human beings.

It's pretty transformative when you train yourself to look at people that way (even if you don't say namaste out loud or bow all the time, which would be weird outside of India). It is such a compassionate approach to life. Even for the fools or dickwads I encounter, on dating sites or in the workplace or in life in general, if I namaste them in my head, their presence becomes more bearable, and the offshoot is that I inevitably feel a deeper connection to the world, which makes it feel less lonely and huge.

This is what I now understand to be true: the universe is alive within each of us.

———

As part of my efforts to "just be" and to fill my life up with things that bring me joy, I decided to learn how to play the sitar. Research shows that music has transformative powers and is good for us. It can reduce stress, ease us into meditation, and awaken us. In *The Power of Music*, Elena Mannes says that music stimulates more parts of the brain than any other human function. Like meditation, it literally changes the way the brain works (in a positive way). Some scholars even speculate that human music may have come before language.

Surely, I am not alone in saying that music was a big part of my life as an adolescent, but then it sort of went away, quietly slipped out of sight like a sunset—one minute it was there, large, glowing, and red, the center of attention, and then: gone.

Many children grow up playing an instrument, which they eventually drop for scheduling, financial, or logistical reasons. Piano was mine. I took lessons for ten years from a series of Russian teachers. One was a neighbor who lived across the street. I would sit in her air-conditioned basement with wall-to-wall cranberry carpeting, and she would write treble clefs in a special lined notebook I toted back and forth from my house to hers. She was stern by nature, and I remember her writing with a Paper Mate mechanical pencil. She pressed down hard and wrote slowly, methodically, but the lead never broke. I never figured out how she did that.

There was also a Russian man who taught me piano at Kitt's Music, a cramped piano shop in a suburban mall in Maryland. He got foaming-at-the-mouth excited when he talked to me about my piano-playing future. "You are so talented, Natashka. Practice, practice!" he pleaded, petting me in a kosher, non-child-molester way. In my unprofessional opinion, I was not talented at all unless we are referring to my special ability to completely freeze up in the middle of every single piano recital, hands shaking, mouth dry, feeling the eyeballs of an audience stuffed with bored parents glazing over behind my back, and wanting to melt away into the acrylic rug.

I abandoned those eighty-eight plastic keys as soon as I got to college, which proffered nonmusical diversions, namely in the form of alcohol and parties and boys. Besides, logistically speaking, piano literally did not fit into my life anymore, nor was I reminded of it every day, because I was no longer stumbling down the staircase in my acid-wash jeans to be confronted with the irresistibility of a satin walnut Young Chang smack-dab in the living room. I forgot about that chapter as if Bach, Mozart, and Beethoven were just a cadre of dead European men who had never been a part of my life.

But now, I wanted more music in my life—to be fed by its centering, grounding power and filled up by it. I thought about my grandmother Bhabhi, who'd played the harmonium, a freestanding organ-like keyboard instrument, which she loved playing, but my grandfather had had to sell it when they thought they were going to get evicted from the apartment for not paying rent, as times were tough.

There was a hunger deep inside me that I'd had no awareness of, like the hunger for nature that started to creep out of its leafy little hiding place when I gave it permission to exist. By removing something from my life that I had allowed to take up so much mental space (the search for a long-term companion, or romantic theatrics in general), I gained all this new space for other things in my ether to show up and have a real presence. Turns out, my soul hungered for music, and I gave myself the freedom to explore this passion as part of my new commitment to doing things that made me feel the fullness of my life. "Sound is God," said the late Ravi Shankar, probably the world's best-known Indian musician, in the epic Beatles documentary *George Harrison: Living in the Material World*.

As for the sitar, well, the sitar called to me at Etna. One night, I'd picked up Maya's sitar, which was inlaid with real ivory, and started improvising. I didn't know what I was doing, but I didn't want to put it down. She said her teacher, Hassan, was from Pakistan and lived in Harlem. I'd actually emailed him that same night to see if he would be around to give me lessons if and when I came back to New York, and decided that if he emailed me back by the next day, it was destiny (which of course he did).

I'd always found the sitar deep, dark, and esoteric. It made me think of caves filled with mystical secrets and prophets burning sandalwood incense. I found its twang deeply relaxing and had been going to sleep listening to it every night for years. I liked that my favorite Hindu goddess, Saraswati, considered the keeper of creative intelligence—authority on all things music and creative arts—is often depicted with a sitar draped across her lap.

The sitar itself is a long-necked classical Indian instrument with seven strings on the playing neck and thirteen resonating strings below. While Ravi Shankar can be credited with bringing the sitar to the West, Vilayat Khan and Nikhil Banerjee are also considered to be the pivotal sitarists of the last half of the twentieth century. There are also famous female sitar players, such as Anoushka Shankar, Ravi Shankar's daughter, who have star power and talent. Few people know that Annapurna Devi, Ravi Shankar's first wife, is also a virtuoso player.

I'm not really sure when I first heard the sitar's twangy signature sound, or how I fell in love with it, but it had the dual ability to comfort and ground me. Sitar elicits the same reaction in some as opera does—you either love it or hate it. It is a special sound and can grate on the nerves of some, though for me it has always had an alkalizing effect. Listening to sitar music at bedtime enables me to glide into sleep more easily. It wipes away anxiety, my clinging to the way I thought life should be. Just by way of allowing me to loosen my grip on things, generally, I have access to greater personal power, so my goal is to find things that deeply unwind me.

Temporarily back in DC, I'd had to go up to New York for meetings, and I booked my first lesson with Hassan. New Yorkers were still heady with summer, yet already feeling a nostalgia for it in spite of the emergence of a sweltering August. My only concern was that if I was back in New York, that would mean I'd have to be back in the office, and I'd become quite comfortable working remotely. The previous few months were the freest I had ever felt, and the happiest in a long time. While it was financially unnerving and I'd had to work hard to make sure I stayed within my budget, I also played hard. I was so focused on the present moment, on the demands of my self-imposed project (and all of its life-affirming activities) that there simply was no space to worry about the future. In a way, I was simply living or being.

That's why I had to lie.

It was a white lie, so it didn't really count. But it was necessary to convey to Mads that I was only "passing through town." If he knew I was staying in New York for a few weeks, he would make me come to the office every day. I wanted to stay on my mission; part of that was having space for as long as I could.

Since I'd given up my place in Brooklyn and all my belongings were still collecting dust in storage in the Bronx, I decided to stay at the two-bedroom apartment in Gramercy Park where my most musically inclined friend resided in all of her bohemian glory. A blue-eyed Buddhist, Cornelia was born in Hong Kong and raised in Holland, Sydney, and rural England. We met at a clammy college bar called Shades of Green back in college at an NYU happy hour, rescuing each other across the long beer-slopped table of drunken sophomores, and quickly became best friends. I liked her accent; I think she was intrigued by my then-unibrow, and the rest was history.

Having trained in musical theater at the highly regarded Hurtwood House in Surrey, and later at the Boston Conservatory, Cornelia developed nodules and transferred to NYU's Tisch School of the Arts to do experimental theater where she and her classmates would roll around the floor and bark like dogs. Meanwhile, down the hall, I was writing unwieldy term papers on Jacques Derrida. She is now a retired actor, ex-vegan, and small-business owner who runs a trendy nanny agency from her apartment, where she takes business calls in a Nutella-stained nightgown from Marks & Spencer. She still sings, but she is no longer belting out earthshaking musical scores. While she has an extensive network of friends and family, music has been her most constant companion since I have known her—through breakups, through everything, music has always been her saving grace, filling her life up so completely that half the time she forgets she is single.

In fact, I was so committed to immersing myself in music, to feeling that sense of fullness in the absence of another, that I paid her roommate, a bike messenger short on cash, to leave for a couple of weeks so that I could have his tiny, claustrophobia-inducing room and plop down in the middle of her world. I woke up one morning to find ten Buddhists seated on the living room carpet. They were chanting *Nammyoho-renge-kyo*, which is a sort of vow, "an expression of determination, to embrace and manifest [one's] Buddha nature."[17] The group was, as usual, rolling *juzu*, or chanting beads, in their hands while reciting this mantra over and over and over (and over). With them oblivious to my presence, I sat on the sofa and joined in.

I wasn't entirely surprised. Cornelia is a member of a Buddhist organization called Soka Gakkai International. Members follow the teachings of Nichiren, a Buddhist monk who lived in thirteenth-century Japan. At her urging, I have chanted with her East Village group a handful of times, knowing that chanting raises the vibrations of the chanter, making one feel peaceful and centered. Of course, chanting is a form of both meditation and music. "The original instrument is right here," Cornelia once told me, pointing at her white throat. "What the Buddha taught was that everything is through sound, because he spoke his sermons. He never wrote them down."

What did she think the world would be like without music? "Well, that's like saying 'What would the world be like without sound?'" she said. Thankfully, I now understand that love, like background music, is all over the place in so many shapes and forms and gestures and offerings; it is not one sentiment that can be summed up in a Hallmark card, but an energy that often soaks into us without us even knowing.

———

I started taking sitar lessons in Hassan's sunny, sparse apartment in Harlem. I liked Hassan. A middle-aged man, he was warm and sweet and possessed the kind of energy that one would expect from someone who plays classical music all day: calm and centered with a clean aura. Usually when I arrived for my lesson in the afternoon, he would tell me that he hadn't left the house all day. At first, I thought that was almost gross, to deprive himself of fresh air when he had an enviable freedom in his chosen career as a musician, but then I realized that he had been in his heavenly cocoon all morning; sitar-playing was not only a vehicle of expression for him, but part of his spiritual discipline. The high vibrational music creates an energetic and peaceful ambiance that is almost palpable. Sometimes I would show up at his apartment, feeling stressed from the day—feeling behind on my writing, something I'd continued to do since Sicily, or frustrated with the many cryptic references Mads had been making about imminent budget cuts, insinuating that the income I had been relying on might soon dry up—and that stress would melt away in Hassan's presence.

At the beginning, I found myself channeling any stress-induced energy into the actual playing. After the first lesson, slightly discouraged, I felt I had bitten off more than I could chew. I went back. I wanted to be good at it; that was my default position: wanting to accomplish something. But slowly, as the days went by, I let go of the need to be good. The sitar didn't respond well to that. It was a *being* instrument.

The ancient Vedic scriptures teach that there are two types of sound. One is a vibration of ether, or air high up. The other, struck sound, is the vibration of air in the lower atmosphere close to the earth. The sound from the sitar would fall into the latter category. Sometimes it took as long as fifteen minutes for Hassan to tune the sitar, and I watched in awe, mesmerized and skeptical that I could ever train my ear to be able to hear the variations in the sounds of the different strings—it was so minute and subtle, at least to my amateur ears. Then he would often play something for me, and sometimes my eyes filled with tears because it sounded so beautiful or sad.

Yet listening to the sitar is very different from playing it. Playing the sitar is not comfortable, at least not at first. I had to contort my body into a pretzel, sitting cross-legged but with the right leg looped over the left knee, and then with the long wooden instrument draped across my lap, poking out high to the left and low to the right—with the gourd, the bulbous heart-shaped part of the sitar, pressed against the arch of my inner foot. Awkward at best. The gourd, which is essentially a hollowed-out pumpkin, is delicate and can crack quite easily from humidity or changes in temperature. I had to balance it over the arch of my left foot while making sure it faced outward but didn't spill forward over my legs, all the while keeping my back as straight as possible. There were several things I had to line up before even looking at the strings, which are plucked with a wire finger plectrum called a *mizrab*, which was squeezed tightly onto my right index finger. My entire first lesson was dedicated to learning how to sit correctly while playing the sitar. It made me really appreciate the fact that Hassan, or any sitar player for that matter, could sit and play for so long. He told me how he used to sometimes play with Ravi Shankar himself, who could sit for six or seven hours without moving his legs. Hassan credited yoga with allowing him to be able to sit like that.

I started learning the ragas—a pattern of notes with characteristic intervals, rhythms, and embellishments. Ragas are difficult to explain in a few words, but essentially they are used as a basis for improvisation. The tradition of Indian classical music is an oral one. It is taught directly by the guru to the disciple, rather than by the notation method used in the West. That means there is no music to read when learning the sitar—I had to use my ears and pay attention to the *dand,* or fingerboard. At first, Hassan made me sing along—*sa da ra da ra da ra da ra sa*—which I felt shy about, but I reminded myself of the saying, "He who sings prays twice." I would get into the flow and forget everything but what I was doing. It was pure meditation.

I felt myself getting slightly better at each lesson, though I reminded myself that that was not the point. "There is no destination with the sitar," Hassan said, to helpfully remind me that I was going in a circle, but also going inward—part of any musical journey. "Don't try to go anywhere." There was something comforting, almost grounding, about that. I still found the position difficult, and my left index finger was almost numb with pain from having to push down on the strings so hard—I had a visible indentation and a callus was forming. It was painful, but as with many things in life, to move forward, to get better, to develop in some way, there is usually pain. Miraculously, I remembered the ragas, and my fingers remembered where to go *without thinking.* Some moments, it felt like we were made for each other, the sitar and I. I told Pramilla how well the lessons were going, and how excited I was about the callus that was forming, and how it would eventually decrease the sensitivity and lessen the pain. Her only reaction was to ask, "How are you going to get a guy with callused fingers?"

When I was on a roll, Hassan would shake his head, close his eyes and say "WOWWOWWOWWOW," which pleased me beyond words. "You're getting so advanced," he would say, encouraging me. I had to remember that this wasn't about accomplishing something; I'd accomplished enough. I no longer wanted to be single-minded about anything—the search for love, the mastery of an art. I was not going to be a professional sitar player. Learning the sitar was about finding deep joy, about nourishing my body and soul through music, about simply being. It made me so happy to play it—blasted all my thoughts to the side of my skull so I could enjoy the rapture of those moments. I thought about my grandmother playing the harmonium, how it must have brought her a similar joy and peace, and how awful it was that things were so financially tight they had to sell it.

According to classical Jungian psychology, what you end up doing in your second half of life is the polar opposite of whatever you did in your first half of life. It is part of the breaking down of the persona, the face we put forth to the world, our ego-infused mask, boundary, or public identity that conceals our true nature. The false identity that covers up the real identity, the truth of who we are. For example, if you had babies early on and were more in touch with the feminine side in your twenties and thirties, in the latter half of life, you would embody your masculine energy and get all Marissa Mayer or Sheryl Sandberg about stuff. It's a polarity thing. We have feminine and masculine in us, just as we have light and dark. My first half of life was marked by ambition and accomplishing—action-oriented and more masculine—instead of being receptive and intuitive, which is considered more feminine not only in Jungian psychology but across various mythologies. But there is a problem with separateness, with duality. Ultimately, the quest for the individual is to become whole. *We are on a quest for wholeness.* Now, what was happening most of this year was that I was tapping into the feminine, a more introspective, still place, but eventually, when I returned to the ordinary world, I would have to integrate the two and keep them balanced.

In Eastern cultures, the Tao symbol with its yin and yang energies expresses the same idea of the individual harboring both the masculine and feminine within them. In the *Tao Te Ching*, these distinctions between male and female are made explicit: "The female always surpasses the male with stillness. In her stillness she is yielding."

The thing about playing an instrument was that it forced me into the feminine; it slowed me down. It forced me into stillness. It was an order: stay put and be. There was something very grounding about the whole process—I didn't achieve or collect anything. On the contrary, it stripped or peeled things away, the facade, my exterior.

It was very interior-oriented.

It homed in on the essence.

Essence is like the whole universe being enfolded into a single drop, and in that single concentrated drop is the destination: now.

After a dozen lessons or so, I decided I did not want to let go of this wondrous landscape of discovering a new form of expression. I had a decent grasp of some of the basics, though I was still a fumbling novice. That didn't matter. I would continue, whether it be with Hassan, or a new teacher if I landed somewhere else. I would continue not because I wanted to see something through, not because I dreamed of one day playing sitar at Carnegie Hall. I would continue because it was teaching me how to *listen*. It was a different kind of listening from what I was used to too—the journalistic type. To play music you have to be able to listen *intuitively*, beyond the ears, the whole body is open and tuning in. That is the only way you know whether you're hitting the right notes. It requires discipline, effort, and intention. It requires patience. In a way, listening is just as much an act of love as it is a spiritual practice. If people begin to heal the moment they start to feel heard—something my work had shown me—then I wondered, What formidable, transcendent things can happen to the people who are truly, truly listening?

———

"Meditation is better than knowledge," says the *Gita*.[18] Although every culture has produced some kind of mental practice that might be termed *meditation*, it is widely accepted that India is the birthplace of many traditions. Now there are countless forms and styles of meditation being practiced widely in both the East and the West, each with their own distinct methods—Zen, mindfulness, loving-kindness, *Vipassana*, transcendental, *kirtan*, Vedic, and mantra-based, to name a few. The objective is the same: to transcend thought and connect with ourselves on a higher level. To free ourselves from the bondage of the body and the mind, mastering them with our breath. To come back full circle to ourselves, which is why I wanted to immerse myself in it at the end of my man fast.

While meditation is popular right now, trendy even, the hardest part is carving out the time consistently. Our lives are sometimes so busy, it's laughable. From looking at my friends, it's clear we're sincerely trying to squeeze the good stuff in—and one day it won't be a matter of squeezing. I once attended a loving-kindness meditation workshop in the East Village alongside a group of strung-out Manhattan women, guided by Sharon Salzberg herself, the cofounder of the Insight Meditation Society. The beloved Sharon, perched on a small stage, led us through *metta bhavana*—which encourages practitioners to unleash compassion for others through what is typically a five-stage process. We started by sending ourselves love or *metta*, and then we sent it to a friend, followed by someone we had neutral feelings about (for example, the guy working at the deli). After that, it got harder—we were instructed to send *metta* to someone we *didn't* like (such as a nemesis) and then, beautifully, to the entire world. As we perched on fancy meditation cushions sipping from little cartons of chocolate coconut water in a gallery adorned with tea lights, I felt completely pretentious but like I had done something good, even though I hadn't actually done or learned anything. I already knew that we should treat people the way we would want to be treated, yet by making a concerted effort to be positive for several minutes, in turn, I *became* more positive. There was an energy shift, subtle but there. No matter what, it was always about coming back to ourselves with kindness.

When I was staying at that ashram in upstate New York years ago, I befriended an interesting man who lived in the middle of a forest with his little dog, Jazz, in a wooden house that smelled like vitamins and mildew. Doug, a long-time meditator, professor of environmental science, and recovering alcoholic, was one of those people you could sit in silence with, and it wouldn't be weird. Out of the blue, he would say things like, "I'm really feeling the crows today." I wanted to be someone who "felt the crows," but he was able to because he had been cultivating *the art of paying attention*, what Mary Oliver is trying to get us all to do, what I'd tried to do on my safari.

"Meditation is my opportunity to press reset," he said. "It is one of the most powerful things humans have available to them, but they lack the patience or don't realize it themselves. By not resetting yourself, you're screwing yourself."

People often say they're too busy for meditation, but according to a Tibetan saying, if you have time to breathe, you have time to meditate.

Even science says meditation is worth taking the time for. Experts have found that daily meditation changes the body's chemistry and the physical structure of our brains. We shed stress, improve our memory and attention spans, and basically become nicer, more patient people to be around. That doesn't mean meditation is easy.

The first time I tried meditating, I was in my twenties, and I literally peed my pants. I was visiting my friend Erika from college, a Birkenstock-wearing vegan who had moved to Rome. A devout Zen Buddhist, she took me to her meditation center, a small spartan chamber in a suburban enclave, where a dour monk in a cranberry robe instructed a dozen of us to sit on the floor with our backs stick straight and do nothing but stare at the wall counting our breaths. No explanation was given except for Erika telling me that at the heart of the 2,500-year-old zazen practice is the study of the self, without the distraction of *thinking*: not allowing our thoughts to get in the way of whatever it was we needed to realize about ourselves. I felt gloomy about spending even a tiny chunk of my time in the Eternal City cooped up indoors. The next hour wore on like a golf tournament. We were not permitted to move an inch, and I regretted my decision to drink two huge bottles of sparkling mineral water on our sweaty tram journey. Not only was it blazing hot, but Erika swore that *acqua leggermente frizzante* was "the key to staying slim in Italy." Unfortunately, every time I slouched (on average once a minute), our monk sternly rapped me on the shoulder—and in sync, out came a tiny squirt of pee. I was mortified and had no idea how to extricate myself from the situation. Keeping a straight back had never seemed so difficult, nor had fixating on a point on the wall. Fortunately, I had found a smashed mosquito to gaze at, though I felt guilty about using its death for my gain. When the gong finally chimed, I tried to untangle myself and, to my horror, couldn't feel my legs at all. Panicking, I glanced at Erika, who looked as if she'd woken up from the most blissful nap, whereas I felt I'd just had a scrappy fight with a stray dog. I started to wonder if I was missing some pertinent gene—why had the experience amounted to torture and boredom for me but been clearly revitalizing for her?

Erika sent me back to Paris, where I was living at the time, with her old copy of *Zen Mind, Beginner's Mind*. "Read this. It'll change your life," she said, handing it over as if it were a freshly hatched chickadee. I delicately wrapped the book in my new 100 percent Italian-leather jacket and snuggled it deep into my duffle bag. It remained unopened for a decade.

Ever since I started working remotely, I'd been practicing meditation more and more, in line with my pursuit of self-development. On a good day I would feel like I'd drifted into a sleeplike state, where my thoughts quieted their relentless, taxing chorus, and I was cloaked in a deep, restorative, quiet field, the restraining order I'd placed on them a success. "The quieter you become, the more you can hear," said Rumi. That's when the obstructions get peeled away, where the bounty lies. On a bad day, time inched slowly. Through meditation, though, I realized how easy it is for us to waste our mental energy on stuff that isn't serving our greater good, beliefs that exhaust us. Failure to manage our thoughts means we end up with hundreds of invisible energy vampires storming around us all day, sucking out our creative juices and depleting our life force.

In the past when I found the sitting-in-silence stuff a bit anguishing, I'd jump at any chance to go to a kirtan. A simple and powerful form of meditation, kirtan is an ancient participatory music experience with roots in India that involves call-and-response chanting in Sanskrit, where simple mantras such as *om namah shivaya* are repeated faster and faster. The goal is the same—to experience release from the daily chatter of the mind (all while chanting the names of Hindu deities). It can be a religious experience, and as there is music involved, using instruments like the tabla, a pair of Indian hand drums similar to the bongos, and the harmonium, some people find it more interesting than plain old meditation. When chanted, Sanskrit is known to set off a special powerful vibration in the body that can affect a person's mind and spirit. Krishna Das, a well-known singer of Indian devotional music, popularized kirtan in the West by performing at various venues, including Dharma Yoga Center where I practice yoga. I've seen him live at a kirtan, and the palpable energy in these rooms during and afterward is pretty astonishing.

While exploring my meditation practice more deeply during my final month of working remotely, I asked Pramilla for any insights, though I was pretty sure she wouldn't have a deep reserve of knowledge to share.

"TV is my meditation," she told me when I broached the subject, waving the remote at the complicated Bose entertainment system my brother and I had bought her for Christmas. "I just watch and zone out," she said. I knew she was afraid of silence, which was why the TV or Pandora was always on.

"That's not meditation," I replied, wondering how my Indian mother could have no interest in the things that are spiritual in nature.

"Well, I have deep thoughts," she said.

"It's when you *don't* think," I explained.

"Most of the time, my mind is blank." She lifted a cup of tea to her lips. "Or I play solitaire on my phone. It helps me meditate. Or I drink a margarita from the Cheesecake Factory, which knocks me out."

I have my doubts over her rather unconventional "meditation discipline," and she really needs one, as she is a total worrywart. Most of her sentences begin with "I just worry that [fill in the blank]." Even when she is watching TV, she is worrying about something. I know her so well I can even read her mind. Whenever I am home, I'll overhear her on the phone talking loudly with one of her Indian friends: "I just worry that she won't have anyone to take care of her." (pause) "I don't know. They say it's really hard to meet a good guy these days." When I ask her why she has always worried so much about my brother and me, since my friends' parents don't behave that way, she says, "Your father and I loved you more than most parents love their children because we loved *each other* so much." Even on the road, she worries. When she is in the passenger seat and I'm driving, even when I am going close to the speed limit, she frantically grips everything in the car—the dashboard, the glove compartment, the doorframe. She seems to have her own set of invisible brakes by her feet (all that anxiety and I've only totaled two cars). Years ago, I bought her Dale Carnegie's *How to Stop Worrying and Start Living*, which she promptly turned into a coaster. I recently found it buried in her closet and put it on her pillow in the hope that she would read it. Because I am an annoying child, I told her that meditation can help her with her anxiety, especially over her unmarried, childless daughter. When I was done with my soliloquy, I asked my favorite question to her, "How annoying am I on a scale of one to ten?"

"Ten," she responded.

We both giggled.

I could see how I was annoying. When I was home visiting, she had to endure what she refers to as my "banana talk," especially as I had all these spiritual epiphanies and unearthed powerful little bullets of wisdom that I felt compelled to share lest I forget them (on a daily basis, she thought I was descending into madness).

"Speak with integrity. Say what you mean and mean what you say," I'd quip, paraphrasing Toltec wisdom from *The Four Agreements*, a straightforward approach to life that I had been practicing.

"Aren't you happy your daughter is so enlightened?" I'd ask her.

"No."

"You know I'm your teacher right? They usually say that children are the teachers to parents, not the other way around."

Even though I teased her, even though I loved her beyond words, I was annoyed that I'd inherited the worrying gene from her. When I was away, if she didn't reply to a text within two hours, I assumed the worst; sometimes I would even cry out of sheer panic. Had she slipped down the staircase? Overdosed on Gatorade? Driven her car under the influence of a margarita from the Cheesecake Factory? My imagination went wild. I was constantly worried about her, obsessed with her health and well-being to the point where I would drive her nuts ("I can't believe you don't use grass-fed butter!" "I can't believe you still eat white bread!" "I can't believe you don't have Himalayan sea salt in the house!") Obviously, she was alone, and with only one parent left I was hyperprotective—she was the most precious thing in my life. I wonder if hormonally at my age I was supposed to be worried about my own children, but as I didn't have any, I worried about her. Even at home, when she was in the house, I worried.

One morning, the phone rang. She answered and started yelling. I assumed it was a call from India (she often yelled into the phone on long-distance calls). As I came upstairs to her bedroom bringing a tray of tea and toast with me, I overheard her say, "One of these days, one of these days, the FBI is going to find you." My stomach knotted as I hovered outside the door listening for any further clues.

When she hung up, I barged in. "Mom, who *was* that? You have to tell me now!"

I braced for something horrible. A terrorist? An angry foreign government?

"That was Microsoft Windows."

"*Why* are you threatening Microsoft Windows?" I gasped. "You live alone. It's probably not a good idea to threaten random people."

"Because they're fake. I can tell because they have a very strong Indian accent, all of them," she said, talking in an affected Indian accent.

I barreled into her room and collapsed on her bed in tears. "Mom, please promise that we will be in every life together. *Please.*"

When I collected myself, I called my brother. "Mom is threatening people with the FBI. Is that normal?"

"She's just getting old," he said nonchalantly.

Pramilla and I were competing with each other over who worried more. I'd decided to do a partial fast for Ramadan, only for a week in a gesture of spiritual solidarity with my Muslim friends, especially in the wake of all the Islamophobia and hate-spewing rhetoric that had bubbled up during the 2016 US presidential campaign. Ramadan, I thought, was the best way to encapsulate what I'd been trying to do over the last several months—that sacred time to focus on the inner landscape. Many major religions encourage or mandate fasting as a means of personal spiritual revival. In Buddhism, fasting is considered one of the most direct ways to acquire wisdom. According to legend, Siddhartha Gautama, also known simply as the Buddha, who lived in India in the sixth century BCE, ate only one grain of rice and one drop of water per day as an extreme form of fasting in order to help him reach enlightenment. Native American Indian tribes incorporated fasting into many sacred ceremonies as a means to experience powerful dreams or visions from the Great Spirit. By and large, fasting can help reveal the things that control us—our negative patterns and addictions—bringing us freedom as we recognize them. As Lalla wrote, "When you eat too much you forget your truth." Aunt Devi used to say something similar: "People who think too much about food are dumb."

"What do you think of me fasting for Ramadan?" I asked Pramilla one day while we were having lunch at the Cheesecake Factory near our house.

"It's a terrible idea," she said. "Why would you fast? You're not even Muslim."

"So you're not worried about my spiritual development?" I asked.

"I'm worried about you passing out on the street," she exclaimed. "Besides, it's not for people like you—it's for people who want seventy-two virgins in heaven."

"Well, I'm going to do it, so please respect my decision."

"Just don't eat anything that's vegan," she whispered to me across the bar, the tequila on her breath mixing with her perfume. I was not about to take health advice from a woman who still smokes—one Salem every day, which she lights, takes a puff from, and then puts out, only to relight again later. I plead with her to stop and have tried everything from hypnotizing to brainwashing to bullying, but it's to no avail.

With the fasting, I was adamant that I try it for spiritual reasons. While I didn't want to do the *whole* month, I was an able-bodied adult in good health, so nothing could go wrong if I did it for a week. Basically, all I had to do was wake up really early (almost like at Etna!), twenty minutes before dawn, so that I could eat something (hard), abstain from eating or drinking during daylight (hard), not have sex (easy), use no bad language (easy), and refrain from smoking (easy), telling lies (easy), and thinking bad thoughts (hard). While the not-eating thing made me a bit hangry, not being able to drink water was the most torturous, especially smack in the middle of summer, as it left my mouth dry and chalky. As an exercise in self-control and discipline, I found it useful. It definitely slowed me down. I found that I was inclined to sit in meditation for longer periods. While fasting, you tend to be more *still*, more serious, because you have less energy. It almost altered my personality, temporarily at least—I was less boisterous, more introspective and quiet, but there were extended moments when I felt high, with euphoria followed by a deep clarity. The effects of detoxing for several months, combined with fasting, had done something to my body, the way my man fast had done something to my spirit. There were parallels between the effects of both detoxes, the diet one and the dating one, that can largely be described as recalibrating and heightening on multiple levels. It was during this time that I felt it had all come back around to why I'd set out on this whole pilgrimage in the first place: to save myself.

Joseph Campbell said, "The world is perfect. It's a mess. It has always been a mess. We are not going to change it. Our job is to straighten out our own lives." There is constant work on this front; it does not go away. We have to continuously save ourselves from ourselves (ego). We have to save ourselves from grief, anger, indifference, monotony, despondency, and fear by owning up to these emotions and taking action to transcend them. We have to save ourselves from feeling weak or run-down by investing in our health and nourishing ourselves in nature. We have to save ourselves from loneliness by getting involved in meaningful communities, by forming deep friendships, by learning to see ourselves as part of a larger ecosystem. We have to save ourselves from what Buddhists refer to as the monkey mind—the unsettled, restless, or confused mind—by meditating. We have to save ourselves from our overachieving pathologies by bringing ourselves into the now.

If there was one message that was bursting to come out of me toward the end of this journey, it was that we are all responsible for saving ourselves and healing the world within our reach as we get stronger and more self-aware. Start inside, at the cellular level, and amplify outward. As we hone our intuition and tap into our innate wisdom, we can help those around us to get on that path as well.

Until we've done it for ourselves, we can't do it for anybody else.

―――

This was my first trip home as a "married" woman. Pramilla thought it was "cute" that I'd married myself in Zanzibar, and she played along with my shenanigan. We were invited to an Indian wedding function at a Latin restaurant in the uninspiring suburb of Rockville, Maryland. A childhood family friend of mine had just gotten married at the age of thirty-three. Of course the subject of my love life would crop up between sips of pomegranate mojitos, but I no longer dreaded it. I had my bling on. At the restaurant, surrounded by cliques of nosy Indians, I confidently flicked my hand in front of them when questions about my marital status arose. "Oh, I am married. I married myself in Zanzibar," I informed them, glowing, while they took in my chunky ring and laughed hysterically. The laughter was like an umbrella sound that, like om, seemed to have everything in it. Mostly, they looked at me like I'd gone nuts.

In the past, I might have felt a bit riled up, but as I stepped further into this new space I was creating, I was cautious and protective of it. Unwilling to fill it with things I didn't want—namely negativity or gratuitous thoughts. It was too easy to slide down that path: no. I was not bitter. I had no reason to be bitter. Beyond that, I didn't care what anyone thought anymore. I wanted to own that liberation, throw off the invisible shackles, remind myself who I wanted to be before the world told me who I should be. I was curious about that space between the labels, the *otherness* out there, not the labels themselves.

Of course historically some women of the East did not marry, though it was considered unusual at the time. Rabi'a al-Basri,[19] an ancient Sufi mystic who lived in Iraq during the eighth century, skipped the whole getting hitched thing. She was considered to be one of the most important among the early Sufi poets, advanced in the ways of meditation and philosophy. After a famine struck Basra and she lost her parents, she was sold as a slave. She lived a hard, ascetic life, but when her master witnessed her devotion to prayer, he freed her. She continued to pursue self-realization and garnered a reputation as a spiritual luminary.

Once, she was asked why she did not marry, and she answered:

"There are three things that cause me anxiety."

"And what are they?"

"One is to know whether at the moment of death I shall be able to take my faith with me intact. The second is whether in the Day of Resurrection the register of my actions will be placed in my right hand or not. The third is to know, when some are led to Paradise and some to hell, in which direction I shall be led."

"But," the people cried, "none of us know any of these things."

"What!" she answered, "when I have such objects to preoccupy my mind, should I think of a husband?"[20]

Widely considered the first proponent of the Sufi approach toward god as the beloved,[21] in her verse you see that Rabi'a didn't see god, or anything, as something outside of herself:

How can you describe the true form of Something

In whose presence you are blotted out?

And in whose being you still exist?

And who lives as a sign for your journey?

She encouraged followers to love god for its own sake, not out of fear. Why fear something that is a part of you? "You are my breath," wrote Rabi'a. In the human body and soul, there is no separation between church and state.

All the wisdom is inside.

———

One of my weaknesses in the past was always looking to others for wisdom. In full disclosure, I've regularly consulted an astrologer, a Mayan mystic, a Reiki healer, an acupuncturist, a tarot reader, a couple of bicoastal psychics, one shadow reader, and a Magic 8 Ball. People are more than happy to dish out advice, often at a cost.

The only time I went to a therapist, he said I was not normal. After my father died, I figured the healthy, responsible thing to do would be to seek professional help to talk about my grief. After combing through Zocdoc.com, I booked an appointment with the least creepy-looking psychiatrist on the Upper West Side who happened to have a slot when I was available. I sank into his leather armchair but couldn't bring myself to actually tell him why I was there. I couldn't say the words without falling to pieces. So we focused on my love life. I told him that my romantic history was colored by a series of short, occasionally meaningful if fleeting encounters and that when I fell in love, I fell in love very deeply. After pouring my guts out for an expensive hour to a total stranger I found on the internet, his feedback was that I was "not normal." In his professional opinion, I would need approximately one million additional sessions to get to the bottom of my abnormality. I never saw him again. While I saw how talk therapy could be helpful, I didn't need some disempowering dick telling me what my issues were, explaining my grief to me. It was mine. I did not need his wisdom when I had my own, something way, way more powerful, but I did not realize that back then.

Whatever these people had to tell me seemed to fall flat. Even the shadow reader could not know what I didn't already know myself. Instead of blowing money, from now on, I'd restrain myself and settle for a thankless "Concentrate and ask again" triangle floating in the Magic 8 Ball's window. Even Mads, who rarely seemed to be thinking about the meaning of life, knew it. "Sometimes we're too busy looking for the next best thing while we have all the answers," he said, one of his recent passing remarks that stuck with me. Maybe he was wiser than I gave him credit for.

I know I used to place too much value on what other people said, wrote, or thought instead of tapping into my own inner wisdom. Bob (my grumpy astrologer) always lectured me about that. "You're giving your power away," he'd say. This is something that I've learned can be further harnessed through meditation and slowing down in general so that I can let life catch up with me. That present-moment thing everyone is always talking about, when you stop and just exist in silence, is a pretty big deal. Solitude can sow a peaceful catharsis, and that is part of its continual allure.

Another way to access this inner wisdom is through writing. Scientific evidence has harped on about the psychological and even physical benefits of externalizing thoughts through journaling. The late feminist Islamic scholar Fatema Mernissi once wrote, "Writing is one of the most ancient forms of prayer." Ages ago, I'd started doing "the morning pages," a tool invented by creativity guru Julia Cameron, author of *The Artist's Way*. She prescribes daily homework: three pages of stream-of-consciousness writing, written in longhand first thing in the morning. It's an exercise in getting out the gunk, so to speak, so that we can get to the real stuff—the insights, the epiphanies, the raw wisdom. The more you write, the more it comes. Nobody sees these pages, of course, so you can write about your secret girl crush, underground socialist antics, or big belly fetish. Periodically, I would succumb to prayerful surges or even ask myself questions, and sometimes a response would flow out: a clarion voice of reason and incontrovertible intelligence. It was like having a divine conversation, but with myself. In a series of books by Neale Donald Walsch, *Conversations with God*, you see the power of this kind of free-flow journaling. The author, overstressed and frustrated with life, hit rock bottom, which propelled him to turn to a legal pad late one night (as one does) where he began scratching out desperate why-oh-why questions to god. And guess what? His hand started writing back to him, answering all of these deep philosophical questions about existence. Through writing, Walsch tapped into his inner wisdom and truth and saved himself from suicidal thoughts. In the end, we have to find that strength inside—no one else can save us but ourselves.

My friend Camila is always going on about gratitude: what a powerful medicine it is and how it's a perception-shifter, the preamble to all sorts of abundance and happiness. I sort of got it. Even if the shit is hitting the fan, it's about homing in on the goodness, the good things that probably still exist anyway. I'd started properly practicing gratitude this year. In spite of the loss and sadness that many of us have experienced, I had a long list of things to be grateful for, and I wrote them down in my journal, even if they were as general as "sunlight." I still felt indebted to the world in many ways, and by documenting these things every day, no matter how small they were, I did feel better.

Generally though, when I tell disgruntled friends to practice gratitude, they sometimes look at me like they want to shoot me in the face. I understand why. Self-help people are annoying as hell. Besides, with gratitude, like the not-feeling-alone thing, it isn't until you fully understand/embody it, that you actually get it. Half the time, I wasn't even sure if I got it, but I knew it was *the* thing, that it shifted my energy frequency in a more positive direction, so I continued to write my lists in my journal. I tried to get Pramilla to do it, since she sometimes has a gloomy tendency to focus on what we lack instead of what we have, but she brushed me off. "There's so much to be grateful for!" I bellowed, rather unhelpfully. In so many ways, I could tell that she felt stripped of her wholeness since losing her life partner. I didn't know how to bring her back around, from emptiness to fullness, to re-emerge the way that I was re-emerging, or at least trying to. Everyone's grieving journey is different, everyone's spiritual journey takes a different shape, and I knew better than to try and impose on her what was working for me.

Encountering myself on the page through writing, I was able to heal myself in ways I didn't completely understand. It oftentimes felt like a direct communion with god. For example, sometimes I played around with asking myself the kinds of questions I used to put to psychics or tarot-card readers: "Why is it taking so long to meet someone?" or "Why do I choose unavailable people?" or "What is my purpose?" I would answer my own questions, and the answers would pour out of me with fluidity, in a way that felt comforting, empowering, and *right*, stripped of any notion that anything was wrong with the way things were. It was almost as if the answers weren't coming from me but from somewhere else. Besides, I was starting to realize that my purpose wasn't something I was going to be doing or was supposed to be doing; it was something I was being called to become.

These days, I see this wisdom, or insight, exhibiting itself in different forms of communication, such as in conversations with friends. The advice I dish out now comes from a calm, wise, and knowing place—three words I would never have used to describe myself in the past. I can confidently say that my most important belief is the following:

All the wisdom we need is already inside of us.

We need to make a little effort to get there, though. This is especially true when we hunger for more than what contemporary secular life has to offer but are eclipsed by the demands and speed of modern-day living. We all have god inside us, but that communication becomes broken when we don't carve out any time for it. I didn't realize it before, but that is what the last several months had been about: surrendering to the need for this journey back home.

Stephen Mitchell, who edited one of the versions of the *Gita* I've been referencing, wrote, "Ultimately [the *Gita*] has nothing to teach. Everything essential that it points to—what we call wisdom or radiance or peace—is already present inside us." That thing that I found when I was drowning in grief, that inner light, the one that Lalla, Rabi'a, and Rumi wrote about so beautifully, that is what he is talking about. That is what the *Gita* is talking about. Meditation, chanting, yoga, fasting, reading sacred texts, taking psychedelic drugs, making art and music, being in nature, *being in love*—these are all ways of peeling back the layers to get to that truth. I felt like I'd reached it, and in self-actualizing, I was ready to re-inhabit the world.

I'd returned to my true self—the child, the poet, the philosopher, the holy warrior of light, the heroine of my own life.

Turns out, I was the one that I'd been waiting for, and I came back to me.

———

I used the excuse of spiritual reasons to self-impose a partial tech detox on the last week of my pilgrimage, which was possible since Mads reluctantly obliged me some time off to go to a writer's residency. I'd put a lot down on paper these last few months and wanted to create something out of it.

"When you're back, I really want you back," he said, pointing out that while I'd stayed on top of my workflow, mentally I had drifted to a different place over the last several months. "You're almost done rebirthing yourself, right? That means it's time to come back to New York."

I pushed the anxiety of those words out of my head and stopped checking my emails, even put an automated "away on a writer's retreat" response in my Gmail, letting emails pile up—all those beckoning, insightful emails from Notes from the Universe, Omega, Kripalu, Spirit Rock, Esalen, and Abraham Hicks, little nudges from the various communities I'd dabbled in, would go unopened. The articles from Pramilla containing headlines like "1 in 50 Finds Love on an Airplane, Study Says" would be ignored.

Besides disconnecting from my inbox, I also logged out of Twitter and Facebook. Not scrolling through my newsfeed was liberating and allowed me to salvage my time and mental space. I also stopped watching the news to protect myself from the noisy discourse—I didn't want to get dragged into any place other than where I was.

I'd cocooned myself in a large ramshackle house as part of a writer's residency in the picturesque Martha's Vineyard, a bucolic paradise I'd never been to before. After all this time floating around, writing alone, it was great to find myself in a community of female writers—a playwright, a novelist, and two short-story writers. An ecosystem of truth-telling and creativity.

I made a pact with myself to stay the kind of person who is questioning and deepening. Maybe that seems strange to some, but there are whole tribes of people out there searching for the truest truths. I've met them: they are everywhere, within every culture.

I spent the days writing and exploring the Vineyard by bike—its beaches, forests, and wildlife reserves—and came back to a community of women who were also living the questions, also navigating the treacherous terrain between who we were, who we are, and who we want to be, all while trying to stay grounded in the present. The truth is, we were all brewing. We were all becoming something. *We are always becoming.*

It makes me think of a funny conversation I had with Filip, Maya's fetching and self-actualized husband. You could tell he was really in touch with his feminine energy. He referred to Maya as a divine sage, and he meant it. I didn't see much of him while I was at Etna, as he had been traveling, and we crossed paths only when I was leaving, but the three of us did reconnect one evening for dinner in Catania. Maya wanted to hear about the rest of my Sicily adventures. I had come back from Pantelleria, where I had practiced being naked, cleansed my soul with special volcanic mud, and had an injudicious fling with a Sicilian man—and they had just come back from taking archery lessons in Sweden. Of course the subject of my man fast came up. Now, Filip is one of those intense men who really holds your gaze and *listens* with his whole soul. It's nice but a little discomfiting, as I'm used to people glancing at their smartphones at least once per sentence.

After I finished blabbering about Tommaso, the possessive Louis Vuitton guy, Filip looked at me and said, "You're not ready." He didn't say for what, but I knew what he meant.

I was defensive. "I *am* ready," I declared, even though, to be honest, I'd felt all this time I was not *quite* ready.

As we were leaving and saying goodbye, he grabbed my shoulders and shook me. With his wine breath in my face and in a strong, stern tone that sounded like it came from the bottom of the universe, he commanded, *"Become ready!"*

I grabbed his shoulders back and said, "I am becoming! I am becoming!"

It was the truth.

———

They say that god, the universe, energy, the Great Spirit has three answers to our prayers:

1. Yes.
2. Not yet.
3. I have something better in mind.

———

I read somewhere that true love means no longer waiting. Love, I was starting to understand, is an ethereal, mysterious thing, something that can't be pursued. It is not a career. Seneca reminds us that whether or not we get to where we want to go in life hinges on a formula of sorts: "Luck is what happens when preparation meets opportunity." In other words, if we want to meet someone, then we must first ready ourselves along the way and have a vision of partnering with someone; by focusing on the things that bring us light and make us feel purposeful, we are heading in the right direction, but we have no more control than that. It is *meeting fate halfway*—setting the intention, having faith, and moving toward where we think we want to be without being so gung ho about it, while trying not to step in what my astrologer Bob calls horse pies. There's the regular way we think of time—the chronology of seconds, days, weeks—and then there is the timing that lines up with our soul's readiness for what we want. My Greek friend told me about a concept from ancient Greece called *kairos*, which translates to "the right time, the opportune moment." Kairos is full of serendipity, where we meet our own desires while meeting the needs of the world at the same time. That is why it is so sacred. In the New Testament, kairos can also refer to God-ordained times throughout history, such as the coming of Jesus Christ. It is not something that humans can force. The timing of things has to be handed over to something beyond ourselves. "To have faith is to trust yourself to the water," Alan Watts once wrote. "When you swim you don't grab hold of the water, because if you do you will sink and drown. Instead, you relax and float."

You relax and float and realize love doesn't involve grabbing or reaching. In Sanskrit, the word for "not grasping" is *aparigraha*; you move through the world with an open heart. In Ayurveda, when we hold on, nothing flows, and we become stagnant. In Sanskrit, *ishvara* (supreme being, god, the ultimate reality) *pranidhana* (dedicate, devote, or surrender)—the yogic act of surrendering to a higher purpose, of self-surrendering—calls on us to approach our practice in the spirit of offering. Life, it seems, can also be approached in the spirit of offering. The notion really resonated with me.

I wasn't going to grab or reach at anything anymore. I was going to offer myself to it. I was going to *become into it*. And one day, I would just *be* it.

I'd sent myself out into the world, an act that began as one thing but then turned out to be something bigger than I could have fathomed, more powerful than healing or learning to trust the universe again or tending to my kundalini awakening or transcending societal and cultural pressures. I realized the deepest gift I have to share with the world.

It's love.

"The only truth is love. Nothing else is real," I told Pramilla after having this profound realization.

Silence. I waited for whatever was cooking up in her head in response to my "banana talk."

But to my surprise, she said, "I agree."

———

And there it was: I did not need to look for love because I was love.

On a practical level, though, would I date again? Sure. But it would be different, somehow. I didn't know how, but I was different, so it had to be different.

Everything felt different. I'd lost my knowing, but I'd found it.

Through that, I'd found true love, and that was enough already.

One supremely beautiful thing happened at the very end of the month. It arrived like a huge, unexpected spiritual delivery, the birth of an underlying feeling that had been present, growing inside me over the course of the last nine months.

I'd bicycled to Lighthouse Beach in Edgartown one morning, unfolded the thin Ganesh sarong I'd bought from Sita in Kerala, and sat there looking out across the white sand, the blue Atlantic. The beach was empty. All of a sudden I felt it: an explosion inside. I started crying uncontrollably. I couldn't figure out why. I didn't feel sad. I didn't feel lonely.

Then I realized what it was: *gratitude*.

It was gratitude for the bounty and beauty of nature; gratitude for freedom; gratitude for space; gratitude for my parents, family, and friends; gratitude for love, the experiences I'd had, both good and bad; gratitude for my health. It was gratitude for the time to engage in this personal project that served me in such a spiritually nourishing and self-indulgent way, that stripped away what no longer served me.

There it was:

The light.

The love.

The awakening.

Would I stay awake? Another question I didn't have the answer to. But I decided to give it one: yes. I could live inside the question and give it an answer too. At least this one. I had control over its outcome. It was true: a little bit of me was more awake than before. It was subtle, but I knew my interior had shifted, and that it had shifted because of me, because of choices I made, and because the seeds inside me had started growing. There was only one way forward: I would have to live this question, and the others, with wholehearted abandon.

That's all we can hope for: to shift a little, to make space within ourselves so we can do that shifting, to make space around us and fill it with the good things that expand the light inside us so that it reaches out and across and beyond everything. It does not take much. It is one breath away at all times.

And it is within that breath that we are invited to continue the incredible, holy, purposeful act of *becoming*.

You must give up the life you planned in order to have the life that is waiting for you.

—*Joseph Campbell*

ACKNOWLEDGMENTS

Writing this book was among the most rewarding experiences of my life. I am indebted to the works of Maureen Murdock, Julia Cameron, Joseph Campbell, Clarissa Pinkola Estés, Kahlil Gibran, Pema Chödrön, Alan Watts, Rainer Maria Rilke, Anne Lamott, Miguel Ruiz, Natalie Goldberg, Simone Weil, Jalāl ad-Dīn Muhammad Rūmī, Rebecca Solnit, Aldous Huxley, Thich Nhat Hanh, Audre Lorde, Krista Tippett, Erich Fromm, Henry David Thoreau, Bri. Maya Tiwari, Joan Didion, Dr. Vasant Lad, Mary Oliver, Bhante Henepola Gunaratana, Mirabai Starr, Jon Kabat-Zinn, Marianne Williamson, Ram Dass, Rudolf Steiner, Caroline Myss, Sue Monk Kidd, and Sri Ramana Maharshi, among many others. All of these great thinkers have informed my writing and made my intellectual and spiritual understanding of the world richer.

I am also grateful for the existence of *The Yoga Sutras of Patanjali*, *Tao Te Ching*, and the *Bhagavad Gita* and for the time I was graced with to delve deep into these sacred texts.

So many wise souls have been with me along this journey, sharing valuable insights and shaping my path in some way. I've relied on the support and advice of innumerable friends, and I couldn't possibly list them all by name. There are certain people in my life, however, who played a particularly important role in the birthing of this book.

A huge thanks to Lisa DiMona, my incredible agent, for believing in me, for letting me write what I needed to write, and for guiding me through the daunting process of getting my first book sold and published. Thank you, Lisa—I am so lucky to have you as a friend, soul sister, and mentor.

A few very dear friends in my community of writers have been exceptionally encouraging and helpful: Sharon Rapose, Dionne McCulloch, and Larry Porges. Thank you for helping me navigate the world of book publishing and for cheering me on. Your support has meant so much.

I owe a special debt to the soul sisters who have gone deep with me. Juana Givens, thank you for being on the same wavelength at all times and for reading my manuscript with so much enthusiasm more than once. Janna Bilski, Annabelle Corke, Sophia Qureshi, Lauren Ohayon, and Belinda Gurd—you have all helped shape this book with your wisdom, love, and encouragement.

A special thanks to Ludo Bok, Rashad Nelms, Kane Luke, David Bolger, Saadia Iqbal, Sabrina Aggrawal, Andy Narraway, Jackie Dent, Anna Jeffreys, Shah Badkoubei, Marcus Prior, Harleen Kahlon, Danielle Thomson, Mark Seddon, Katya Svirina, Andrea Manni, Alex Brunais, Kimberly Williams, Ruchi and Rajiv Dadlani, Trente Hargrave, and Renata Bacci Sed for your friendship and support during this period, especially to those of you who opened up your homes to me when I was homeless and wandering.

Thanks to the readers who read early drafts of the manuscript and took the time to provide valuable constructive feedback: Cristina Ascone, Sheetal Dhir, Athena Russo, Sherna Khambatta, Sofia Diarra, Saumya Roy, Vanessa Manko, and Jennifer Thomson. This was hugely helpful for when I tackled the revision. A special thanks to Ceci Sturman for her much-needed assistance with fact-checking, research, and other crucial tasks.

Thank you to Ronit Wagman for her skillful editorial eye and for being the perfect "midwife" for my manuscript, and to my wonderfully encouraging editor at Amazon, Little A—Erin Calligan Mooney.

I also want to thank the community of seekers at Ananda Ashram in Monroe, New York. My time there was transformative and healing. A special thanks to Janaka Daly and Dmitry Khoronji for your infinite wisdom and for standing by as I walked through the darkness.

I owe thanks to my astrologer T. C. Eisele for keeping it real with me and for constantly reminding me to trust my own intuition over anything else.

Thank you to the Noepe Center residency program in Martha's Vineyard and to the inspiring community of female writers I had the chance to get to know there. I would also like to thank the community of special women I met at Mirabai Starr's *Writing Your Story of Loss and Transformation* retreat at Ghost Ranch in New Mexico. Your support has been so wonderful.

I also want to give a shout-out to the extraordinary community of women I've met through Emerging Women as well as the community of mindful change-makers I've met through Wisdom 2.0. I've been introduced to so many powerful ideas at these conferences.

Thank you to my family, in particular my uncle Kumar Kishinchand for valuable information about our family history and Partition.

And finally, thank you to my beloved mother, Profulla Scripture, a fearless goddess without whom this book would not exist.

NOTES

Chapter 1

1. Jon Wilson, *The Chaos of Empire: The British Raj and the Conquest of India* (New York: Public Affairs, 2016). The English ruled territory in India starting in the 1600s. The East India Company rule in India effectively began in 1757 and lasted until 1858. The British Crown took over control until 1947, when India won independence.

2. "If there is meaning in life at all, then there must be a meaning in suffering. Suffering is an ineradicable part of life, even as fate and death. Without suffering and death human life cannot be complete." Viktor E. Frankl, *Man's Search for Meaning* (Boston, MA: Beacon Press, 2006).

Chapter 2

1. Inspired in part by a section in *A Return to Love*:

> Our deepest fear is not that we are inadequate. Our deepest fear is that we are powerful beyond measure. It is our light, not our darkness, that most frightens us. Your playing small does not serve the world. There is nothing enlightened about shrinking so that other people won't feel insecure around you. We are all meant to shine as children

do. It's not just in some of us; it is in everyone. And as
we let our own lights shine, we unconsciously give other
people permission to do the same. As we are liberated from
our own fear, our presence automatically liberates others.

Marianne Williamson, *A Return to Love: Reflections on the Principles of
"A Course in Miracles"* (New York: HarperCollins, 1992).

2. Joshua Foer, *Moonwalking with Einstein: The Art and Science of
Remembering Everything* (New York: Penguin, 2011).

3. "Marriage and Divorce," American Psychological Association,
http://www.apa.org/topics/divorce/. Another reason why couples
may choose not to go through with a divorce is because it's so
expensive.

4. "Family structures of a married couple and their children were present in [Western Europe] and [New England] in the seventeenth
century, influenced by church and theocratic governments." James
M. Volo and Dorothy Denneen Volo, *Family Life in 17th- and
18th-Century America* (Westport, CT: Greenwood Press, 2006).

5. Helen Fisher and Krista Tippett, "This Is Your Brain on Sex," April
20, 2017, in *On Being*, produced by On Being Studios, podcast.

6. Stephanie Coontz, *Marriage, a History: From Obedience to Intimacy,
or How Love Conquered Marriage* (New York: Penguin, 2005).

7. Mandy Len Catron, "To Fall in Love with Anyone, Do This,"
New York Times, January 9, 2015; Arthur Aron et al., "The
Experimental Generation of Interpersonal Closeness: A Procedure
and Some Preliminary Findings," *Personality and Social Psychology*

Bulletin (rev. July 21, 1995): http://journals.sagepub.com/doi/pdf/10.1177/0146167297234003.

8. "Anthem," *The Future*, Columbia Records, 1992.

Chapter 3

1. "No one today is purely one thing. Labels like Indian, or woman, or Muslim, or American are not more than starting-points, which if followed into actual experience for only a moment are quickly left behind." Edward W. Said, *Culture and Imperialism* (New York: Alfred A. Knopf, 1993).

2. "Memorable Albert Einstein Quotes," A.S.L. & Associates, accessed October 16, 2018, http://www.asl-associates.com/einsteinquotes.htm.

3. Dr. Vasant Lad, *Ayurveda: The Science of Self-Healing* (Twin Lakes, WI: Lotus Press, 1985).

4. Erich Fromm, *The Art of Loving* (New York: Open Road Media, 2013).

5. International Organization for Migration (IOM), "Humanitarian Emergency Response to the Libyan Crisis: Seven-Month Report on IOM's Response," 28 February 2011–27 September 2011. https://www.iom.int/jahia/webdav/shared/shared/mainsite/media/docs/reports/MENA-Seven-Month-Report.pdf.

Chapter 4

1. United Nations High Commissioner for Refugees (UNHCR), "Response to the Somali Displacement Crisis into Ethiopia, Djibouti, and Kenya, 2011," *Refugees*, http://www.unhcr.org/4e172ba19.pdf.

2. Brené Brown, "The Power of Vulnerability," TED Talk, June 2010 at TEDxHouston.

3. Neil deGrasse Tyson, *Death by Black Hole: And Other Cosmic Quandaries* (New York: W. W. Norton & Company, 2014).

4. Neil deGrasse Tyson, "Session 2: Discussion with Tyson, Weinberg, Krauss, Harris, and Shermer," *Beyond Belief: Science, Reason, Religion, and Survival*, presented by The Science Network at the Salk Institute, November 7, 2006, http://thesciencenetwork.org/programs/beyond-belief-science-religion-reason-and-survival/session-2-4.

5. Defined as a person who prefers to be single rather than settle and who waits for the right person to come along rather than dating indiscriminately.

Chapter 5

1. *Bhagavad Gita: A New Translation*, trans. Stephen Mitchell (New York: Three Rivers Press, 2000), chap. 10, verses 36–40.

2. The *Bhagavad Gita*, which translates to "Song of the Spirit" or "Song of the Blessed One" is in the *Mahabharata* and consists of 18 chapters and about 700 verses.

3 *The Bhagavad-Gita: Krishna's Counsel in Time of War*, trans. Barbara Stoler Miller (New York: Bantam Classics, 1986). Most scholars agree that the *Mahabharata* was composed between 400 BCE and 400 CE.

4. While I can take issue with how Lord Krishna persuades Prince Arjuna to fight, *Gita* scholars say this is an allegory of the battle between the good and evil tendencies within all human beings.

5. Krishna is also known as the Lord of Love.

6. Some Hindus consider Krishna in the *Gita* to be a full incarnation of Vishnu, which consists of three gods who are responsible for the creation, maintenance, and destruction of the world as part of the Hindu triumvirate. The other two gods are Brahma (creator) and Shiva (destroyer).

7. Sri Swami Satchidananda, *The Yoga Sutras of Patanjali* (Buckingham, VA: Integral Yoga Productions, 2012). In his updated version of this ancient text, he outlines the art and science of traditional yoga meditation for self-realization.

8. Yasmin Nair, "Gay Marriage IS a Conservative Cause," *Gay Marriage Hurts My Breasts* (blog), February 26, 2013, http://www.yasmin-nair.net/content/gay-marriage-conservative-cause.

9. The *Gita* presents a secular path to enlightenment and offers several paths to achieve it. It was composed for the common people who found it hard to understand the more esoteric teachings of the Vedas and the Upanishads.

10. A species of *Psilocybe*.

11. Mikal Gilmore, "Beatles' Acid Test: How LSD Opened the Door to 'Revolver,'" *Rolling Stone*, August 25, 2016, https://www.rollingstone.com/music/music-news/beatles-acid-test-how-lsd-opened-the-door-to-revolver-251417/.
Lysergic acid diethylamide (LSD), also known as acid. As Harrison told *Rolling Stone*, "I had such an overwhelming feeling of well-being, that there was a God, and I could see him in every blade of grass. It was like gaining hundreds of years of experience in 12 hours."

12. A respectful way of saying "using nonsynthetic drugs" (without the stigma of the word *drugs*).

13. Miller, *The Bhagavad-Gita: Krishna's Counsel*, chap. 17, verse 3.

14. Masaru Emoto, *The Hidden Messages in Water*, trans. David A. Thayne (Hillsboro, OR: Beyond Words Publishing, 2004).

15. Mitchell, *Bhagavad Gita*, chap. 2, verses 67–71.

16. Mitchell, *Bhagavad Gita*, chap. 10, verses 18–21.

17. "The Meaning of Nam-myoho-renge-kyo," Soka Gakkai International, accessed October 16, 2018, https://www.sgi.org/about-us/buddhist-concepts/the-meaning-of-nam-myoho-renge-kyo.html.

18. Mitchell, *Bhagavad Gita*, chap. 12, verse 12.

19. Also known as Rābi'a al-'Adawiyya.

20. Claud Field, *Mystics and Saints of Islam* (New York: Cosimo Classics, 2011).

21. Camille Adams Helminski, ed., *Women of Sufism: A Hidden Treasure* (Boston, MA: Shambhala, 2003).

ABOUT THE AUTHOR

Photo © Maggie Marguerite Studio

Natasha Scripture is an author, poet, humanitarian, and former aid worker. As a spokesperson for the United Nations, she covered humanitarian crises around the world. Before the UN she worked for a variety of organizations, including the BBC, CNN, Al Jazeera English, the World Bank, TED, National Geographic, and Condé Nast Publications. She has been published in the *New York Times*, the *Telegraph*, *Glamour UK*, the *Sydney Morning Herald*, *Huffington Post*, *New York Post*, and the *Atlantic*, among other publications, and has been featured in *Marie Claire*, *Women's Health*, and the *Sunday Times Style* magazine. Natasha has lived in several different countries, travels frequently, and seeks to inspire and empower women everywhere with her writing and storytelling. To learn more, visit the author at www.natashascripture.com.